£2.99

£14

DAVID
LIVINGSTONE

DAVID LIVINGSTONE

Trail blazer

John Waters

Inter-Varsity Press

INTER-VARSITY PRESS
38 De Montfort Street, Leicester LE1 7GP, England

First published 1996

British Library Cataloguing in Publication Data
A catalogue record for this book is available from the British Library.

ISBN 0–85111–170–X

Set in Palatino
Typeset by Avocet Typeset, Brill, Aylesbury, Bucks
Printed by Cox & Wyman Ltd, Reading, Berks

Inter-Varsity Press is the book-publishing division of the Universities and Colleges Christian Fellowship (formerly the Inter-Varsity Fellowship), a student movement linking Christian Unions in universities and colleges throughout the United Kingdom and the Republic of Ireland, and a member movement of the International Fellowship of Evangelical Students. For information about local and national activities write to UCCF, 38 De Montfort Street, Leicester LE1 7GP.

Contents

List of maps

Preface

Biographies of Livingstone are legion, but none gives a satisfactory account of his life or character ... A balanced assessment of a man whose life was even by the coolest reckoning a most extraordinary one has yet to be written.[1]

This was the sobering assessment of Timothy Holmes, as late as 1990, of all previous attempts to encompass the life of a man who, in the late twentieth century, became a highly controversial figure. This factor is reflected in Holmes's comments on specific biographers, covering the whole range from 'Blaikie's saintly tone'[2] to Jeal, who 'tends to the opposite extreme'.[3] Holmes subsequently went on to contribute a biography of his own, presumably (although he nowhere makes this claim) to restore some of the balance that he feels has been lost.[4]

Dr Andrew C. Ross, Senior Lecturer in the Department of Ecclesiastical History at New College, Edinburgh, credits Holmes's biography with being a genuine attempt to find the 'real' Livingstone. He describes it as 'a good study and one very sympathetic to the David Livingstone that I think existed as opposed to the Livingstone that all sorts of people have reshaped for their own ends, ends that were often opposed to everything that Livingstone stood for and believed in.'[5]

That Holmes's biography is a determined attempt to find the 'real' Livingstone is reflected in its title, *Journey to Livingstone*. Its subtitle, *Exploration of an Imperial Myth*, suggests a concern to cut his subject's character free from anachronistic accretions. Livingstone lived under the authority of African chiefs, with many of whom he enjoyed relations of mutual respect, a far cry from colonial conditions which to some extent he predicted but never saw. 'His polemic against the Portuguese statesman Sá da Bandeira hints that Livingstone in 1862 anticipated the 1880s partition of Africa among the colonial powers.'[6]

Livingstone was motivated by a mission which aimed to draw in not only missionaries but committed Christians of all walks of life into the regeneration of Africa. His appeal to all sorts and conditions of people made him a statesman who had a lasting impact as much on future generations as on his own. It is the very breadth of his influence that has exposed his life and letters to microscopic examination. His journals and field notebooks are compared (and contrasted) with his published works. Literary conventions are examined, such as the deathbed scene in the Victorian edition of his last journals. Here Dorothy Helly distinguishes fact from fantasy by referring to the editor's notes from interviews with two of the men who carried Livingstone's body out of Africa.[7]

Many lines of investigation have still to be followed up, such as the contemporary context of *Missionary Travels*[8] and the editorial demands it was expected to meet.[9] There is no call for biographers of Livingstone to repeat each other; his own writings amount to millions of words and much of the material he wrote has yet to be quoted.

A study of this kind depends a great deal on those who have transcribed, edited and published Livingstone's original writings. Here again, however, Holmes does not find a high standard. Many of Livingstone's editors have, he says, been guilty of 'deliberate suppression ... It is regrettable that these editors did not have the scholarly principles of Professor I. Schapera to guide them. His editions ... are models of thoroughness and objectivity which many will strain to emulate.'[10] Schapera has given reliable access to many of Livingstone's journals and letters which are quoted in this present work.[11]

Given the wide range of Livingstone's interests and the vast output of both his pen and his biographers, it is inevitable that some principles of selection need to be followed. The key elements highlighted here are those identified by Holmes as 'two frequent motifs' in the letters he has edited: 'Livingstone's dedication to Christ and his determination to see an end to slavery. An understanding of his approach to these matters is essential to any appreciation of his life.'[12]

We may ask: if these are indeed the dominant themes in Livingstone's life, why is it that he is controversial and how did his biographers come to such contradictory conclusions about him?

To these questions there is no short answer – except the invitation to read on, and come to your own conclusions about this extraordinary character. Yet one thing springs to mind.

It is well known that he was a diminutive man of indomitable courage; the name 'David' fitted him well. It is axiomatic that Livingstone had both demanding ideals, great gentleness and respect for Africans, a good deal less patience with Europeans, and a dark side to his nature. This darker side some biographers have denounced as being inconsistent with his profession as a Christian. Yet as a Christian, Livingstone professed to be of no account, a 'poor poor imitation' of his master.[13] The more he trod his lonely path the more he saw obstacles and pitfalls, and the more he doubted that the 'divine favour' was with him. But he felt strongly that whatever our human failings,

All will come out right at last. We are not alone, though truly we deserve not His presence; He encourages the trust that is granted by the word, 'I am with you always, even unto the end of the world.'[14]

Whether we succeed or fall flat on our faces, Livingstone believed that God's overarching plan would be fulfilled in the end.

It is common enough in Christian biography to find that the closer a person comes to the end of their pilgrimage, the further they feel from the character of God; the more aware they become of their own darkness in comparison to the light of Christ. They plumb the depths of their souls. So it is with Livingstone and his journals. In the end, it is hardly possible to write a 'balanced biography' of a man who has become a spectacle to the whole world; a fiery Scot, made to feel his frailty in the crucible of Africa; a man who spoke his mind, yet also kept secrets. I am reminded of the words of a kindred spirit who has spent his life in cross-cultural mission and traversed many countries in pursuit of it. Paralleling Livingstone's attitude to his Scottishness, Martin Goldsmith calls himself English without being bound by the constraints of Englishness. (He is, in fact, a Messianic Jew.) 'What has Aristotle's golden mean got to do with mission?' he asked. 'I don't want to be balanced' (holding his arms up high and pointing them away from each other);' I want to be *extreme* in both directions, both Fully emotional and Fully rational and theological'.[15]

Professor Andrew Walls, formerly of New College, Edinburgh, provided inspiration and some fresh pointers in my quest for Livingstone. I am also grateful to Geoffrey Warhurst of Cheltenham for information on Boer and Nguni-Zulu history; to the University of Natal for providing verification on place-names in south-central Africa; to the librarians of Rhodes House, Oxford, for their untiring assistance in making available many volumes of Livingstone literature; and to the British Library, London, for making their resources available.

My wife, Rachel, not only provided vital maps without which Livingstone's journeys would be unfathomable; but also lived through this project from the very beginning of our marriage. The time given to the work was all the more precious to the family since it was done during relatively short leaves in Britain during our service with the Church Mission Society.

November 1995   *John Waters*

1
The clans

The strangeness, the 'otherness', of Africa was not what had impressed itself on the mind of the young Scot when he came to the Cape in 1841. The Xhosa people he had met with there reminded him so much of the Highlanders of his grand-parents' generation: the border tensions between settled and less settled clans, the cattle 'lifting' that was not seen as theft, yet could lead to outbreaks of fighting that transformed the landscape. Tribes would be forced to shift to new areas, yet their close ties of kinship would still keep them together.

Tales told by the Xhosa around the campfire reminded David irresistibly of his grandfather, who recounted the lives of his ancestors going back six generations.[1] His grandmother used to sing the Gaelic songs of the Western Isles, and he had learnt Gaelic in order to read the Bible to her. So the young Livingston[2] was alive to the folklore of the clans, the last tribal system in Europe.

Arriving at the Cape on 15 March 1841, four days before his twenty-ninth birthday, David had stayed with Dr John Philip, a fellow Scot who had been a superintendent of the London Missionary Society in southern Africa since 1820. Finding him to be a 'vigorous and outspoken champion' of the interests of the Coloured and African communities,[3] David took his part from the pulpit – somewhat perhaps to the senior man's embarrassment – in a controversy with the colonists.

It was not that Livingston thought that contact between the Cape people (such as the Xhosa) and the colonists was a bad thing; in fact, he wanted to encourage it. Not just missionaries, but traders too, could benefit Africa. He was fired by the vision of spreading the gospel through the agency of the Africans themselves. To achieve this vision, there had to be a change in conditions among the warring tribal groups: the Zulus (Nguni) of northern Natal, the Xhosa of the eastern Cape, and the Tswana of the dry country to the north, where

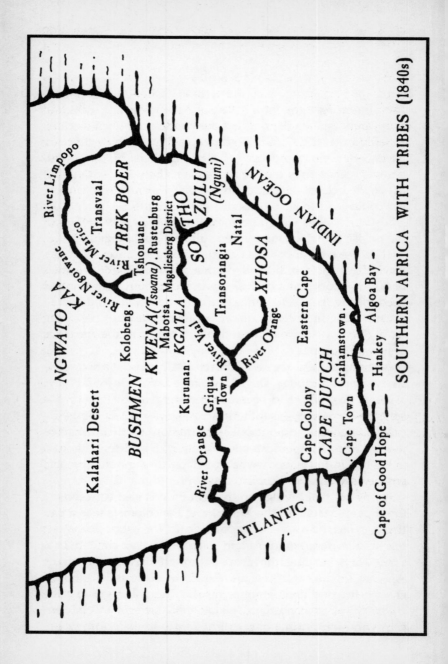

SOUTHERN AFRICA WITH TRIBES (1840s)

River Limpopo

NGWATO KAA

Kalahari Desert

River Ngotwane

River Marico

Transvaal

TREK BOER

Tshonuane

Kolobeng.   .Rustenburg

BUSHMEN   KWENA (Tswana). Magaliesberg District

Mabotsa.

KGATLA

SO THO

ZULU (Nguni)

Natal

Transorangia

Kuruman.

Griqua Town

River Vaal

River Orange

River Orange

XHOSA

Eastern Cape

CAPE DUTCH

Cape Colony

Grahamstown.

Cape Town.

Hankey

Algoa Bay

Cape of Good Hope

INDIAN OCEAN

River Orange

ATLANTIC

12

he was headed. David trusted that traders, by stimulating peaceful commerce between the tribes, could help to bring about that change.

He had heard the idea forcefully presented the previous year at a packed meeting in Exeter Hall, London, on 1 June 1840. There Thomas Fowell Buxton, an evangelical reformer and campaigner against the slave trade, had proposed an expedition to West Africa. The aim was to reach the interior via the Niger River and find out what resources Africans could call on to trade with the industrializing West. The motive was not profit so much as the desire to free African chiefs from the temptation of selling fellow Africans into slavery.[4]

Buxton was the ally and successor to William Wilberforce in the fight against the slave trade. To these men Dr John Philip, David's new-found friend, had sent information in the 1820s about the activities of farmer-settlers in the Cape who took both forced labour and land from Africans along the borders of the colony.[5]

The result was a Parliamentary resolution in 1828 calling for steps to guarantee 'to all the natives of South Africa the same freedom and protection as are enjoyed by other free persons residing at the Cape, whether they be English or Dutch'.[6] The Dutch had settled at the Cape since 1652 when Jan van Riebeeck had established vegetable gardens to supply the crews of Dutch East Indiamen on their way to the Spice Islands of what is now Indonesia. They were followed after 1688 by Protestant emigres or Huguenots, fleeing persecution in France. There came a flowering of Reformation culture, fine architecture and settled urban life.

By 1750 the 'Cape Dutch', living within 100 to 150 miles of the coast, were as different from the frontier farmers further north as they are today. In the 1790s the 'Trek Boers' or nomadic farmers emerged, moving north-east into the Eastern Cape where they reared cattle and adopted a lifestyle similar in many respects to the gun-toting American frontiersmen of the Wild West. Like the Xhosa, whom they came into contact with, they were cattle-breeders who needed small fields for subsistence crops. In a few years the land would be denuded and they would be forced to move on, inevitably clashing with the Xhosa who followed an identical economic pattern.

When Livingston reached the Eastern Cape by ship from Cape Town, on the second leg of his journey to the mission centre he had been assigned to in the north, significant changes were underway. More Boers had tried to take land there after the banning of slavery by the colonial authorities at the Cape. 'Ordinance 30' of 1830 had made every person of every race equal before the law; to the Trek Boers this was anathema. Up to then, they had been able to treat their workers as they liked and, although they had had few slaves, the compensation which they got for them was small.

Trying to get beyond the reach of English law, the Boers who headed north-east to the Eastern Cape had collided with the Xhosa, sparking off what were known as the 'Kaffir Wars'. Many Boers then trekked north, defusing the situation in the Eastern Cape enough for mission work to go on.

A fruit of this work was the LMS mission centre at Hankey, which Livingston was especially interested to visit. Here were Hottentots, descendants of the original inhabitants of southern Africa, the Bushmen, who had intermarried with Bantu tribes from the north. The Bushmen had been hunted by both the Bantu and the Boers until the early nineteenth century, but now their Hottentot descendants were living here as free citizens, able to trade with their neighbours and at the same time keeping up a high standard of spiritual life, meeting for prayer at four in the morning.

Livingston could see change coming for Africa, just as it had for his own family. In three generations, Scottish Highlanders had become lowland farmers, or crofters, and crofters had become factory workers. David's grandparents, who had farmed on the Isle of Ulva, off the coast of Mull in the Western Isles, left their croft in 1792 when the farm could no longer support a growing family. They moved to an industrial cotton-mill complex on the River Clyde, near Glasgow. There, at a mill tenement in Blantyre, David was born in 1813.

David's parents, Neil and Agnes, were from Scottish Calvinist stock and from them he had learnt of past religious movements. It seemed to him that the Hottentots of Hankey were in a state somewhat similar to his Scottish forefathers 'in the days immediately succeeding to the times of the Covenanters'.[7] Their family worship was striking and uplifting. 'Sitting round a fire in the bush, they made the rocks re-echo to their beautiful singing. They knew all the hymns by "heart".'[8] A Boer family whom he visited at the same time wanted medicine for a child, and were kind to the Scot. They were in a condition different from the Hottentots. Indeed, some of the more settled Boers or Cape Dutch reminded David of his father Neil, with their Dutch Calvinist background and tradition of hard work. Yet they knew little of the gospel and had formed curious ideas of Africans, whom they saw as 'sons of Ham', born to serve them.[9]

The further north Livingston went, the less settled the Boers became and the more inclined to impose forced labour on Africans. The Trek Boers had crossed first the Orange and then the Vaal Rivers, perhaps moving as they did further and further from the original ideals of Jan van Riebeeck and the Huguenot-influenced colony at the coast. It was said of the Trek Boers that they hated to see even the smoke from their nearest companion's hut. As a group of them had recently entered the south-west Transvaal[10] a little to the east of the area David was assigned to, he could expect to have irascible neighbours.

The journey from Algoa Bay on the coast to Kuruman, the northernmost centre of the LMS, was a 500-mile trek by ox wagon. Livingston finally arrived on 31 July 1841. He was warmly welcomed by Robert Hamilton, an artisan, and Rogers Edwards, who helped Moffat with printing and was a carpenter by training. David was keen to take their advice to join a trip into the interior. It would be a good orientation. Meanwhile, he looked about him. The countryside around Kuruman struck him as bleak: it was barren scrubland, pockmarked with thorn-trees known as 'wait-a-bit', from their habit of hooking into the unwary traveller and holding him back.

Within a day or two Dr Livingston got the chance to put his

Glasgow medical training to the test. It had taught him nothing about tropical diseases, but quite a lot of chemistry. He was a pharmacist-physician, able to make his own medicines. The first prescription succeeded, and 'an unsuccesfull [sic] case since has not in the least abated their confidence'.[11]

Medicine made friendships, but it was not David's main aim. Eleven weeks later, he was glad to go on reconnaissance with Edwards, searching for a suitable site for a new mission centre. Edwards spoke the language, SeTswana, and a Tswana Christian called Pomore, the son of a chief near Kuruman, came as a guide. The tribes were thinly scattered and between them they had to cross large tracts of burning sand. The sun was 'so hot in the middle of the day that centipedes coming out of their holes are roasted alive'.[12]

Wild horses, giraffes, ostriches or antelopes occasionally broke up the monotony of camel-thorn trees and bushes. The six-week survey of territory up to 250 miles north of Kuruman revolutionized Livingston's ideas of evangelization. He concluded that 'an extensive native agency is the most efficient mode of spreading the gospel'.[13] He had visualized missionaries radiating out from Kuruman to reach the surrounding tribes; Robert Moffat, the founder of the centre, had given David the impression that it was strategically located for this. He had met Moffat in London, six months after offering to the LMS to go to South Africa. Moffat, who was in Britain to get his SeTswana translation of the New Testament printed, had failed to emphasize the fact that the Tswana were nomadic. It was obvious now that in order to find grazing grounds for their cattle, they were moving steadily away from Kuruman. The vital question was where to start a new centre. During the 700-mile round trip, it became apparent that it was the most northerly tribes on the route that were most open to being visited. Among these were a group that had split off from the Kwena tribe.

They had found this splinter group living in a village 15 miles south of Shokuane, at that time the capital of the most powerful Kwena chief, Sechele. The village was called

Lepelole, after 'a cavern of that name' nearby.[14] The chief man, Bubi, was very welcoming. Edwards' discussion with him showed that the people knew nothing of the gospel, but were quite open to it. Seeing their situation and feeling his own deep need to learn SeTswana and get to know their way of life, Livingston resolved to return. He meant to cut himself off from all European society for six months, in order to bond well with Kwena culture and concentrate on SeTswana. He now realized that the language which Moffat had chosen for his New Testament translation was spread over a vast area.[15]

The following year, on 10 February 1842, the Scot again set off from Kuruman, taking with him Pomore, whom he hoped would stay with the Kwena long term and teach them. It was clear to him that the only way the far-flung tribes could be reached effectively was through African workers.

The native teachers are really the most efficient agents in the dissemination of religious truth, and if we had two with each of the Interior tribes ... as much would by the Divine blessing be effected by them ... as would be effected by any two Europeans for the first half dozen years at least.[16]

Livingston found Bubi as friendly as before, and his Scottish instinct for the clan system helped him understand kinship relationships. For example, he quickly grasped the fact that Africans use kinship words much more broadly than Europeans. When one of Bubi's wives brought him some beans and a kind of beer, he called her 'sister', and this simple touch pleased her. It showed he recognized their customs: within the clan, there was no need to distinguish between a sister and a more distant relative, such as a cousin – all were brothers and sisters and mothers and fathers.

'Every evening since', David wrote to his 'real' sister, Agnes, 'she sends me a huge bowl of sour porridge or beans or some sweet reeds with the message, "Sister sends you this, as she ought to take good care of her brother."'[17]

The Scot won the confidence of Chief Bubi[18] and persuaded him to support a project to build a dam and canal to irrigate the land, thus making it possible for Pomore to have a garden and grow his own food while working among the Kwena. The chief was delighted with the idea of the foreign medicine-man 'making rain' in this way and gave him sixteen men for the work, including his own rain-maker.

A blistering red sunburn soon put Livingston out of action as a labourer, but the bantering relationship he kept up with the rain-maker and his crew kept the Kwena faithful to their task. '*Namane e tona e kgolo tirô e,*' they intoned as they dug; 'a great calf of a work is this!' 'He is making us oxen now,' was another little ditty; 'we shall see our wives no more.'[19]

The teasing, rhythmic songs lifted the spirits of the men, so that they stuck to their task despite serious setbacks. 'Although the dam was twice swept away by floods, and I was unable, in consequence of getting both legs and arms severely sunburned, to stimulate them by my example, they did not seem in any way discouraged, but laboured on to the end.'[20]

Seeing the work was well under way, the budding language student decided to make a further journey to the north. Seitlhamo, a guide given him by Bubi, respected his abilities but some companions they picked up on the way did not suspect that he could understand SeTswana.

'He is not strong,' they said, sizing up the stocky Scot. 'He is quite slim, and only seems to be stout because he puts himself into those bags' (a reference to Livingston's thorn-proof sail-cloth trousers). 'He will soon knock up,' was their verdict.

Overhearing these comments made the Highland blood boil. For days afterwards, he kept the party at the top of its speed, until he heard them expressing 'proper opinions' of his walking ability.[21] They had had to leave their wagon since the oxen got bogged down in the sand, but by skirting round the fringe of the Kalahari desert they finally reached the Ngwato tribe, about 350 miles north of Bubi's.

The Ngwato chief, Sekgoma, welcomed Livingston with choice portions of rhinoceros meat. 'You have come to us just like rain,' he exclaimed. 'If you had brought your waggon [*sic*] I should have detained you at least a month looking at you.'[22]

Walking on to the Kaa tribe, situated 24 miles to the east of

Sekgoma over ravines of basaltic rocks, Livingston found for the first time that he could speak about Jesus with freedom and without notes. The Kaa, perched like eagles in their mountain lair, were reclusive. A trader who had visited them died of fever, and since the neighbouring tribes suspected them of poisoning him they were taken aback by the gusto with which the Scot ate their porridge, and even more so when he lay down to sleep. By the trust he showed in them, he won a hearing for the gospel. 'I had more than ordinary pleasure in telling these murderers of the precious "blood which cleanseth from all sin".' It was also the first occasion he had addressed a group of Tswana 'in their own tongue without reading it ... I felt more freedom than I had anticipated.'[23]

David returned to Sekgoma[24] to find him deep in thought. After sitting in silence with the Scot for some time, the chief suddenly sighed.

'I wish you would change my heart,' he said. 'Give me medicine to change it, for it is proud, proud and angry, angry always.'

Startled, Livingston picked up a New Testament, but Sekgoma cut in: 'Nay, I wish to have it changed by medicine, to drink it [and] have it changed at once.'[25] Abruptly, the chief got up and went away.

Sekgoma's relationship with Livingston was always going to be contradictory.[26] Yet this meeting was the start of a spiritual awakening in his tribe that would lead to the conversion, not of Sekgoma, but of his son, Khama.[27] The house of Khama was to become vital to the progress of the gospel 'in the whole of the Tswana-speaking area of southern Africa'.[28]

The only inkling Livingston had of this was the fact that one Ngwato tribesman had the beginnings of an understanding of God's nature, and the missionary was able to add to that the good news about Jesus and the resurrection. This ray of light was sufficient to persuade the Scot to return. Meanwhile, Sekgoma gave him some Ngwato companions for the long journey back.

At Bubi's village things were not going so well. Pomore had become feverish, and it seemed the dam-building and canal-digging would go to waste. A healthier site for a mission centre would be needed. At the same time, rumours of war were in the air. Bubi introduced Livingston to the emissaries of a chief who lived in the Kalahari with his cattle. The chief, Sebego, wanted to come out of the desert to plant corn, but the missionary sent a message warning him that the time was not right.[29]

Sebego, however, came out anyway. Thirty-six of his people were murdered in an incident which set off a chain reaction of inter-tribal raids. During these Sebego was able to repulse Sechele, chief of the Kwena, but was then robbed of his herd by tribes jealous of his cattle wealth. 'So poor S. is now, from being the richest in cattle in the whole country, reduced to wander up & down the wilderness with only a handful of people, scarcely any women & children, & only his shield to sleep on at night.'[30]

It turned out that Christians from Kuruman were visiting Sebego at the very time he was first attacked. They were blamed for complicity in the plot and it was not until 21 February 1843 that the Scot could find anyone brave enough to accompany him from Kuruman to see Sebego. In the end Bubi's man, Seitlhamo, volunteered to be the guide.[31]

Twelve days later they found Sebego. 'He demanded why I had attacked and destroyed all his people. I replied by asking why he had refused to listen to my advice ... Did the messengers he had sent to me last year fail to deliver my message, or did he discredit my words?' Some of the surviving messengers then recognized Livingston and Sebego was won over. He had not heeded David's warning, 'being entirely ignorant of the power of guns'.[32]

This restoration of trust enabled Livingston to speak to Sebego's people. 'He himself listened with great attention when I told them of "Jesus and the resurrection", and I was not unfrequently [sic] interrupted by him putting sensible questions on the subject.'[33] Yet for all his valuable cultural exposure the Scot found it hard to get through to them. He was convinced as never before that he needed to be 'baptized by the Holy Spirit' if the Word were not to be made ineffective by his 'mode of presenting it to the mind'.[34]

Passing on from Sebego's, Seitlhamo guided their ox wagon a few hours to the north-west, into a valley set in an amphitheatre of mountains. There, Livingston saw a river suitable for irrigation, and came to a group of eight villages mining for iron ore.[35] The people were called 'Kgatla', and their first contact was friendly.

It seemed a healthy spot for a new mission centre, and after several return visits with Mr Edwards, culminating in a grand *pitso* or assembly of the tribe, they agreed to have missionaries among them. Accordingly, in August 1843, Livingston moved there with Edwards, the carpenter-builder, and Mebalwe, a deacon from the church at Kuruman. They set to work on building a canal and houses.

The only drawback to the project was that the place seemed to attract more than its fair share of lions.

2
Mary goes north

Meanwhile, on 10 April 1843, the Moffat family had sailed into Table Bay at the Cape. Their twenty-three-year-old daughter, Mary, was thrilled to see Table Mountain again, with its fleecy white tablecloth of cloud, overlooking the Bay. Memories flooded back of the three years she had spent in Cape Town training to be an infant-teacher. She had expected to go back to Kuruman at the end of her course.

Instead, five years ago, her parents had come and taken her from the Mediterranean climate of the Cape into the snow of four English winters. She had spent those years staying with friends of the family, while her father Robert spoke like a prophet to vast audiences. Telling Britain of the plight of Africa, he also managed to get printed a large number of SeTswana New Testaments.

This precious cargo was loaded, with other supplies, on to a ship at Cape Town. The party, which included two new missionary couples, the Ashtons and the Inglises, sailed for Algoa Bay in the eastern Cape. It proved difficult, once they had landed their large cargo, to find enough oxen to haul their wagons north. During the long delay, Mary would have had time to revisit Salem.

Salem was the site of the Wesleyan mission school to which Mary was sent at the age of ten, in 1831. At that time it called itself the 'Athens of Africa', and the teaching had certainly been good. Nevertheless, Mary's thoughts were tinged with sadness as she recalled how the local settlers had hated missionaries. Salem and nearby Graham's Town had been founded as buffers against the pressure of tribal migrations of Xhosa from the north-east. The frontier colonists frowned on Mary's character and Kuruman upbringing, calling her a 'white African'.[1]

Feeling herself to be a foreigner among the white settlers, she had learnt to hide her deeply tanned face from them. In fact, she knew herself that she got on much more naturally with Africans. As the ox wagons finally rolled north from Algoa Bay, she felt reassured by familiar territory.

Mary was a child of the dust, and 100 miles or more from the Cape the landscape already began to remind her of the north. They crossed the eastern edge of the Great Karoo, a very dusty plain lying in a rain shadow. In spite of the dry climate, some agriculture was possible and very occasionally the convoy of wagons would pass a farm. The land rose gently until they reached the border of the Cape Colony, the Orange River.

Crossing the river, they entered a region formerly overrun by the great Zulu general, Tshaka.[2] A kind of Genghis Khan of the Nguni people, he welded the Zulu armies out of a confederation of their tribes, based in the eastern coastal kingdom of Natal. When Mary was a girl, Zulu attacks had pushed the Xhosa into conflict with the colonists in the south, and at the same time sent waves of invasion armies to the north-west.

Mary had been born in Griqua Town, in the north-west, and brought up in an African village. She had grown up chatting with other children in the language of the Tswana cattleherders. She had even picked up the clicking tongue of the San or Bushmen, who inhabited the Kalahari Desert; her nurse, Sarah, spoke one of at least thirty-two languages and dialects to be found there.[3]

Sarah had been rescued as a child by Mary's mother, called 'Mma-Mary' after the African custom of naming the parent after the first-born child. Mma-Mary had stopped Sarah's Bushmen relatives from burying her alive with her dead mother. Mrs Moffat was an indomitable figure, and many instances of her resourcefulness came to Mary's mind as familiar places passed by.

Early in the 1820s a Nguni leader, Mzilikaze, rebelled against the Zulu general Tshaka. Tshaka, who had called his capital *Ungungundhluvu*, or 'the place of the stamping of elephants' (the royal animal for the African), was not recognized as emperor by all the Nguni. The warrior chief Mzilikaze was able to lead away from Natal an army of fighters trained in the

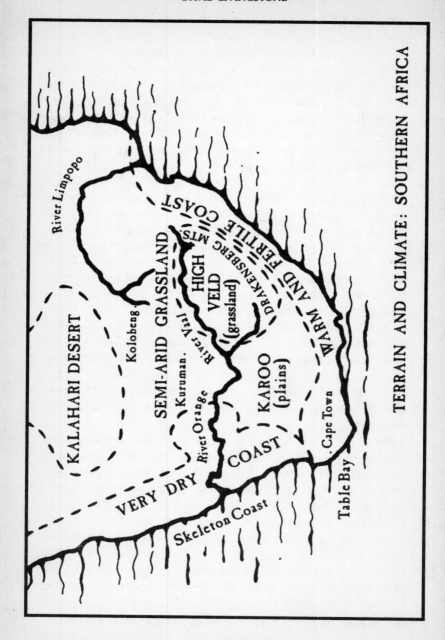

TERRAIN AND CLIMATE: SOUTHERN AFRICA

River Limpopo

KALAHARI DESERT

SEMI-ARID GRASSLAND

Kolobeng.

Kuruman.

River Vaal

River Orange

HIGH VELD (grassland)

DRAKENSBERG MTS.

FERTILE COAST

WARM AND

KAROO (plains)

.Cape Town

COAST

VERY DRY

Skeleton Coast

Table Bay

tactics of Tshaka, and gain authority over other disaffected groups of Nguni who were heading north.[4]

The first disaffected groups to cross over the dry, red earth of Transorangia into the High Veldt were little more than bandits. Mary remembered being bundled out of bed in the small hours, wrapped in a *kaross* or skin cloak and sent off by her mother in a wagon to Griqua Town, 90 miles to the south. Sometimes (if Robert were away, as he often was) she would see Mma-Mary go out in her nightgown to rally the people of Kuruman to face the invaders.[5]

In 1823 three groups, set on the move by the depredations of the Nguni, reached the very gates. They were led by a woman warrior, Manthatitsi, wielding an axe. This time Robert Moffat was there, and, looking very tall next to the courageous but diminutive commandant from Griqua Town, rode out coolly between the battle lines. His courage won the respect of both sides. Not only was Kuruman saved, but Moffat also won a hearing for the gospel from the Tswana.[6]

Mzilikaze, as overlord of the renegade Nguni, heard of this encounter between his enemy, Manthatitsi, and Moffat. Moffat was able to visit Mzilikaze and became his personal friend. This relationship had a mellowing effect on Mzilikaze and in time Robert was able to exercise a moderating influence. Moffat's family (and those connected closely with them) were able to travel in safety without interference from Mzilikaze's followers.

When they were still 150 miles from Kuruman, and the column of ox wagons was fording the Vaal (or Yellow) River, Mary noticed a cloud of dust in the distance. Zizagging over the veldt, avoiding the thorn trees but pressing on towards the wagon train, was a lone horseman. As he grew closer, she could make out the figure of a man of average height who held himself straight up in the saddle. His shoulders were well set. When he reined in, and removed his riding-hat, she could see that his head was unusually large but well-proportioned, the features strong and rugged. His chin and mouth were heavy and broad, his hair brown and eyebrows bushy.

Mary's little brother, John, thought the man's made-up suit

a bit odd, but nobody else minded. The whole family was pleased to see David. Mary had met him only briefly in London, when he had come to ask her parents questions about Africa. Now he was answering *their* questions.

During the rest of the day, Robert Moffat found out from Livingston the situation in the Tswana area and the state of the new work among the Kgatla. The tribesmen were moving nearer the centre where the missionaries were building with Mebalwe, and his wife Mapoleane. Ashton and Inglis, the newcomers, were also interested to hear of progress. It seemed to David, however, that Ashton was sympathetic towards the idea of working with African evangelists. He was pleasantly surprised to discover that Robert Moffat (contrary to reports) was quite positive too. 'He is not, as I was informed by some who knew him, in the least opposed to Native agency. He is a warm friend to them, but his character has been sadly traduced by many who ought to have known better. He told me the reason of the slander brought against him was his having got an unworthy character turned out of that office.'[7]

It was encouraging for David to meet again this man who had made the desert 'blossom like a rose' at Kuruman by finding in some caves nearby a never-failing spring, called the Eye of Kuruman. Moffat had created a great fountain with irrigated gardens and brought from a distance the timbers to build a church and stockade.

Moffat wanted to know what the new mission centre was called. Livingston explained that the Kgatla had named it Mabotsa after one of the surrounding hills. Moffat, of course, knew the meaning: *mabotsa* is the SeTswana word for marriage feast.

David got the chance to chat with the ladies later on. Mma-Mary would never come out of the wagon with her girls until the end of a day's stage of eight to twelve hours. First the oxen were 'spanned out' or unyoked, then the men would get the camp fire lit and put on the kettles. Next the women would come down from the wagons, drink coffee, cook supper and sing hymns with the men around the fire.[8]

Mary noticed that David's eyes shone with an unusual brilliance. To one who had been cooped up in the humid atmosphere of a mill for twelve hours a day from the age of ten until the end of adolescence, to be under the stars was exhilarating. The sun had made his complexion darker than Mary remembered – more like hers, in fact. There was plenty of time to get re-acquainted, for the wagons moved slowly (about 3½ miles an hour) so that there was a whole week of these evenings before Kuruman came into view.

David was struck by the pint-sized, black-haired daughter of the Moffats. At twenty-three, she was a sturdy traveller, somehow retaining a fresh and neat appearance even after hours on the trek. He decided that 'Mary was the best spoke in the wheel'.[9] She had, after all, been riding ox wagons since the age of three.[10] Her matter-of-factness and practical nature appealed to Livingston. She did not show her feelings easily, but then neither did he. This facet of her character no doubt sprang from the very source of his admiration for her, that she was so African, and had been treated as such by the colonists of Salem and Graham's Town.

By the time the column of wagons rumbled into Kuruman, to be greeted by many of the Tswana with tears of joy, Livingston knew that he had a special affection for Mary. He noticed particularly how fond of her the African children were; her accent reflected theirs perfectly. David knew that his voice still sounded foreign to the Tswana, yet he was not treated as a foreigner by the people of Kuruman, who were glad to see him 'bring back' the Moffats. The family had been away for nigh on five years; the Tswana had thought they would never return. David was struck by the sight of an emotional reunion between Robert Moffat and a Bushman. 'One poor Bushman who has been brought up by him wept aloud when he approached him; and as I had gone to meet [Moffat], I recieved [sic] many thanks for bringing him. They had believed he should never return.'[11]

Returning to Mabotsa, Livingston was soon busy working on the irrigation ditch with the Kgatla. He found them so deterred, however, by the lions prowling in the vicinity that he felt the only way to counteract this fear was to encourage the Kgatla to kill one.

So it was that his tartan-jacketed figure could be seen standing on a low rise under the hot afternoon sun. He was stooped over a smoking gun, struggling to reload. As he was ramming a bullet down the second barrel, he caught sight too late of a huge tawny shape hurtling through the air.

Starting, he turned half round just as the lion hit his shoulder, spinning him around. They crashed to the ground together, the lion growling horribly close to his ear. The enraged beast shook its prey violently.

Eleven infected teeth sank into the upper arm, crunching the bone into splinters. Yet there was no pain, no feeling of fear; the shock of impact had numbed his senses. There was only the crushing weight of a massive paw holding down his head.

Twisting round to free himself from the load, he looked up at the lion's eyes and saw them fixed on his African friend. From 10 metres, the African aimed his flint gun and fired, but the spark failed to ignite the charge. Quickly, he squeezed the trigger again.

Round the corner of the hill came a crowd of Kgatla tribesmen; they had tried to encircle the lion, but it had broken through. Now they were confronted with the sight of their quarry turned hunter. Leaping on the rifleman, as the flint gun again misfired, the lion bit him on the thigh.

A hunter ran forward, lunging with his spear at the lion's flank. Whirling round, the animal caught his assailant by the shoulder. The onlookers held their breath, expecting the *coup de grâce*. Poised over the prone bodies of its prey, the beast suddenly crumpled.

'He is shot, he is shot!' the cry went up. 'He has been shot by another man too; let us go to him!'[12] shouted others. The Kgatla surged forward, converging on the spot where the three casualties lay.

Carefully, they carried them to their huts: Mebalwe, who was the man with the flint gun, to his wife Mapoleane; the spearman, to his friends; and the Scot to his lodgings with the carpenter-builder and his wife, Mr and Mrs Rogers Edwards. There he had to give instructions, through a mist of pain that grew more intense as the shock wore off, on how to disinfect his wounds and set his arm in a splint.

The next day, the Kgatla made a huge bonfire over the carcass of the lion. By this they hoped to take the 'charm' out of it which they supposed had stimulated the lion and its troop to attack their cattle herds in broad daylight. This was unheard of, and made them believe themselves to be 'given' by the curse of a neighbouring tribe into the power of the lions. That is, they had believed it until David had encouraged them to kill a lion.

The incident gave him pause for thought. Mr and Mrs Edwards, who had been 'kind to a fault'[13] to the bachelor Scot while he was in their house at Kuruman, now found it more difficult to look after him as a lodger with serious wounds. Forced to rest until the splintered fragments of bone could heal up, he chafed at his confinement.

It didn't help his frustration to be forced to watch fleas dancing a reel across his sheets. He couldn't help but contrast the lackadaisical housekeeping of his hosts with the hygienic if miniscule home back in Blantyre, where he had always had clean linen. Seeing that his convalescence was inconvenient to the Edwardses, he began to wish for a household of his own.

David's family had already paired him off once mistakenly. 'So you thought I was married, did you?' he had chided his sisters, Janet and Agnes, seventeen months previously. 'I am not afflicted in that way yet.'[14] But Mary had got under his skin, and as he slowly recovered from the lion attack (which had happened so soon after his return from Kuruman in January 1844), he had plenty of opportunity to reconsider his views on matrimony.

David's arm healed steadily, probably because his tartan jacket had wiped all trace of virus from the lion's teeth before they sank in. As soon as he was fit enough to move about, Livingston tumbled into a wagon, without so much as a clean shirt to change into. In 'spanning in' the oxen once again, he was following the example of Mebalwe, his fellow worker who had helped to save him from the lion.

Mebalwe had gone off with Edwards on a tour of villages to the east. In June 1844 David too set out, having written to the

London Missionary Society that he was going to contact villages north-east of Mabotsa, to the east and north of the Marico River.[15] But he was still thinking of Mary, and somehow contrived to pass through Kuruman by the end of the month, even though it was to the south-west of Mabotsa – in the opposite direction.

Just catching glimpses of Mary while on the move was getting too tantalizing. David finally arranged a proper visit to Kuruman in July, lasting three weeks. Without waiting more than one week, he sent her a confidential note.

Kuruman 15th July 1844

My Dear Miss Moffat

You may feel a little surprised at the liberty I take in addressing you, and the more especially as the appellation with which I commence implies something of familiarity more than may be agreable [sic] from a stranger. But having felt a growing affection for you ever since we met, and you having been familiar to my thoughts in consequence, I cannot help now first speaking as I feel.

I have a strong desire to become better acquainted with you than merely seeing you moving about enables me to be. And the object of this note is to ask whether you will object to it or not. May I hope for a candid statement even though you decline acquaintanceship? I won't think the less of you if you only let me know that your objections are conscientious ones. And if you have none let it be between ourselves for the present. And I solemnly assure you there will be no insincerity on my part.

I write instead of speaking in order that you may not answer without having had some time to think. And I hope whatever the result may be we shall both in all our future conduct seek the glory of Him whom we profess to follow. You may answer by pen or otherwise, whichever is most agreable. I hope you will answer and not suspect that I am trifling for

I am yours sincerely

David Livingston.

David received the answer he hoped for, and committed himself to preparing an independent household. He laboured with his own hands to build a house, despite the limited mobility of his left arm. The bone had been damaged and a false joint developed which would not allow him to lift anything above the level of the shoulder.

As David and Mary made their plans for their first home, the only cloud that appeared on the horizon came in the form of a note from Mrs Edwards. Her husband, she said, had felt aggrieved ever since a disagreement broke out between herself and Mapoleane, wife of the African worker, Mebalwe.

Mapoleane had the impression that, following a quarrel between herself and Mrs Edwards over some meat, Mr Edwards had banned her from communion. David, without knowing the details of the case, thought that Mr Edwards had only meant to rebuke Mapoleane and not to exclude her. Talking with Mapoleane, Livingston found that she had apologized twice to Mrs Edwards for using strong words and also explained the situation to those who had overheard their quarrel. As Mr Edwards did not want to speak directly with Mapoleane about it, David 'warned her to be more circumspect in future' and invited her to take communion again.[17]

The incident seemed trivial enough to Livingston, and Edwards made no allusion to it himself. Feeling a slight uneasiness, however, David told Mary about the quarrel. 'I hope as little of that will occur to us as can be,' he wrote; '... you are as dear to me as ever, & will be so long as our lives are spared.'[18]

3
A tale of three cities

On a South African midsummer day, 9 January 1845, David and Mary were married at Kuruman, amid vigorous and vibrant choruses of praise rising up to the thatched roof of the church. The air was 'heavy with the scent of syringa, the mimosa golden in the hard, bright sunlight'[1] as they stepped outside to receive the congratulations of their Tswana friends.

Their homecoming to Mabotsa, however, was anything but congratulatory. The young couple had hardly had time to move in when David was sharply criticized by his colleague, Rogers Edwards. It seemed that he had been holding his feelings in check for months. Edwards made it clear, however, that he considered Mebalwe and Mapoleane to be unofficial workers, since he had not agreed to Livingston's hiring them. He felt that the Scot had failed to defer to his seniority and had taken too much credit for founding the mission centre.

Livingston had mentioned Edwards's role in founding the centre in a letter to LMS Director, Arthur Tidman.[2] In publishing an extract of this letter, however, the LMS editor mentioned only the role of 'our intrepid Missionary, Mr. Livingston' in his foreword.[3] Evidently Edwards had taken offence, but had not thought to ask his colleague what he had originally written. He also accused him of pinching a plot in the gardens. David had, in fact, come to a private arrangement with Mebalwe and a convert from Kuruman called Kobay-upudi, by which all three of them had moved their gardens.[4]

Sadly, it all reflected a failure of communication between the two men: the taciturn Englishman, bending over backwards in an attempt to hide his true feelings for the sake of appearances; the rather brusque Scotsman, unable to understand a man who was not 'honest outspoken' as he was. 'You never speak out,' Livingston complained to Edwards, 'notwithstanding all your boasts of honesty, unless your temper boils over & compels you.'[5] Yet he himself had not told Edwards 'the principal reason' for moving his garden, which was that Edwards 'had spoiled the lower part of the water ditch'.[6]

Perhaps, underneath it all, Edwards felt insecure because of Livingston's close rapport with the Tswana, made even more intimate with the arrival of his African-born bride. For Livingston, the incident marked the beginning of a pattern that can be seen throughout his career, of having a much better working relationship with Africans than with Europeans.

David and Mary resolved to uproot themselves from Mabotsa. Mebalwe and Mapoleane asked to go with them.[7] They also planned to take Paul, who had become a Christian under the ministry of Robert Moffat, and his family.

This decision, although hastened by circumstances, was not a sudden one. Livingston was keen to take the gospel to a tribe no-one else had worked with. Less than three weeks after his wedding, while still at Kuruman, David had written, 'At Mabotsa matters go on pretty well. But I don't expect to remain there long. The sphere is too small for two missionaries. As I am the younger I propose to go on to … either Bubi or Sechele.'[8] As long ago as 1843 he had met with Sechele. As the most powerful chief of the Kwena people, he had been angry with David for fraternizing with Bubi's splinter group.

Sechele was a remarkable man. Robert Moffat had found no evidence that, before he came to the Tswana, they had had any idea of relating to an eternal God. 'No fragments remain of former days, as mementoes to the present generation, that their ancestors ever loved, served, or reverenced a being greater than man.'[9] Sechele had met Moffat when the latter was a young man. The fact that he had taken in little from the encounter might well have been due to the fact that Moffat was still learning SeTswana. Certainly, when Livingston came to discuss the gospel with Sechele in 1843, the chief had asked 'striking' questions, such as this:

'Since it is true that all who die unforgiven are lost forever, why did your nation not come to tell us of it before now? My ancestors are all gone, & none of them knew anything of what you tell me. How is this?' (I thought immediately of the guilt of the church, but did not confess.) I told him multitudes in our own country were, like himself, so much in love with their sins my ancestors had spent a great deal of time in trying to persuade them, and yet after all many of them by refusing were lost. We now wish to tell all the world about a Saviour, and if men did not believe the guilt would be entirely theirs.[10]

David now contacted Sechele at his town of Tshonuane, 40 miles north of Mabotsa. Sechele made the most of David's visits. The chief 'acquired a perfect knowledge of the alphabet, large small & mixed, in two days.'[11] He invited David's team to move to Tshonuane.

Mary kept busy teaching children at Mabotsa while David built their second home. He wrote to her father:

The house is 64 feet by 20, the kitchen 8 feet, a lean-to at one end. As the wall will be much lower than that of the house, it will be little more trouble than the verandah would. Nasty water, but I shall make a well. There is one already made by some animal, but it needs deepening. The water in it is excellent. I have remedies for everything in my head, but alas, they all need time. Hope however is a blessed thing. We enjoy the future in the present.[12]

Mary's sister Ann came to visit her from Kuruman with a maid and two wagon boys. On the way back from Mabotsa they had to stop in the hills where the lions were still lurking. An attack in the twilight dispatched one of their oxen, and Ann had to hide in the wagon all night listening to the lion chewing bones.[13]

Livingston came back to Mabotsa when Mary was due to have a baby. Robert was born in December 1845, and from then on Mary was called 'Mma-Robert'.

When Mary moved to Tshonuane, an unforeseen period of drought began which made it difficult for the Kwena to cultivate the land. Worse still was the discovery of the attitude of the Boers to the east. In February 1846 a message arrived from them asking for 'an explanation of our intentions' and hinting 'that they had resolved to come and deprive Sechele of his firearms'.[14]

Livingston found their commandant Potgieter to be 'a well-informed man' and convinced him that action against the Kwena 'would break up our Mission, and that he ought to delay the execution of the orders of [the Boer] Council untill [sic] I should lay the whole matter before it. This I did by letter, and likewise stated my intention of introducing the gospel amongst the Eastern tribes by means of native agents.'[15]

Threats from the east and drought at Tshonuane were not enough to deter Mrs Moffat from coming to the rescue. 'Mma-Mary' trekked up from Kuruman in September 1846. As well as news from there she brought with her food to make up for the dried-up state of David and Mary's garden. She found that their next baby was on the way. Robert was by now nine months old. A family conference ensued, in which they agreed that it would be best for the new baby to be born at Kuruman.

As soon as the mission team was established at Tshonuane they set to work on building a school, 15m x 6m, which was completed 'in less than two months'. Paul was put in charge of the teaching programme.[16] By November 1846 he had got it underway with the assistance of his son, Isak. Mary was now able to travel with David and Mebalwe on a six-week survey of the country to the east of the mission centre.[17]

On their way back they visited Commandant Potgieter and were told that his council had received Livingston's representations favourably. This encouraged them to call on Mokgatle, chief of a Tswana tribe about 90 miles east-south-east of Tshonuane, who had asked to have an African Christian teacher. Mokgatle confirmed to them that he would be happy to have Paul placed with him.[18] However, a Boer who lived near the chief had twice demanded to know 'why he had not killed "that missionary" according to previous instructions'. Mokgatle had answered, 'I avoid that which you avoid. I took him to your chief, and he did not kill him.' Livingston felt he could not leave Paul in such a situation without first going to see the Boer to try to turn him from his 'enmity'. Yet he could not go then as they had been away from home for over two months.[19]

It seemed that neither Paul nor Mebalwe would be able to survive in the Transvaal without special protection. The Boers wanted cattle and were competing for the same resources as surrounding African tribes. They acted as a rather unruly white tribe, often unwilling to defer even to their own council and commandant. Following 'a misunderstanding', some of the Boers ordered three African tribes to help them attack Moletsi, chief of one of the Kwena tribes. 'These formed a living bulwark in front of one hundred mounted whites. The ill-fated tribe was driven back by the battle axes of their own countrymen ... On asking ... why they had been so foolish as to assist in the murder of their countrymen, their reply was that they feared that, had they refused to go, they themselves would have been attacked.'[20]

David and Mary took Robert (in the troublesome process of teething) and left Tshonuane for Kuruman at the beginning of March 1847. On 8 March David was at Dikgatlhong, 100 miles south-east of Kuruman, to attend the fourth meeting of the LMS District Committee. It had so far refused to follow up the idea dear to David's heart of promoting and training African evangelists and teachers.

Robert Moffat had personally opposed the idea when it had been proposed in 1845. Now, however, he seconded a new motion put forward by his son-in-law. This called on all overseers of churches in the south to report the names of African members whom they could recommend for missionary service further north. At the same time missionaries in the north were to find out the feasibility of working with tribes troubled by the Boers.[21]

Livingston was encouraged to see the motion passed unanimously, but he was under no illusions about the mixed feelings of his older colleagues on the subject of a training institute for African evangelists. He felt, however, that William Ashton, who had come to Kuruman from England with the Moffats in 1843, would make a good tutor for African agents. The Directors of the LMS in London were as keen as David to promote this scheme and appointed Ashton to the task.[22]

Mary and David's second child was born at Kuruman early in May 1847. They named the girl after David's mother, Agnes, and David told her in a letter of 4 May: 'Have been favoured with a little girl, name Agnes; not a pretty name, but it is that of My dear Mother. All doing well. Thanks to God.'[23] The news of the delivery was added as a postscript at the head of a letter about the family (Robert had finished teething). The melancholy idea that he would not see his mother again made David reminisce about her.

I often remember you, how you used to keep us all cozie and clean. I remember you often assisted me, my dear Mother, to put on my clothes in dark cold winter mornings, and later in life made a good breakfast for me on Monday mornings before I went away down to [medical] College. A thousand things rise up in my memory when I think of you. May God bless you. Sometimes when I see a word in Scotch I remember it as it came from your mouth.[24]

It was not only Gaelic that attracted David's attention. On the way back to Tshonuane he kept his ears open as always for SeTswana words that were new to him. He now had a special motive for recording them. On the banks of the Ngotwane River, a tributary of the Limpopo which he had to cross beyond Mabotsa, David found time for a letter to his father, Neil. He told him of his plan to write a new grammar of the SeTswana language.[25] All previous attempts had been based on classical or Indo-European grammars. Livingston intended to analyse SeTswana on its own terms, and by so doing was to produce a method much closer to modern versions.[26]

Soon after their return to Tshonuane, Livingston proposed moving from that site to a healthier one. Chief Sechele agreed immediately. Although there had been limited success in growing African corn and pumpkins, the water had grown more and more brackish. About 40 miles north-west of Tshonuane, a free-flowing stream called the Kolobeng came out of the mass of hills. This was chosen as the new site. Before the middle of August 1847 David and Mebalwe were at work there building huts, Mebalwe as 'thatcher' and Livingston as 'architect'.[27] The Kwena were completely unused to making anything square-shaped; all their huts were round and roomless. To Mebalwe, however, the idea of making them square got less mysterious as he watched Livingston at work.

Paul and his family had stayed behind at Tshonuane to protect Mma-Robert and the children. This did not prevent a feeling of insecurity in an increasingly deserted place. 'Mary feels her situation among the ruins a little dreary, & no wonder, for she writes me yesterday that the lions are resuming possession & walk round our house at night.' To come to Kolobeng too soon, however, would not be so very soothing. 'Kolobeng means "the haunt of the wild boar", but it seems to have been the haunt of everything else. Hyaeanas [sic] abound exceedingly, buffaloes in immense herds, and zebras quite tame in the thickly wooded country around. Elephants too have left their traces on what will, we hope, for the future only contain marks of the "pleasant haunts of men".'[28]

Noting, perhaps, that lions were not on the list, Mary and the children joined David in temporary accommodation at Kolobeng in September 1847. One consolation for the hazards of hyenas was the beauty of their surroundings. A panoramic view of low, rounded hills rising out of rolling plains pleased the eye, and the sound of rushing water delighted the ear. The family now enjoyed 'tolerable health, but the setting in of the hot season seems to try our stamina. Mary is troubled with shooting pains in the chest.'[29]

As soon as the huts were finished, David turned his attention to a different kind of architecture. 'Our plan was to get up temporary houses & a temporary meeting house as soon as possible, in order that teaching might go on regularly during the time we should be occupied in making gardens.'[30] This plan took priority over building permanent housing, not only in David's mind but also in Chief Sechele's.

'The chief without any suggestion from me told me it was his desire to build a house for God, that I should be at no expense whatever with it. He even thought that we should do nothing in the work, but to this latter we objected, as it was for the work of the God of all. I think sometimes that he expects God will bless him for his good work, yet he expresses himself occasionally quite in the orthodox style.'[31]

Sechele thought of building 'a very fine house', but was advised to opt for speed and simplicity. A meeting-place 'of pole and reed' was built in double-quick time. 'He employed all the males in cutting reed, & sent them a good distance to select the straightest wood they could find. We began it on Saturday morning & met in the walls on Sunday. Many hands make light work. Here it was not light work to prevent them from doing too much.'[32]

David and Mary decided to hold a public service in the church three nights a week, with the help of Paul and Mebalwe. Mebalwe was a hard worker and had greater firmness of character than Paul; but Paul was the better speaker, and became something of an African theologian in his own right. 'We cannot part with Mebalwe. He works so hard he is our right hand. Paul has never been accustomed to work, but is the best theologian by far.'[33]

Now that the 'house for God' was built, however, Sechele felt free to propose 'an exchange of work'. The essential job of digging a watercourse was due to begin in October, and the mission team was ready to join in. Sechele, however, suggested that his people would dig the canal if the mission team would build him a European house. David agreed. 'We are glad to do this, for we are but few in number,' he wrote to his father-in-law.[34]

As it turned out, once they had built the chief's house he made that, too, a house for God. '[October] 14. Sechele sent his brother today with the request that I should give him assistance to establish an evening prayer meeting in his house … Paul & I began, & we have arranged that one of us go every evening. Always when affected his eyes glisten. We wish it may be the beginning of conversion. His eyes glisten tonight.'[35]

David used to come into the town to talk after sunset. He would speak to anyone in the tribe who was interested, on general, sometimes scientific, subjects using pictures and specimens. A favourite technique was the magic lantern, the slide projector of the day.

Sechele was a fluent speaker and, like many African leaders, an effective orator. Powerful words held a great attraction for him. Now every time he saw the Scot coming into town he pressed him to hear some chapters of the Bible.

Livingston had given him a Scripture portion which Moffat had recently published at Kuruman. It was a SeTswana translation of Proverbs, Ecclesiastes and Isaiah. David was aware of the special virtues of Moffat's translation of Isaiah. 'Isaiah is certainly an improvement on Proverbs,' he told his father-in-law. '[It] has many new words, at least new to me.'[36] It was from the book of Isaiah that the chief especially loved to read aloud.

Mary meanwhile held Bible studies with Sechele's five wives, and some of them proved to be attentive scholars. In November David was able to write, 'The prayer meeting in Sechele's house is usually well attended. I make a few remarks on the portion read. He rings a small bell for all within hearing to come.'[37]

If the meetings at the chief's house were encouraging, the effects of the climate reminded them that they really needed a house of their own. It was not too healthy living 'in a little hut through which the wind blew our candles into glorious icicles (as the poet would say) by night, and in which crowds of flies continually settled on the eyes of our poor little brats by day.'[38]

Before starting work on their third house in succession, however, David felt that he needed a change. Early in February 1848 he set out with Paul and his son, Isak, on a journey among the eastern tribes, 'one object of which is to recruit & remove the languor of body & mind which affected me before I begin the erection of a permanent dwelling'.[39]

If it was excitement he was looking for, he certainly found it. On the return journey,

it was necessary to cross a dry river, the banks of which were very steep. Paul & I jumped down to look for a ford, the waggon [*sic*] continuing its course along the bank abreast of us. We came into a part with grass longer than ourselves & full of game paths. I was thinking, 'this is a very lionlike place', when Paul proposed mounting the waggon ... I turned my face waggonwards, and when within 20 paces of it found a female black rhinoceros, having just calved ... The beast, enclosed by us & the waggon, had its attention providentially directed towards the latter, & Paul & I ran into a rut. The animal made a furious attack on the waggon. Its horn glanced on a spoke & split it up as if it had been a boiled carrot. The felloe split too with the shock ... [Isak] was in the waggon & thinks he shot the beast, but it went away with its little red calf. We heard its snorting as we stood in the rut, & our guns being in the waggon expected every moment to be visited, but we were down the wind.[40]

During the journey they set up a temporary hut at Mokgatle's, preparatory to starting a school there. They also took a detour to meet a Boer farmer, Johannes Pretorius, to canvass his support for the project. He 'had gone to cut wood, but his wife was very kind. Pressed us to remain, & we should have complied, but we saw 4 Mapela children in the house, stolen slaves. My heart grew sick & I left.'

David was prepared to put Pretorius's support at risk for the sake of freeing African children from forced labour. 'My people by my advice tried to steal them by telling them where we should spend Sunday. They said they had often run away, but [Mokgatle] caught them & returned them to their owners.'[41]

After this reconnaissance David felt able to get down to the work on the new stone house. Apart from the doorframes, iron and nails available at Tshonuane, the Scot had to have all the materials specially made. Two Boers sawed beams, and a team of nine Kwena, one of whom had learnt the craft at Kuruman, made bricks for the interior walls. David also got the window ready.

By 23 March an old wagon arrived with presents from the Moffats of tree seeds and fruit. The apples were 'a great treat' for all the family. David was already growing ginger and an olive tree. The most successful experiment, however, had been with potatoes; a large crop was harvested. With the old wagon now available ('we do not like to spoil the new one'), they were able to fetch the roof for the new house.[42]

Now that winter was upon them, coughs and colds prompted the Livingstons to move from the hut into their new home on 4 July 1848, even though David was still making doors. He fitted temporary ones, but these had their drawbacks. One night a hyena came 'and took away a buffalo's skin from the door. Mary wanted me to go and see whether the room door were fastened, but ... I advised her to take a fork in her hand and go herself, as I was too comfortably situated to do anything of the sort.'[43]

Mary was enterprising enough to rise to the challenge. She knew how to adapt to their conditions. She had learnt to make soap out of ash, a process that could take up to six weeks. All she had to bake in was 'a flat-bottomed pot', which she heated 'by putting coals on the lid as well as under'. This method was, however, improved on by putting local materials to maximum use. 'We had an ant hill near, so having made an iron door we made a large hole in the ant hill and put on the door, and there we had a good oven in a twinkling.'[44]

They would get up early, have family worship and breakfast, and from seven until eleven teach both adults and teenagers. David would then work as a smith, carpenter or gardener until lunchtime. After siesta in the afternoon, sixty to eighty young Kwena came to Mary's infant school. 'The Native children are fond of her,' David wrote to his brother Charles in America, 'and maybe, so am I.'[45] David's one regret was that he was too busy during the day, and too tired at night, to play with Robert and Agnes.[46]

4

Sechele's decision, David's dilemma

The news that Sechele had actively encouraged the building of a school and meeting-house in his town spread far and wide. Perhaps the most famous chief who tried to turn him away from his chosen path was Moshesh, a renowned general and shrewd diplomatist who was to found the Sotho federation of tribes.[1]

Sechele had sent men to Moshesh with *karosses* to buy a horse. Moshesh gave them two horses, and ten head of cattle. He sent a private message to Sechele, offering him guns and ammunition, with this rider:

> Tell him to allow his people to believe if they like, but he (Sechele) must never believe. 'I am a king ... & I won't put myself under the authority of another (*viz.* God); I have my kingdom as well as He, & people would laugh at me if I believed & put myself under the power of another. Tell Sechele that.'

Sechele told David, 'I treated [his message] with disdain, because he did not know what he was saying, for he said that God is a chief like himself.'[2] Far from taking Moshesh's advice, Sechele 'opened his mind' to Livingston.

> Sunday 6th August [1848]. Sechele remained as a spectator at the celebration of the Lord's supper, and when we retired he asked me how he ought to act in reference to his superfluous wives, as he greatly desired to conform to the will of Christ, be baptized, and observe his ordinance. Advised him to do according to what he saw was written in God's book, but to treat them gently, for they had sinned in ignorance and if driven away harshly might be lost eternally.[3]

Sechele went and spoke to his wives, each of whom had their own individual huts arranged around his. Assuring them that they had not offended him in any way, he explained that his conscience did not allow him to live with more than one wife.

Next day an eerie silence descended on the town. The entire tribe stopped work and the women stayed at home instead of going to the gardens. Two of Sechele's wives were daughters of his underchiefs, who had helped him succeed to the chieftainship after his father had been murdered. Fearing that they had lost their hold over their chief, they held *pitsos* or tribal assemblies at night to try to intimidate him.[4]

Many of the men cursed their chief – all the more bitterly since they knew he would no longer shoot those who showed him disrespect, as he had done in times past. Sechele was taken aback by their vehemence. 'Next morning he resolved to call the people together generally and explain his conduct, and say if they wished to kill him to do so immediately.'[5]

David, meanwhile, went to see Mma-Kgari, who had become Sechele's wife by running off with him when he was visiting her first husband, Sebego.[6] Mma-Kgari had become one of Mary's best Bible students.

> Poor thing, she was melted in tears, could not speak but with a choking voice. Offered me back her book, 'as she must now go where there is no word of God'. Wished that they could have remained in the town that they too might be saved, but [Mma-Kgari] has no relations. She was much loved and worthy of it. We shall not cease to pray that she may be saved.[7]

At the next meeting of the tribe Sechele's chief headman failed to sway the men by saying that he too would send away his wives. The men asked the chief not to send the women away even if they were no longer to be his wives.

Sechele did decide to allow one young mother who had no other home to stay in her hut. His senior wife, Mma-Sebele, remained with him, but the other three he sent back to their families, each with a new set of clothes and all their property. David and Mary expected a backlash, but found that most of the Kwena bore them no ill will personally.

> Opposition exists, but not towards us. It manifests itself in hatred to the gospel. Some woman or other wished the lion which bit me were here to finish me. But all are civil. We cannot detect a particle of difference in the conduct of the mass of the people towards us, which is a cause for gratitude ... The children are returning to the schools, & the meetings are improving.[8]

Sechele asked to have his second son by Mma-Sebele baptized with him. He intended to rename him Setefano, or Stephen, indicating that Sechele wanted his youngest child to be, like him, 'the first follower of Jesus in this country'.[9] During the build-up to the baptismal service rumours spread that those who became Christians were made to 'drink the brains of men'.[10] When the day of baptism came, on 1 October 1848, onlookers were genuinely surprised that only water was used. 'I expected to see something green in it,' said one man to Livingston.[11] If the audience were pleasantly surprised about the baptism, David was unpleasantly surprised to discover what they thought of the Lord's Supper, which until then had been held only in private. 'Discovered in the evening that a horridly Satanic idea had long been promulgated among the people generally "that the Lord's supper was a scene of impurity".'[12]

At his baptism Sechele renounced not only polygamy, but also his power and prestige as rain-doctor of the tribe. This role had involved him in a kind of sympathetic magic whereby the making up of potions or medicines would, with the use of certain rituals, command the clouds. This second renunciation made Sechele's position doubly difficult. 'He endures a good deal of trial from his people at present. We have no rain, one good shower alone this year, while all around us the rains have been abundant.'

As early as March 1847 Livingston had noticed that the

ground was not holding the moisture from the rain, and now the river itself was drying up. 'Last year at this time we could not make our watercourse contain its water, but two dry seasons following each other seems too much for it.' The merry sound of the midnight frogs – music to the ears of any traveller, as they croaked only near water – died away.

Forgetting that the drought had begun before Sechele's decision, the people blamed this trouble on the gospel. 'This is the fourth year of scarcity. [Yet the people say] They had always abundance of corn untill [sic] the Word came ... If the prince of the power of the air has no hand in it we feel unkindly towards the old rogue.'[13]

By January 1849 there was very little food left in the scorched gardens. The men therefore went away hunting, the women to collect locusts. Attendance at the school and the church dropped. As Kolobeng became more and more deserted, Chief Sechele considered moving 9 miles downriver to a place called Dimawe.

Livingston too pondered over his next move. The drop in attendance at the school and church caused by the drought concentrated his mind on the area to the east of him. Even this avenue of service, however, seemed to be blocked. In December 1848, when he was ready to send Paul to settle with Chief Mokgatle, the Boers 'made me aware of a strong undercurrent of opposition'. Anxious for Paul's sake, David called off the move to Mokgatle's 'until our arrangements at home were such as would admit of my spending a few months with him at the commencement'.[14]

This plan came to the ears of the local Boer commandant, Potgieter. When he realized that David and Paul really meant to settle with Mokgatle, and not just visit him, 'he suddenly altered his tone, and threatened in a most furious manner to send a commando against the tribe with which we meant to settle'. He claimed that Livingston was trying to take over the area for the English government.[15]

On a previous occasion when David had gone to appeal to Potgieter not to proceed against Sechele, the commandant had asked him to inform on the Kwena. At that time he had 'distinctly refused from being in any way connected' with the local Boer government, on the principle that the work he did for Christ he did under the authority of Christ. David reminded Potgieter of this and pointed out that by the same principle, he would hardly connect himself with the Cape government either. In saying this he was not being disingenuous; he disapproved of the Cape Colony's wars against the Xhosa (on their eastern border) as much as he disapproved of Boer attacks on the Tswana. He also put it to Potgieter that if he obstructed the work of the gospel 'by driving the people away, the blood of their souls would be required at his hand'. The commandant, taken aback, offered to accept Livingston's plan – if he would teach the Africans that the Boers were 'a superior race to them'![16]

Livingston and Paul pressed on with their preparations, but when they heard that some ministers of the Dutch Church were within travelling distance, David decided to seek their mediation. He found a delegation of their Synod at the farm of Gerrit Kruger, Boer commandant in the Magaliesberg district .

In the presence of their clergy the Boer commandants were very conciliatory. They promised to win over their followers to mission work if only Livingston would give them a month's grace to try their influence. To build a school at Mokgatle's now would be to force the issue. The Dutch ministers prevailed on Livingston to accept this compromise.

Potgieter later claimed that Livingston had left him in a hurry, without answering all his questions. Perhaps this was not surprising, since the last words Livingston heard from him were: 'If a deal of blood is shed you will fall in the midst of it, and I cannot protect you.' David and Paul took this to mean that the Boers intended to attack the very tribe they were about to visit.[17] This was the Tswana tribe of Chief Mmamogale, living about 35 miles east of Rustenburg. They sent him a warning and then returned to Kolobeng to help Mebalwe build his house.

Livingston was still unaware of undercurrents that were running in the Boers' minds in that encounter at Kruger's. As the previous year's newspapers had still not reached him from the Cape, he was unaware that the Boers had recently suffered a defeat at the hands of the English.

In February 1848 the British had annexed Transorangia and in July the Boers there had rebelled, backed by a force led by the Commandant-general of the Transvaal, Andries Pretorius. He was defeated at Boomplats on 29 August. The Governor of Cape Colony had then offered a reward of £2,000 for his arrest. This same Pretorius was present at Kruger's farm when Livingston made his sudden appearance there.

It is scarcely surprising then that the Boers suspected Livingston's motives. They knew that if his reports on their activities reached the Cape government they would be in trouble. Recent events had done nothing to dispel the memory of what happened when John Philip of the LMS communicated with the British Parliament (via Buxton in the 1820s) about their treatment of Africans. The subsequent ban on forced labour had set off the northward migration of the independent Boers.[18]

As soon as the Scot was out of the way Potgieter wrote to the LMS District Committee demanding that they withdraw Livingston. If they did not, the Boers would attack the Kwena and expel him by force.

Although Potgieter did not state this in his letter, he and all the Boers believed that Livingston himself had armed the Kwena, and would arm all other tribes in the vicinity through his African agents. Potgieter wrote to the LMS that Sechele not only possessed many guns but had 'even obtained possession of a cannon!'[19] The Boers could not tolerate the fact that Sechele, unlike other tribes in the area, was independent and might yet inspire other Africans under their sway to break free of their rule.

The Boers were ready to admit that the Kwena had never attacked the Boers, but after hearing of Sechele's travelling around with a long iron object they had convinced themselves that it was a cannon. In fact it was a long-legged cooking-pot lent him by Livingston!

David enjoyed the joke and wrote a satirical paper on it. Yet at Kruger's he had done nothing to disabuse the Boers of their exaggerated estimate of Sechele's armoury, put at 500 guns. He felt that this misinformation might act as a deterrent to a Boer attack. To Robert Moffat, however, he had confided that the Kwena did possess eighty guns, which he had seen them fire off into the air to scare cattle-raiders.[20]

Sechele had access to rifles from itinerant traders and other chiefs, such as Moshesh. He had no need to depend on the mission for them. Nevertheless, David did buy the site of his house from Sechele with a rifle, and he was prepared to mend the guns that the tribe possessed when necessary. Drought conditions had reached the point where the vegetables were burnt off the land; the tribe needed guns, above all, for getting meat. Livingston's references to a 'seven-barreled [sic] gun' which 'Sechele is very anxious to get'[21] are more obscure, but there is no evidence that such a weapon was ever delivered to the Kwena. If it had been, its purpose would have been deterrence, not attack.

> The tribe would never have enjoyed the gospel but for the firearms. The moral suasion of their presence here goes a great way with the Boers. I am thankful for it. No one has ever been killed by them; they are just like the painted guns you see in some ships and called by sailors 'Quakers'.[22]

In any case, the Scot saw no reason why the rifles should not be used in self-defence against the Boers. He was prepared to rebuke Sechele for any act of aggression on other tribes. He had disapproved of a raid Sechele made without his knowledge on Bubi's successor, Khake, and he successfully protested against an intended raid on the Ngwato of Sekgoma. Even though this earned him the curses of the Kaa, who had asked Sechele to attack Sekgoma on their behalf, the Kaa themselves eventually came to take refuge with Sechele since they had heard he had embraced the 'word of peace'.

Livingston was nevertheless perfectly ready to support Sechele in improving the defences of the town.[23] Indeed, as Boer threats increased and Livingston's exasperation with them grew, he told his brother Charles how he had stood up for the Kwena politically before the Boers, while the tribe armed itself for its own defence.

> The Boers or Dutch emigrants oppress these tribes and treat them almost as slaves. They would have contrived to do so to Sechele too, but I succeeded in freeing the [Kwena]. A considerable number of guns were purchased, and as this is the source of the power of the Boers over the other tribes they began to be afraid that the other tribes would follow his example.[24]

In these circumstances of gathering tension Livingston had to send his family out of harm's way while he considered where to move. 'My poor lady is away out crying all the road in the full belief that I shall not be seen by her again.'[25]

Another circumstance that had caused pain to Mary was a message brought to Kolobeng on 14 March by Sam, the son of Rogers Edwards. It informed them that a woman from the church at Kuruman had died in childbed – and that the man who had got her pregnant was Isak, the son of Paul. Paul had noticed that for some months Isak had not been speaking with him, but only with his mother. He had not known why.

Even this paled into insignificance in comparison with the revelation that Chief Sechele himself had fallen. Mma-Bantshang, the young mother who still lived in her hut next to the chief's, was pregnant again. Early in January 1849 Sechele had received a visit from a chief who would certainly have asked to see her (since her sister was his stepmother). Sechele accompanied him and at some point was alone with her. Neither she nor Sechele attempted to deny what had happened. 'The confession loosened all my bones,' wrote David. 'I felt as if I should sink to the earth, or run away, two very opposite states.'[26]

Sechele nevertheless averred, 'I shall never forsake Jesus or his word, we shall stand together before him.' He felt he had laid himself open to temptation by 'not making it known' before his baptism 'that any one who chose might have [Mma-

Bantshang]'. Since she had no parents it was essential to find her a husband.

David felt that Sechele was genuinely penitent. At a meeting with Paul and Mebalwe it was decided to suspend the chief from the church 'for a time, in order to see the fruits of repentance'. Sechele sent Mma-Bantshang away immediately. Despite the great difficulty of anyone accepting her, David saw that 'she must have a husband'.[27]

As for Sechele, 'after the first paroxysms of grief' had subsided the church began to hope that his state was very different from Isak's. There was no evidence that what the chief had done was part of a general pattern of behaviour, 'nor have we heard anything else, or anything to make us disbelieve his frequent declaration, "I shall never *tloboga* [give up] Jesus."' By contrast, Isak's true character had been known to the tribe for some time. When it was exposed he absconded, '& then laughed at his mother wife father &c running into the field after him'.[28]

Livingston could be forgiven for thinking that in mission work with the Tswana he had gone three steps forward, only to take two steps back. He wrote to the LMS:

There are no elements in the [Tswana] character calculated to encourage the belief that conversions will occur precipitously. They are truly *slow* of heart to believe. It is therefore imperatively necessary to endeavour to extend the *gospel to all* the surrounding tribes. This, although it involves a great many weary journeys [*sic*], is the only way which permits the rational hope that when the people do turn to the Lord it will be by groups.[29]

The aim, then, was to spread the net wider. The question was, where?

5
The lake and the desert

Looking around him, Livingston could see that the only way forward now was to the north. Kolobeng was cut off by the desert to the west and menaced by the Boers on the east. Such a position seemed to make further progress impossible. Perhaps if he had been patient, more good could have been done; Sechele offered to build David and Mebalwe a house for free if they would move with him to Dimawe. Yet even Sechele's own tribe had little faith that the new site would be any more fruitful. They would certainly still be out, hunting and gathering.

At this point two signs pointed Livingston northwards: a goal, and a friend to help him achieve it. Sechele told him of a great chief called Sebetwane, who had saved his life when a rebel faction had murdered his father. He had come to surround the Kwena town, but before doing so ordered his men to spare the dead chief's children. Sechele was clubbed down but not speared. Sebetwane took Sechele and his mother with him to the Ngwato. The Ngwato chief of that time offered to redeem Sechele. Sebetwane asked Sechele whether he would accompany him or go back.

Sechele's mother was footsore, so Sechele said to him, 'You see my mother is unable to go any farther, and though you offer to treat me kindly in your country I should like to live in my own land. Let me save my mother & return. I shall consider that kindness enough.' [Sebetwane] said, 'Very well, since you don't like to come to me, take these nine head of cattle & return.'[1]

Sebetwane, chief of the Kololo, ruled a vast region to the north of the Kalahari Desert. No foreigner had ever succeeded in crossing the Kalahari. Even the half-caste Griquas had repeatedly failed, running out of water. Yet on 1 May 1849

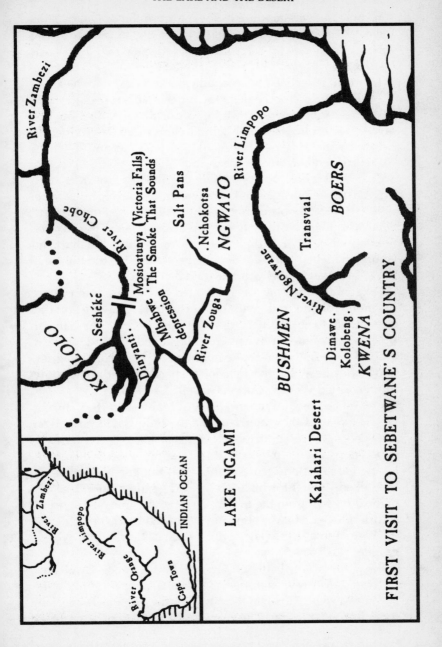

FIRST VISIT TO SEBETWANE'S COUNTRY

seven messengers reached Kolobeng from the Kalahari. They were a deputation sent by the chief of the Tawana to invite Livingston to visit him. Their chief lived, they said, by a great lake.[2]

Livingston declined to accept them as guides, since he knew the direct route over the desert was unsuitable for wagons. He had already been preparing to go north before the Tawana arrived. Their invitation only made him more determined to push on with the expedition as soon as possible, and so widen his field of endeavour for the gospel.

Two days after the coming of the Tawana, the Kaa tribe arrived at Kolobeng to take refuge from the Ngwato tribe, whose chief was oppressing them.[3] Sekgoma was the Ngwato chief who lived on the edge of the desert nearest the Kwena. Hearing that Livingston wanted to cross the Kalahari, he complained that the Scot would be 'killed by the sun and thirst' and that he, Sekgoma, would be blamed.[4]

Sekgoma's warning was motivated by his desire to protect his monopoly on trade with the north. In fact, Livingston did not intend to go right across the desert. Only the San, or Bushmen, could survive there. He aimed instead to skirt around the edge. Even so, he might easily have come to grief, had it not been for the help of a special friend: a wealthy hunter, called William Cotton Oswell.

Oswell had met David and Mary at Mabotsa in 1845, during the first year of their marriage. At the time David had given him good advice about which route to take on his hunting expedition. The Livingstons did not approve on principle of killing game for any reason other than hunger. Nevertheless, they liked Oswell for his friendly and gentle nature. He was on health leave from the Indian Civil Service, recovering from a bout of fever. He was slim and agile, and had won from the Bushmen the title of 'Tlaga' which means 'alert, wary' – like a gazelle, perhaps.[5]

Being financially better off than the Livingstons, Oswell and his friend, Murray, equipped the Kalahari expedition. David saw it as a chance to open the north for the gospel; Oswell was more interested in the lake that was reputed to exist north of the desert, where there was bound to be game. They recruited as guides some Hottentots, and a man named Ramatobi who had spent his youth in the southern part of the desert. He had fled from the Ngwato tribe of Sekgoma, who was going to try to stop the expedition getting through.

David said goodbye to Mary on 1 June 1849. She had had to give up her infant school,[6] as she now had a three-month-old baby to care for. Thomas Steele was born on 7 March at Kolobeng. The birth had gone very well, and been followed by an unwonted shower of rain. But the corn had by this time withered in the fields. The food supply was so scarce that Mary had agreed to go to Kuruman with the family while David was in the desert. Mary's younger sisters, Bessie and Jane, helped to look after Robert and Agnes. Mma-Mary, of course, was delighted to have them, although Robert may not have reacted well to his grandmother's strict discipline.[7]

Meanwhile, Livingston's party had found the way ahead cleared of helpful informants. Sekgoma had sent men to force the Bushmen out of their track. By doing this, the Ngwato chief hoped the party would not find enough water for themselves, their horses and their oxen; only the Bushmen knew where to dig for it. Nevertheless, they dug for water in dried-up river beds and managed to get beyond Sekgoma's sphere of influence.

Ramatobi, the guide, though very good in the earlier part of the journey, began to get lost, since the scenery was almost featureless. Oswell managed to find water – by mistake. Seeing in the distance what he took to be a lion, he galloped after it. In fact, as David realized, it was

a Bushwoman running away in a bent position, to escape observation ... She thought herself captured, and began to deliver up her poor little property, consisting of a few traps made of cords; but, when I explained that we only wanted water, and would pay her if she led us to it ... she walked briskly before our horses for eight miles, and showed us the water of Nchokotsa.[8]

There they found sufficient water to drink, although being far from fresh it could not entirely take away their ever-present sense of thirst. Moving on through a belt of trees, they were startled to see Oswell throw his hat up in the air. He gave such a shout that the Bushwoman and Kwena thought he had gone mad. In the soft light of the setting sun, both Oswell and Livingston could see a beautiful blue expanse.

The waves danced along above, and the shadows of the trees were vividly reflected in such an admirable manner, that the loose cattle, whose thirst had not been slaked sufficiently by the very brackish water of Nchokotsa, with the horses, dogs, and even the Hottentots, ran off towards the deceitful pools.[9]

What seemed to be a magnificent lake was merely a blue haze caused by the sunlight reflecting off incrustations of white lime; they had reached the first of the great Kalahari salt-pans, measuring 20 miles in circumference. In fact the real lake they were aiming for was still 300 miles further off; they were only half way.

On 4 July they set off again on horseback, frequently tantalized by mirages. Their perseverance was rewarded, when, to Livingston's great excitement, they came upon a real river – no illusion, but the River Zouga, lined with towering trees and running north-east. The result was that they were able to sail in the direction they wanted to go (since the river ran into the lake) using the dug-out canoes of the peaceable Yeyi tribe.

The Yeyi had never been known to take up arms, and relied on their knowledge of the river for protection. The Tswana called them *Koba*, or slaves, because of their pacifism, but Livingston saw them in a different light. 'We greatly admired the frank manly bearing of these inland sailors. Many of them spoke [SeTswana] fluently, and while the waggon [sic] went along the bank I greatly enjoyed following the windings of the river in one of their primitive craft and visiting their little villages among the reed.'[10] Though SeTswana was only their second language, they 'seemed to understand the message of mercy delivered better than any people to whom I have preached for the first time'.[11]

However, when they reached Lake Ngami, they were met by a barrier more obstinate than the desert: the Tawana, led by Chief Letsholathebe. Though he led only a splinter group of the Ngwato, he was young and ambitious. He had actually invited Livingston to visit him, but 'the chief … prevented me getting a boat at the ford. They don't like one to go past them to the other tribes.'[12] Letsholathebe wanted to hold on to his share of the Ngwato monopoly of trade with the north. He refused to give them guides to get to Sebetwane.

The lake itself at that time was a fine sheet of water, never seen before by Europeans. It contained a number of islands, inhabited by a tribe of fishermen. But Livingston was less interested in exploring it than Oswell. To him, what mattered was the river route to the north. However, Letsholathebe had vested interests to protect. He forced the Yeyi not to give them boats, and they had to turn back.

For Mary's sake it was a good thing that they did. She had taken the family from Kuruman and gone to Kolobeng in August, at least two months before David could get back from the desert. Eventually, she sent a message north, telling David that they were all ill. He hurried back without taking a day to rest, reaching home on 9 October 1849. The family by then were on the mend, and David was pleased to find Robert able to speak quite well in both English and SeTswana, while Agnes talked in a mixture of the two. Thomas was 'a fine little fellow'.[13]

It was now their father's turn to suffer from impaired speech. David had a lump between the tonsils, caused by an extended soft palate. Freeman, an LMS director, visited the family with Moffat and Mary's sister, Ann, over the New Year. He suggested that David go down to the Cape for an operation, but he was unwilling to go south at that point.[14] He was again thinking of the north.

News meanwhile reached England of the existence of Lake Ngami, and the river beyond it. It caused great excitement. Up to that time, it had been thought by the highest geographical authorities that the centre of Africa – from the Kalahari to the Sahara – was simply a burning desert. Due to the difficulty of access from the coasts, which were unhealthy, few European travellers had penetrated far inland. So the knowledge that there could be a vast, fertile region in between was a revelation.

For putting the lake on the map, the Royal Geographical Society voted Livingston twenty-five guineas – news which did not reach David and Mary until later in 1850. The Society failed to acknowledge immediately the contribution of Oswell, who was slow to send them the observations he had made of the lake. In fact, they were more detailed at that stage than Livingston's; David's focus was on the river flowing into the lake from the north, and all that this might mean for opening up Africa to Christian mission.

Excited by that prospect, Livingston left Kolobeng again in April 1850. Originally he had agreed to rendezvous with Oswell, who was bringing up a boat from the Cape to try to break the blockade of Chief Letsholathebe. For some reason, the Scot did not believe that Oswell could be relied upon to arrive with the boat. Being impatient, perhaps, to reach Sebetwane and the north before the Boers could interfere, he went ahead with Mary and the family. Mary could not be left behind with the Kwena, who were deserting Kolobeng and leaving it open to attack by the Boers.

In any case, Mary had caught David's vision for the north, and, as an experienced wagon-traveller, gifted with a rare understanding of the language of the Bushmen, she could enjoy the trek. She sat with Tom, who was by now one year old, high on the mattresses in the wagon. Robert and Agnes either played in the back or walked along the track with their father. As well as the family, David also had the companionship of Mebalwe and Chief Sechele. Sechele's brother was with Sebetwane, so this was a special incentive for him to come.

They changed route at the Zouga in order to avoid some patches of tsetse fly, whose bite was fatal to oxen. Apart from high winds, the desert crossing was easier than before. It was such a pleasure to reach Lake Ngami and let the toddlers paddle there. But the place turned out to be unhealthy. Just when Livingston had got the agreement of Chief Letsholathebe to let them cross over into Sebetwane's country, the children caught fever.

Mercifully, their father had had the foresight to bring with him some quinine, the only remedy at that time for malaria. 'Thomas had it in the remittent form, & Agnes in the intermittent.' Malaria was also attacking the porters and the oxen were dying from the bite of the tsetse fly. The only course open was to get the wagons back into the purer, drier air of the desert.

[Mary] behaved like a heroine. Takes after her father. Waggon [sic] turned clean over in a pitfall, an event she often feared, but when it came could not help saying to herself, 'Is this all?' Thomas though much reduced is quite himself again & walks alone. Agnes is not so robust as formerly. Robert picked up a shell on the banks of the ... [Lake Ngami] and said, 'I shall give it to Grandma.' I felt proud to hear it.[15]

Meanwhile, Oswell had reached Kolobeng with the promised boat – only to realize that the boat was useless because the heat had warped its planks out of shape. The Livingstons were too far ahead to catch up, so Oswell decided to go hunting along the Zouga. He aimed to follow the south bank of the river to the lake, then go round the lake and back along the Zouga, this time following its north bank.

In May he heard that David's party was within 60 miles, and he hurried to overtake it. By the time he caught them up, the family was recovering from its bout of malaria. Yet Mary was very grateful to Oswell for coming and escorting them. Not only did he bring gifts from her father, but he accompanied the family all the way back to Kolobeng.

There Mary awaited the delivery of her fourth child. In August little Elizabeth was born. She was 'a tiny thing no bigger than [Mma Mary's] middle finger', wrote Mma-Robert.[16] Yet the birth was untimely. An epidemic of bronchitis was at that time raging among the Kwena, and Elizabeth caught it.

Her father could use only the mildest of medicines with such a tiny patient. She lived less than six weeks. David could not forget the piercing cry with which she died. He buried her among the mimosa trees. The grave is still there, carefully marked but now covered over by the thorn bushes. Mary must have been devastated. She developed a rare form of paralysis of the face, called Bell's palsy, with persistent headaches. In October, Mma-Mary came to the rescue of the dispirited couple. She found them in a near-deserted village, eking out an existence in a house with windows that had been broken by hail.

At Kuruman they recovered, the paralysis receded and Mma-Mary was able to send them back to Kolobeng in February 1851 'with roses in their cheeks'.[17] David made one of his regular visits to Sebubi, an African teacher working 40 miles south-west of Kolobeng.

It was a great joy to Livingston to see an African taking responsibility for a mission; 'to see [Sebubi] come forward & choose a station for himself is quite exhilarating,' he had written. 'I felt inclined at once to go over & help him with his house, but thought afterwards it would be better not. Let all the praise of the commencement be given to whom it is due.'[18]

Sechele then took a definite decision to move his people the 9 miles downriver from Kolobeng to Dimawe. There the earth was red and might hold moisture, and the rocks could be used in defence against the Boers. David did not, however, think it worthwhile to begin building a house all over again with his own hands, for the fourth time. There was no certainty that the Kwena would stay there for long. Mma-Mary was shocked to hear that he was thinking of taking Mary and the family north again.

Mrs Moffat would have been prepared to hear of a trip to the 'mountains of the moon' if she felt it had a genuine missionary purpose. The sedentary idea the Moffats had of mission work is shown by her readiness to accept such a journey, had David *'found a place'* to go to 'and commence missionary operations'. But she saw it merely as 'an *exploring* expedition'.[19] Oswell may have described it as such to the Moffats; but he improved the prospects for the journey by offering to go ahead of the Livingston family to open up the wells. David and Mary gratefully accepted his offer and set out on 24 April 1851.

Mary's commitment to exploration as a means of preparing the way for the gospel can be seen in three ways. First, she had agreed that the twenty-five guinea gift voted by the Royal Geographical Society should be spent by David on a special watch. It was 'for observing occultations of stars by the moon'[20] or, in other words, finding longitude so that David could map their way. This gift could easily have been used to help the household budget, but Oswell had generously financed the expedition.

Secondly, she knew her presence on the expedition would be invaluable for winning the acceptance of African chiefs, particularly Sebetwane. As the daughter of Robert Moffat, the only man to tame the marauder Mzilikaze, she had an aura of political authority around her. Where she went, Mzilikaze would not invade.

Thirdly, by bringing the children they would dissipate suspicion. To the Africans, this was a mark of trust, a gratifying token of sincerity in relationships.

Yet having travelled to Ngami before, Mary knew it would be a 'weary way'.[21] This time they crossed the bed of the River Zouga after the salt-pans and went due north, avoiding the lake. At first the new country was hard and flat, with plenty of springs. Yet after that they entered what David called 'the worst piece of country in Africa for sand drought and dreariness'.[22]

Not an insect, not a bird, broke the stillness of the desert. Three days went by with no sign of water. Their ears ached for the croak of a frog, their eyes searched for the spoor of rhinoceros or elephant. The guide tried to follow old elephant trails, lost his bearings and 'on the morning of the fourth day ... vanished altogether. We went on in the direction in which we last saw him, and about eleven o'clock began to see birds; then the trail of a rhinoceros.'

This was the signal to unyoke the oxen and let them rush off to the west in search of water. While everyone else followed in the wake of the oxen, Oswell and the Livingstons stayed with the wagons. The water supply there had been allowed to run low. 'As is always the case the children drank more than usual as the water became less, and their mother sat crying over them as she saw the precious fluid drawing to the bottom of the bottle.' The suspense of waiting for water and wondering whether it would ever come, coupled with bitter anxiety about the children, was unbearable. It would have been a relief to David if Mary had actually opened her mouth to complain, but not one word of blame passed her lips.[23]

To their immense relief, on the afternoon of the fifth day, Oswell and David met the men returning with a little water – just enough to save their lives.

The worst was over. They reached a brook called the Mababe and ran into a patch of tsetse fly. Pushing on from there they came to the Chobe River, an important tributary of the Zambezi. Here Mary agreed to stay with the wagon party while David and Oswell took a canoe.

Paddled by five strong men, it took them 30 miles. As they got closer to Sebetwane, they were told of his reputation. 'He has a heart! he is wise!' the people said.[24]

Sebetwane was a thin, wiry man about 5ft 10ins tall. He was intensely gratified to find that David had brought his wife and family with him, and actually gave orders to move his town down to their wagons. Meanwhile, he repaid this mark of trust by telling the newcomers all about himself.

Oswell describes how late into the night Sebetwane came alone to them and 'sat down very quietly and mournfully at our fire', wrote Oswell. He and David 'woke up and greeted him, and then he dreamily recounted the history of his life, his wars, escapes, successes and conquests, and the far-distant wandering in his raids. By the fire's glow and flicker among the reeds, with that tall, dark, earnest speaker and his keenly attentive listeners, it has always appeared to me one of the most weird scenes I ever saw.'[25]

Some of Sebetwane's people, the Kololo, had been with him and Manthatitsi at the battle for Kuruman in 1823.[26] The old men asked David why white men had opposed them and he explained to them Robert Moffat's intention in riding out to talk to the warring parties. 'Then we killed ourselves by not understanding their [the white men's] language,' the elders replied.[27]

Oswell went back to the wagons, but Livingston stayed on. He had been able to explain some of the Scriptures to Sebetwane and now held a service for him. This turned out to be the great chief's only chance to hear the gospel. For, on 6 July 1851, he caught pneumonia.

It seemed that there was an overruling plan in the events of Sebetwane's life. He had come up from the south and pacified a large number of tribes, spreading his own language in a region larger than France. He had stood up to Mzilikaze but fell, finally, to disease, dying the very next Sunday after David's arrival.

Yet he had heard the gospel, and the language he had brought to the north was a dialect of SeTswana – at the very time that Robert Moffat was completing the translation of the Bible into that language. He ruled from Dinyanti, a centre south of the River Zambezi.

Waiting for permission to make a brief survey of the country from Mma-Motsisane, the daughter and successor of the dead chief, David began to plan and dream. On 31 July 1851 a messenger came from Mma-Motsisane commanding that Livingston and Oswell 'should be treated exactly as if [Sebetwane] were alive, and that we should be taken wherever we wished to go'.[28] Since the country was intersected with many small rivers, it was unsuitable for wagon travel. Mary and the children stayed at the camp by the River Chobe under the protection of the headman, while Livingston and Oswell went forward on horseback.

After three days of riding they came in the afternoon to Seshéké in the centre of the continent. 'All we could say to each other was ... How glorious! How magnificent! How beautiful! And grand beyond description it really was – such a body of water.' David estimated it to be 300–500 metres wide, and deep. 'The town of Seshéké appeared very beautiful on the opposite bank. The waves were so high the people were afraid to venture accross [sic], but by & bye a canoe made its way to where we stood … In crossing … the waves lifted up the canoe and made it roll beautifully.'[29]

The 'River Seshéké' turned out to be the Zambezi. Its rolling waters seemed to beckon as the authentic 'highway to the interior'[30] of which Thomas Fowell Buxton had dreamed. Soon afterwards, however, Livingston was told of the existence of a huge waterfall, called Mosioatunya, 'the smoke that sounds'. Oswell, however, had already stayed much longer than intended and they did not go to see it. Time would tell what bearing it would have on the 'highway'.

On the way back, Mary gave birth to a son, on the River Zouga. They called him William Oswell, in honour of their great friend and benefactor, William Cotton Oswell, who was soon to leave Africa. David also nicknamed his son 'Zouga', after the river which had been for them a highway through the northern desert.

Yet he could not contemplate exposing Zouga or any of his family on any further hazardous journeys into unknown territory. David and Mary decided together that, for the sake of the children and their education, she would take them to Scotland.

David felt the call to the interior inescapable. His mission would be to find healthy areas for evangelistic work beyond the reach of the drought, and the Boers. First, however, he had to take Mary and the children – Robert, Agnes, Tom and Zouga – down to the Cape. They took ship for Scotland on 23 April 1852, aiming to stay with David's parents at Hamilton, near Glasgow.

Mary was born to the dust and the desert; she was going to a foreign land. For David, parting with the family was like tearing his heart out.

6

Do or die

As Mary watched the bleak, barren desert of the Skeleton Coast slip by to starboard, David wrote her what was (for a Victorian) an impassioned letter.

Cape Town
5th May 1852

My dearest Mary,

How I miss you now and the dear children! My heart yearns incessantly over you. How many thoughts of the past crowd into my mind! I feel as if I would treat you all much more tenderly and lovingly than ever. You have been a great blessing to me. You attended to my comfort in many many ways. May God bless you for all your kindnesses!

I see no face now to be compared with that sunburnt one which has so often greeted me with its kind looks. Let us do our duty to our Saviour, and we shall meet again. I wish that time were now. You may read the letters over again which I wrote at Mabotsa, the sweet time you know.

As I told you before, I tell you again, they are true, true; there is not a bit of hypocrisy in them. I never show all my feelings; but I can say truly, my dearest, that I loved you when I married you, and the longer I lived with you, I loved you the better.[1]

There were few 'kind looks' for David now. When he wanted to send off the mail, a postmaster threatened to bring a lawsuit against him for claiming that the price was too high. When he tried to get ammunition, which he needed to kill game for meat *en route* to the north, the Scot fell foul of the colonial bureaucracy; only a court order could get the permission.

This was not, however, a case of personal discrimination. On 17 January 1852 the British had signed a treaty with the Boers, known as the Sand River Convention. The treaty banned 'all trade in ammunition with the native tribes' and stipulated that 'every waggon [sic] containing ammunition and fire-arms, coming from the south side of the Vaal River, shall produce a certificate, signed by a British magistrate ... to the nearest magistrate north of the Vaal River, who shall act in the case as the regulations of the Emigrant Farmers direct'. In effect, anyone travelling north would be subject to search and inspection by the Boers.[2]

This development seemed ominous enough. When taken with the Boer threats in the past against Sechele and the mission centres, it made Livingston think twice before putting into action his plan to get to Sebetwane's country. However, by applying to Lieutenant Governor Darling of the Cape Colony he was able to get all the gunpowder he needed.[3]

Livingston left Cape Town on 8 June. The journey gave him the chance to try out some astronomical observations, based on the instructions of Thomas Maclear, Astronomer Royal at the Cape. He had been one firm friend David and Mary had made on their visit to the Colony. Maclear was vitally interested in his fellow Scot's plans to open a way to the north. For it was still true that, as Jonathan Swift put it,

> Geographers in Afric maps
> With savage pictures fill their gaps.[4]

While Maclear wanted to improve the accuracy of the maps that Livingston would send back to the Royal Geographical Society, David wanted to build on his boyhood hobby of astronomy to pinpoint promising sites for mission centres.

This dream appeared to be banished by news which reached him at Kuruman. He was kept there a fortnight by the need to repair a wagon wheel that had broken on the journey. The delay kept him from going to the Kwena at a time of crisis. On 28 August he heard that the Boers had attacked Sechele and completely destroyed Kolobeng. The holdups at the Cape and at Kuruman now seemed providential to David. Yet he was shaken by the news. 'Am I on the way to die in [Sebetwane's] country? Have I seen the end of my wife and children? The breaking up of all my connections with earth, leaving this fair and beautiful world and knowing so little of it? I am only learning the Alphabet of it yet, and entering on an untried state of existence.'[5]

In October 1852 Sechele's wife Mma-Sebele arrived at Kuruman with a letter addressed to Robert Moffat. It was written in Sechele's own, unidiomatic style of SeTswana. The chief had been confronted with Boer demands that he surrender to them Mosielele, the chief of the Kgatla at Mabotsa, who had taken refuge with him.[6] This he had refused to do, and still other demands were made:

Dimawe [on the River Kolobeng]

My friend of my heart's love and of all the confidence of my heart, it is I, Sechele. The Boers have been too much for me. They attacked me though I had done them no wrong. They wanted me to be under their rule, but I refused. They said I should stop the English and Griquas and Thlaping (southern Tswana) [from proceeding into the Interior]. I replied, All these are my friends, I cannot stop any one [of them]. Then they said I must go and speak with them. I replied, I do not understand your language; but I said, If you bring Mr Edwards to interpret, then I shall speak with you.

They came on Saturday and prepared to fight on the Sabbath; but I besought them not to fight on a Sabbath, and they listened. They began on Monday at break of dawn. They shot with all their power, they set fire to the town, and they scattered us. They killed sixty of my people and captured women and children and men; they also took ... all the cattle and [other] wealth of the Kwena. And they plundered Livingston's house, taking all his goods.[7]

The house was probably broken into first by the Kwena guards Sechele had posted there, then by the Boers (who used Livingston's dictionaries as wadding for their guns) and finally by Griquas on a hunting expedition.[8]

To have to write to Mary about the fate of the family home, when she was trying to settle with her in-laws in wet and wintry Scotland, was scarcely pleasant. To hear that the Boers were out for his blood, because they blamed him for their own casualties, was chilling. Griquas who had been to the scene told Sechele that about thirty of the attackers had fallen. In fact only three of these were Boers; the rest were almost certainly Bantu auxiliaries, who had to take the brunt of the fighting.[9]

Fearing to go north in case of a revenge attack, David bided his time.[10] In gathering information about the attack, the Scot was able to meet Sechele. The chief gave him the names of 124 Kwena children who he said had been carried off for forced labour by the Boers. To Livingston this was tantamount to enslaving them. His LMS colleagues, Edwards and Inglis, shared this opinion and wrote to the Boer commandant, Pieter Scholtz, 'protesting against what they called the enslavement of young captives. He considered their letter libellous, and after trial in court at Rustenburg they were expelled from the Transvaal (November 1852).'[11]

Chief Sechele, against Livingston's advice, decided to go to the Cape to protest to the colonial authorities (and if necessary to Queen Victoria). The Sand River Convention had technically promoted the liberty of travellers and outlawed slavery,[12] but in practice the British had given the Boers a free hand. By it the Cape Colony had not only recognized the independence of the Boers beyond the Vaal River,[13] but had also disclaimed all alliance with 'coloured nations' in the region. On 25 January 1853 Sechele 'was informed in reply ... that, in terms of the Sand River Convention, the British Government could not interfere in the quarrel between him and the Boers.'[14]

Although he wrote letters to the authorities, including Lieutenant Governor Darling, Livingston had no desire to go to the Cape. He was determined to go in the opposite direction, northwards to Sebetwane's country, to open up the way for mission beyond the war-torn area. Setting off on 14 December 1852, he hoped to go through Kolobeng but was put off by the presence of Boers. He never did get to see at first hand the damage done to his house.

Pressing on to the north, he was grateful for the fact that on the long trek the attacks of fever that afflicted other members of his party did not affect him. Still, it was not a healthy area that Sebetwane had chosen for the Kololo capital, Dinyanti.

When they reached it on 23 May 1853, the Scot could not help thinking that a better site would have to be found if there were to be a mission among them.

Sebetwane's daughter, Mma-Motsisane, had assigned the chieftainship to a youth of eighteen, called Sekeletu. He welcomed Livingston with a present of eleven valuable tusks, saying he was willing to trade with ivory, but 'these they gave to their father, and they were just as any present'. However, the principal men then reiterated a request for a secret 'gun-medicine'. David 'offered to show Sekeletu how to shoot, and that was all the medicine known'.[15]

Grateful for the provision for his work that the tusks represented, Livingston now got down to his essential purpose of teaching the way of salvation through Christ. This he did to audiences of up to 600 people by the banks of the Zambezi. Always choosing one subject only for an address, he took care to make it short, clear and applicable to those he spoke to. At the end, there would be a short prayer, for which the women with children had to be told to remain standing. For when they knelt, they would squeeze the offspring wrapped close to their bodies, and set up a skirl of wailing (like the bagpipes), making the prayer impossible to hear.[16]

Sekeletu was not slow to perceive that the presence of the son-in-law of Robert Moffat, friend of Mzilikaze, would be an asset to his foreign policy. To claim friendship with Moffat's kith and kin would protect the Kololo from attack. From the day they met he had called David his 'father'.[17] He asked a lot of questions, especially on the issue of monogamy. Having taken several wives, he was afraid that reading Scripture would change his heart.

When Sekeletu heard that Livingston planned to leave him to go in search of a fever-free site for a mission centre, he was very reluctant to agree. By now this was not merely a matter of foreign policy; he had a genuine sense of family relationship with David.

Finally however, on 16 June 1853, Sekeletu agreed to let his father-figure go. He promised to help Livingston in every possible way and to be his companion while he travelled through the country ruled by the Kololo.[18] In doing this, the young chief was putting himself in grave danger.[19]

They had gone 60 miles together when they met Sekeletu's half-brother, Mphephe. This man was secretly plotting to kill Sekeletu. Three times that day the plot was foiled by unexpected obstacles.[20] Once Livingston himself unconsciously saved the chief's life by blocking him from the view of a spear-thrower.[21] The plot was disclosed by Mphephe's own people, to whom Sekeletu gave the responsibility to execute the would-be murderer.

The party, numbering 160, continued on up the broad Zambezi, which Livingston had first seen on his visit to Sebetwane. In time they came to the village where the unsuccessful assassin's father lived. The father was questioned along with a village headman, by Sekeletu. Then, to David's horror, both men were cut down by the axes of Sekeletu's warriors. The pieces of their bodies were then fed to the crocodiles.[22]

Shocked to find himself the unwilling and unsuspecting spectator of such a scene, David was concerned that his presence there might be taken to mean that he was involved in the slaughter. In remonstrating with the Kololo he found that only by telling them of the last judgment, when God would call them to account and punish violent deeds, could he 'make any impression' on them.[23]

After this they visited Mma-Motsisane, who was living on the south end of an island in the Zambezi called Loyela. She revealed that the requirements of being a chieftainess had been hard to bear. Among them was the expectation that she should engage in a kind of serial polyandry. Married women of the tribe were bitter about having to send their husbands to her. Mma-Motsisane wanted to stop the custom and have a husband of her own. After hours of debate, a man stood up in the assembly and said, 'I have married her.'[24]

Leaving Mma-Motsisane, the party, now increased to fifty canoes, travelled for two hours to Naliele. This had been the capital of the Lozi, a large and influential tribe on the upper Zambezi, before they were conquered by the Kololo. Here on 14 August 1853 Livingston held a service for 1,000 people. He was about to begin when a man caught a boy about 6 years of age who was passing accross [sic] the square with his mother, and after shouting at the top of his voice in praise of the son of [Sebetwane] said, I thank you, and led off the boy, whose heart seemed bursting with agony, to his own house.

I asked Sekeletu to give the man to me, as I wished to purchase a new jacket with him. The man laughed at first, but when I persisted he began to think it serious and said, surely the son of [Sebetwane] won't part with an old servant? I answered he was old and useless, whereas the boy was young and would make a good soldier. I think by the remarks made all saw that I regarded his act as odious. He afterwards told Sekeletu he was afraid I would kill him.[25]

Only two days before, the Portuguese trader Antonio da Silva Pôrto had passed by with 'a large company of slaves'.[26] Pôrto had come from 'the farthest inland station of the Portuguese opposite Benguela'.[27] In the Lozi country he had built a stockade at Katongo, with the blessing of the recently executed Mphephe.

Livingston heard that 'frequent and long conferences were carried on in Senor [sic] Pôrto's house' between Mphephe and Pôrto, through an interpreter. Mphephe had sought Pôrto's aid in a scheme to secede from Sekeletu and establish an independent kingdom in the country of the Ila. Pôrto's party had given Mphephe a large gun which was mounted like a small cannon. If Mphephe had 'succeeded in destroying Sekeletu their arms would have been employed in bringing all the [Kololo] into subjection and establishing the slave trade on a firm footing in this region'. Pôrto later denied that he had agreed to take part in Mphephe's plot.[28]

Livingston had first met Pôrto at Dinyanti and 'thought of going Westward in company with this merchant'. However, when he visited the stockade (on a ridge east of Naliele), he had been confronted with 'the sight of gangs of poor wretches in chains'. This was one factor which made him 'resolve to proceed alone'.[29]

David still thought of following the same route as Pôrto's

party, while keeping a long distance behind them. However, on 27 October Sekeletu visited Livingston to tell him that on leaving the Lozi Pôrto had 'caught two men and a woman and bound them among his gangs of slaves'. When Pôrto reached Naliele, however, he was intercepted by a company of Kololo warriors who forced him to give up his captives before he could cross the river. 'It is well he did something to shew his real character to the [Kololo] and enable them to decide whether slavers are the proper sort of visitors.'[30]

'This affair made me alter my resolution again,' Livingston wrote to the LMS Director, Arthur Tidman, on 8 November 1853. 'For if I followed [Pôrto's] footsteps the different tribes through which we have to pass would naturally believe me to be of the same clan.' Livingston had also 'sent men to the Westward in order to examine if there is any strip of country free of tsetse in that direction. Their report was unfavourable.' Consequently he decided to take a detour northwards up the Zambezi until they reached the Lunda people and then 'proceed Westward by land' to Luanda on the Atlantic coast. The Lunda people occupied an area which now includes eastern Angola, north-west Zambia and Katanga, Zaire.[31]

Before leaving Dinyanti on 11 November 1853 Livingston sent back in the company of a trader all the people who had come with him from Kuruman. Travelling with twenty-seven Kololo and Lozi, he eventually found that a box 'containing my whole stock of ammunition and prepared medicines' was missing. It transpired that it had been taken from his wagon by Thebe, a cook from Kuruman. David sent back 'about a hundred miles' to the wagon for a fresh supply of ammunition.[32]

Every morning the party would get up a little before 5.00, dress, and drink coffee. By 5.20 the canoes would be loaded and they set off, the coolest part of the day being the pleasantest for paddling. After stopping at 11.00, 'the heat is oppressive. We cower under umbrellahs [sic].'[33]

At Ngonye men from the village carried the canoes clear of the falls there 'by means of poles on the shoulder'. They did so with great good humour, and made a special request to see the pictures of Livingston's magic lantern. The pleasure of this part of the journey was lessened by Livingston's languid condition, since his 'last most severe attack' of fever.[34]

Then 'to our sorrow' came news of a raid sanctioned by Sekeletu's younger brother, Mpololo, on an area which included four villages of the Lunda people to the north. This was precisely where Livingston's party were heading. 'As this is in direct opposition to Sekeletu's policy, who sends by our hands presents in order to secure the friendship of these tribes, and a fresh foray was in preparation, we sent forward orders to Mpololo ... to disperse the expedition immediately.'[35]

On 7 December Livingston boldly confronted Mpololo in front of his mother, Mma-Sekeletu. She 'suggested that all the captives taken ... should be returned by my hand, to shew ... that the guilt lay not with the superior persons of the [Kololo], but with a mere servant.' Mpololo agreed and the decision was confirmed at a *pitso*, or mass meeting, of the tribesmen at Naliele. So it was that the Scot had the great pleasure of liberating slaves so early in the journey. 'We return eighteen souls from captivity, a thing never before performed in this part of Africa.'[36]

At Naliele, on 12 December 1853, Livingston met an Arab called bin Habib. He was the leader of a trading party which had travelled from Zanzibar off the east coast to Benguela on the west coast, arriving in April 1852. Bin Habib and his companion Manoel had been left by Pôrto at his stockade. They had no more goods to exchange for food and begged beads from Livingstone, before setting out for the west.[37]

Another Arab of bin Habib's party, named bin Chombo, was meanwhile escorting the agents of Pôrto eastwards to Mozambique.[38] Although such journeys were being made both by Arabs and Portuguese, none had mapped their path with anything like the accuracy that the Scot was aiming to achieve.

Sickness hindered Livingston from responding to spiritual need, but it did not stop him altogether. Even if he was too ill to preach on a Sunday, he would find an opportunity to use a magic lantern to illustrate God's Word. At Shinte on Saturday 21 January 1854, the chief man, Kabompo, was, David wrote, 'very anxious to see the pictures, but I am too ill to go to the town at night. The fever is very severe and makes me quite lean, yet the heart beats violently when I move, causing a buzzing in the ears.'[39]

Livingston did manage to show the slides on the Monday. Africans had never seen pictures projected before and reacted to them in interesting ways. 'The pictures of the magic lantern were shown to Kabompo to his great delight. He manifested great composure, listened very attentively to the explanations; but his people when they saw them coming out on one side with the extracted slide thought those on that side would now be caught by the figures, and made a precipitate rush away. Some said these were certainly liker [sic] gods than their pieces of wood smeared with medicine.'[40] Despite the panic, this was 'the only service he was ever asked to repeat'.[41]

Sekeletu had presented Livingston with four riding-oxen for the overland stage of the journey. Yet they set off without sufficient stores of food and gifts to pacify the many hostile chiefs that barred their path to the coast. All they could offer was a small amount of coffee, cloth and beads and some of Sekeletu's elephant tusks. The moments of greatest danger, demanding clear-headedness and calm courage, could come just after David had had an attack of fever.

The chief of the Chiboque demanded more tribute than he had been given. When this was refused, the Kololo camp was surrounded by men 'flourishing their weapons and pointing their guns at us. When I got the chief to follow my example and sit down, I asked what guilt we had that he came armed in that way.' He replied that one of the Kololo, by spitting on the ground, had made a spark from the campfire touch 'his servant, & this guilt we [must] wipe out by paying a fine of a man, ox, gun, or other valuable article'.

'To the demand for one of our number we were all determined never to submit.' Livingston agreed to 'pay a small fine', which the chief seemed willing to accept. But his young men and counsellors wanted more, 'and at every demand all his armed men rushed about brandishing their weapons. One young man made a charge at me from behind, stopping his sword just over my head.'[42]

'... I quickly brought round the muzzle of my gun to his mouth, and he retreated. I pointed him out to the chief, and he ordered him to retire a little.'[43] He made peace by giving up an ox, but he was determined now to avoid the tribes that were on the path of slave-traders. 'We were determined to die for each other rather than deliver up one of our number [to slavery].'[44]

Their new course involved passing through increasingly dense forests. Climbing plants hung down over the path and had to be 'quickly lifted over the head or ducked under with dexterity, for the ox invariably rushes on more quickly if there is any difficulty. He sometimes leaves the path without any apparent cause except for the purpose of hanging his rider like Absalom among these tough and strong climbers.'[45]

Once Livingston was crossing a river in the local style, by holding on to the tail of an ox, when he lost his grip and sank. Immediately, twenty of the porters given him by Sekeletu dropped their loads on the bank and plunged into the water to rescue him. Great was their joy to find him up and swimming. As Livingston reached the bank one porter was holding him by the arm and another around the waist. These Kololo carriers were the best he ever had, faithful and patient. Yet they were so afraid of losing their way that they were 'faint-hearted' if a local guide threatened to abandon them.[46]

Nevertheless, peaceful defiance was sometimes necessary. On Sunday 2 April 1854, a chief called Sansawe demanded 'a red jacket and a man' or they would have to go back. David told the chief he could kill him if he liked, but God would judge him for it. The next day they set off soon after dawn in drizzling rain, and Sansawe's men were nowhere to be seen. 'We were sincerely thankful for our deliverance, and some remarked, "We are children of Jesus".'[47]

After going for more than three months through thick forest, with only a few glimpses of the sun, it was a relief to come out into the parkland and scenery of the western region (now known as Angola). There was still no relief, however, from the demands of the chiefs. Livingston had by degrees to surrender his shirts, his razor and other personal property.[48] At times he could hardly resist ordering his men to fight – and it was the Kololo who were patient.

Sometimes I was furious and would have fought, but my companions were more pacific, stripping themselves of their [copper] ornaments & paying for passage. At other times they were on the bloody key and I was quakerish, and we rose up by night and passed our enemies, expecting an assault in every thicket and glen we came to. And, after all, I thank God sincerely in that he prevented us from shedding human blood.[49]

Patience was unexpectedly rewarded. They had been stopped by a wide river, refused canoes and told to hand over a slave for payment. Livingston, exhausted by weakness, was on the point of parting with his precious coat when a Portuguese sergeant arrived from a garrison across the river. Cypriano de Abreu got them ferried over the River Cuango.[50]

Then they were fed. It was Livingston's first proper meal for months. He was ashamed to appear greedy and had his host not been present he would have bought more food to eat at night. This sharp hunger was also the result of fever. Livingston had to endure another 500 miles of travelling before the party finally reached the coastal port of Luanda. They were escorted by a corporal of militia sent by the Portuguese.

As they approached the strange town they wondered what sort of reception they would get. The Africans feared that they would be kidnapped. Livingston knew that it was only in recent times that Luanda had given up being a slave-trading port, by a treaty with the British. To comfort them David promised to stay with them, so that what happened to them would happen to him.

On the journey he had suffered no fewer than thirty-one attacks of fever.[51] He was now so weak that he could not sit on his ox for more than ten minutes at a time.

7
The promise

After 1,500 miles and two years of travelling from Cape Town, Livingston entered Luanda on 31 May 1854, 'labouring under an attack of fever and diarrhoea'.[1]

Help was at hand. 'Edmund Gabriel, Esqre, Her Majesty's Commissioner for the suppression of the slave trade, and the only Englishman I know in this city, most generously received me and my 27 companions into his house. I shall never forget the delicious pleasure of tumbling into his bed after sleeping six months on the ground.'[2]

Hospitality, however, could not prevent another very bad attack of fever, quickly followed by dysentery. Livingston's condition was getting worse. 'I soon became reduced to a skeleton.' David's Kololo companions feared that he was dying. At this point, however, the Navy came to the rescue. On 1 July Commander Phillips of HMS steamer *Polyphemus* arrived in port. 'He at once sent for his surgeon, Mr Cockin, by whose judicious treatment I was much relieved.'[3]

Livingston's convalescence gave him leisure to find out more about the role of his host in this Portuguese penal colony. Gabriel was 'British arbitrator (and later commissioner) in the Mixed Commission Court for the suppression of the slave trade'.[4] These courts, established at Luanda and elsewhere under a treaty of 1842, dealt mainly with ships seized by naval forces because of their use, or suspected use, for transporting slaves to America.[5] The British and Portuguese were represented on each by a commissioner, an arbitrator, and a secretary: 'when the two commissioners cannot agree, they draw lots which of the arbitrators shall act, and his vote decides'.[6]

'The unwearied attention and kindness through a long sickness which Mr G. invariably shewed' were essential to David's recovery. 'May God reward him,' he wrote later.[7] At least two naval captains offered to take Livingston to

England,[8] but he had little hesitation in declining. The sicknesses that he had suffered showed that he could not rely on the western route via Angola as a way of opening south central Africa to mission. So his work was not finished. He did, however, send off his notes, observations and maps with Lieutenant Bedingfeld, a naval officer travelling on the *Forerunner*.

David had promised the Kololo that he would see them back to their homes. Plunging back into the forest must have been a daunting prospect, knowing how unsuitable the route was for regular travel. It was also a cheerless one, since in two years he had still not heard from his family. No-one, apparently, had expected him to make it to the coast. On 20 September 1854 he and the Kololo marched out of Luanda to face danger and sickness all over again.

When they had travelled 200 miles, news came from the coast; the ship that Livingston had refused to go home on had sunk. His determination not to give up his task may have saved him from drowning. 'The letters which I sent by Lieut. Bedingfeld have all been lost, the steamer in which he sailed having struck on a rock near Madeira and went down in a few minutes afterwards. Fourteen lives were lost. I feel so glad [at] the escape of Mr Bedingfeld I am reconciled to the labour of rewriting my letters.'[9]

The *Forerunner* had been wrecked on 25 October, and Livingston received the news on 23 December at Pungo Andongo. There he stayed until 1 January, rewriting his notes.[10] With this news came a note from Lord Clarendon at the Foreign Office, enclosing a cutting from *The Times*. The newspaper called his journey to Luanda 'one of the greatest geographical explorations of the age'.[11]

Yet Livingston's purpose was not primarily geographical. 'The end of the geographical feat is but the beginning of the missionary enterprise,' he later wrote, in explaining the purpose of the transcontinental journey.[12] This is a key principle for understanding Livingston.[13] Exploration would show what places might be healthy bases for mission and what products might replace traffic in human flesh.

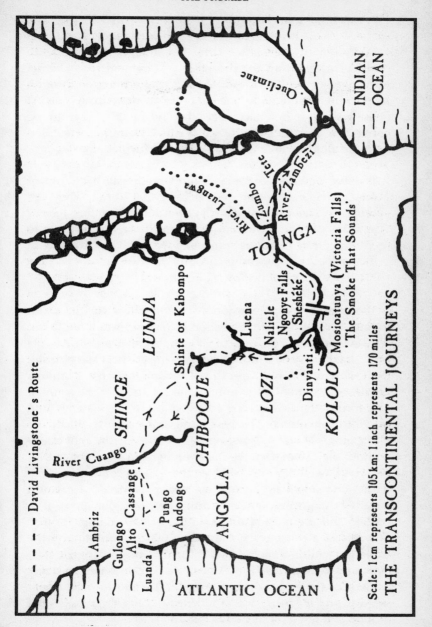

THE TRANSCONTINENTAL JOURNEYS

Scale: 1cm represents 105 km: 1 inch represents 170 miles

- - - David Livingstone's Route

Livingston was becoming increasingly aware that the success of mission centres would be inextricably linked to the suppression of the slave trade. He thought he could see positive results from the proactive role men such as Gabriel were playing in this regard. On his way eastwards through Angola Livingston had done his bit to promote this cause. At Gulungo Alto he had met the hospitable Portuguese gentlemen, Senhores Canto and Castro, whom he persuaded to invite all races to listen to a speech on free labour.

The Portuguese gentlemen expect anxiously a supply of fresh American cotton seed from Mr. Gabriel. They are prevented by our cruizers [sic] from following their former nefarious traffic in human flesh, and now turn eagerly to coffee, cotton, sugar, as sources of wealth. They are now in the transition state, and if encouraged will percieve [sic] the vast superiority of licit over illicit trade.[14]

The process of persuasion was going to take time, but Livingston's optimistic prediction is to some extent borne out by the evidence. The case of Flores, an emigrant to Angola from Brazil, may be cited. He became the greatest slave-dealer in the colony and was later expelled. On his return to Angola he turned his attention to mining the resources of the country. The fortune he had gained from slave-trading was put into providing an alternative to his former means of livelihood.[15]

A change like that, however, was not to be brought about without the use of coercive force. Livingston's mentor in this, Thomas Fowell Buxton, 'believed that lawful commerce alone would be inadequate to counteract the slave trade – it would require both government naval intervention against the slave traders and the only lasting solution of Christianity itself'.[16] The role of a proactive naval policy was exemplified by the exploits of HMS *Philomel*, which on 25 and 27 August 1854 blew up two launches from Ambriz, 'a notorious nest of slave-dealers', at the mouth of the Congo.[17] Yet while the blockade at sea was proving more and more effective, the situation on the ground still left a lot to be desired.

Despite the naval patrols on the Atlantic seaboard and the work of the commissioners ashore, David found disturbing evidence that the slave trade was spreading inland faster than ever before. 'Formerly the trade went from the interior into the Portuguese territory; now it goes the opposite way. This is the effect of the Portuguese love of the trade: they cannot send them abroad on account of our ships of war on the coast, yet will sell them to the best advantage.'[18]

David describes to Mary (and Nannie, nickname for their daughter Agnes) a dealer paid by a Portuguese trader.

This agent is about the same in appearance as Mebalwe, and speaks Portuguese as the Griquas do Dutch. He has two chainsful of women going to be sold for the ivory … These women are decent-looking, as much so as the general run of Kuruman ladies, and were caught lately in a skirmish the Portuguese had with their tribe; and they will be sold for about three tusks each. Each has an iron ring round the wrist, and that is attached to the chain, which she carries in the hand to prevent it jerking and hurting the wrist. How would Nannie like to be thus treated?[19]

More of Livingston's men were carrying guns on this return journey, but happily they did not need to use them. The party had made a good impression when they had first passed that way and the tribes were generally friendlier than before. 'We have passed two chiefs who plagued us much when going down, but now were quite friendly. At that time one of them ordered his people not to sell us anything, and we had at last to force our way past him. Now he came running to meet us … The alteration in this gentleman's conduct – the Peace Society would not credit it – is attributable solely to my people possessing guns. When we passed before, we were defenceless.'[20]

Nevertheless the going was slower this time. It was now the rainy season and the travellers had to force their way through tall grass which was heavy with water. In a flooded plain the ground was swampy and they had to sleep in the wet, as they had to do for months afterwards. This led to Livingston having an attack of rheumatic fever and losing a lot of blood.

The whole party was suffering from malaria. Despite his own illness, David took care of the Kololo and nursed them through all their fevers. By day they were exposed both to heavy rain and to the direct rays of the sun, with the temperature above 96°F (33°C) in the shade. For food, they had to live on cassava roots. All the money the porters earned while at the coast was lost and their clothes became rags. At last, on 25 July 1855, they reached their own province.

As they marched down the Lozi valley people welcomed them with dancing. David wrote with gratitude of one reception which was typical of many villages.

They gave us two fine oxen to slaughter, and the women have supplied us abundantly with milk and meal. This is all gratuitous, and though I feel ashamed that I can make no return my men explain the total expenditure of means in the way hither, and they remark gracefully, 'It does not matter, you have open[ed] a path for us and we shall have sleep.' Strangers from a distance come flocking to see me, and seldom come empty-handed. I distribute all presents among my men.[21]

On 29 July 1855 they held a service of thanksgiving. 'I told them we had come that day to thank God before them all for his mercy in preserving us in dangers by strange tribes and sicknesses,' David wrote.[22]

He was surprised to find that Sekeletu had not come to meet him. Perhaps the chief's conscience had been troubling him. In Livingston's absence, he had been raiding his neighbours. 'We hear the bad news of Sekeletu having gone on a marauding expedition against the people of Sebolamakoa. By the advice of an uncle he goes, expecting them to flee at once ... This opens a bad prospect for me, for this foray is in the direction I expected to take, but it is just what I expected from his character and the advice he recieved [sic]. His wish is to be great, and he knows greatness only as reflected in his father's deeds. My people pronounce the whole affair as "bad, bad".'[23]

At Naliele on 9 August Livingston reflected on the natural barriers to establishing a regular route into the interior. 'The waterfalls of Mosioatunya, Kabompo, & others, explain why commercial enterprise never entered the interior of the continent except by foot travellers. I am sorry for it. My dreams of establishing a commerce by means of the rivers vanish as I become better acquainted with them. But who can contend against nature? Can these cataracts not be passed by placing boats on frames with wheels? Difficulties are not always insurmountable.'[24]

Leaving Naliele on 13 August, Livingston's party was 'proceeding along the shore at midday' when 'a hippopotamus struck the canoe with his forehead and nearly overturned it'.[25] Despite this misadventure they got to the Ngonye Falls on the 20th and Seshéké on 25 August, only to find 'that Sekeletu had left this yesterday with his ill-gotten goods; but he will be lauded by all, so that if I were not here to lift a warning voice he would have no chance of knowing the true nature of his deeds.'[26]

It was an inexpressible relief on 6 September to get news and letters via his father-in-law. 'The goods sent by Mr Moffat from the country of [Mzilikaze] came to hand on the 6th in pretty fair condition, seeing they had remained on an island near Mosioatunya a whole year ... A whirl of thoughts rushed through my mind as I opened my letters, but thank God I had no cause for sorrow ... Letters and newspapers have been a great treat, as may easily be imagined by any one remembering that three years have elapsed since I heard from my family.'[27]

This parcel of mail may have been the one which contained within it a letter from David's father, Neil, asking the whole family to change their name from Livingston to Livingstone. David took time to get used to the change but began to sign himself 'Livingstone' with more frequency, for example in a letter to William Thompson of the LMS from Dinyanti, dated 27 September 1855.[28]

Next to news from his loved ones, it must have been gratifying to read this testimony from the Astronomer Royal, Maclear. 'I do not hesitate to assert, that no explorer on record has determined his path with the precision you have accomplished.'[29]

There was also some encouragement on 2 September 1855 when people were 'more attentive and decorous at the services'. At night, this could be attributed to their fascination for 'the pictures of the magic lantern, and explanations founded thereon'. By day, however, the headman played his part. 'Moriantsane, who acts as a sort of churchwarden ... got up silently last Sunday and hurled a club at the heads of some who were behaving improperly.'[30]

They did not meet Sekeletu until the party reached Dinyanti on 11 September 1855, two years after leaving it. The following day David 'delivered the presents of the Government of [Luanda], *viz.* a general's dress coat, trowsers [*sic*], sash, sword, and cocked hat'. A horse which was also sent had died on the way. 'The tail of the horse was shewn by my companions as proof of its death.' They also handed over gifts from the merchants of Luanda.

Great satisfaction was expressed, and yesterday we had a pico in order to discuss the question of removal to [the Lozi area] in order to be nearer the market. Some of the older men objected to abandoning the line of defence afforded by the [River] Chobe against their southern enemies, the [Ndebele]. Sekeletu at last said, 'I am perfectly satisfied of the superiority of the path for trade which you have opened, and when you return with [Mma-Robert] you will find me there.' A party has been sent with [bin Habib] with ivory for [Luanda]. My companions are allowed to rest meanwhile, and it is probable when the others return they will be ready to start. The trade is fairly set agoing.[31]

Although David let the chief know what he thought of his raiding, their friendship stood up to this test. Meanwhile the Scot took every opportunity, during a three-month 'rest' period from August to October 1855, to hold 'large meetings' to sow seeds of transformation among Sekeletu's people. He was only too well aware that many could listen with delight one night and yet show no sign of change the following day. Yet he was encouraged to see 'many of the elders' paying 'marked attention to the addresses'. He found 'great difficulty in preparing them' because of the need 'to make the truth plain enough'.[32]

As well as working through how to present the story of the 'love of Christ' cross-culturally to the Kololo, David also considered how to reach those whose activities opposed his message. 'If I am permitted to enter on this large and interesting field I shall get copies of the Arabic Testament, of the edition furnished to Mungo Park, and distribute them among the Arabs, and copies of the New Testament in Portuguese,' he confided to his journal. He felt that one of the most remarkable effects of the character of Christ on his own heart was the desire to reach out to 'all the tribes of men', no matter what they had done. He felt sympathy even for the Boers whom he believed to have sacked his house and sought his life. They 'knew nothing of my feelings towards them. I never spoke to or thought of them but with feelings of deep commiseration.'[33]

Opposition to mission, however, inevitably led him to think of ways of circumventing it. He began to prepare for another journey, this time to the eastern coast along the River Zambezi, which seemed to be an easier way to the sea than the western route. Sekeletu promised his friend an escort of over 100 men, ten cattle, three riding-oxen, stores of food and the right to receive taxes from the tribes under the chief's control.

Before setting out, however, Livingstone made one last effort to get his message across.

Sunday, 28th October 1855. Feeling it might be my last opportunity with this people, I felt very anxious to convey to them a clear view of Christ's holy gospel and their need of his mercy and love in view of our future state (John iii:16–19). This precious message cannot & will not, I firmly believe, fall to the ground. May Almighty God command a blessing.[34]

Livingstone left Dinyanti on 3 November 1855 'accompanied by Sekeletu and 200 followers, who are of course all fed at his expense'.[35] The chief, in fact, 'took cattle for this purpose from every station we came to'.[36]

One night the two of them had to settle under a tree during an electric storm.

We passed through the patch of tsetse by night, and had some of the most vivid lightning I ever saw. When absent it was so pitchy dark the horses and men were completely blind, and a new flash would reveal all taking different directions. The horses trembled and cried out, the men laughed and stumbled against each other. The pelting rain came on and completed the confusion. Having passed several fires we were at last compelled to go to one.

All Livingstone's boxes had been sent ahead and the only item they still had with them was Sekeletu's blanket. This prompted an act of compassion which touched David deeply.

It felt miserably cold after the intense heat of the day. Wet to the skin, we lay down under a bush, and Sekeletu kindly covered me with his own blanket, lying during the remainder of the night uncovered himself.

Conscious as he was of the genuine humanity of his Kololo friends, Livingstone wondered how they would fare in the future. He thought of the Xhosa people, far down on the eastern border of the Cape Colony, who were being invaded and their land parcelled up. He compared their treatment to the contemporary case of a debtor who killed his creditor.

All shew great kindness. It is a pity that such men must perish by the advance of civilization. God grant that ere the ruthless Colonists advance so far the saving gospel be recieved [sic] as a solace for the soul in death. If they must perish, as certain races of animals, before others, by the

decree of Heaven, we would seem to be under the same
'terrible necessity' in our [Xhosa] wars as the American
Professor of Chemistry said *he* was to dismember the man
he murdered.[37]

8
No Man's Land

Leaving Seshéké on 12 November they sighted, nine days later, what looked like a huge bush fire. They saw smoke-like vapour

> arising exactly as when large tracts of grass are burned off. Five columns rose and bended in the direction of the wind against a low ridge covered with trees, and seemed at this distance (about 6 miles) to mingle with the clouds. They were coloured white below and higher up became dark, probably as the vapour condensed and returned in showers.[1]

When they got closer, David was amazed to see the River Zambezi drop out of view with a tremendous roar, into a great crack in the earth.

> The falls are singularly formed. They are simply the whole mass of the [Zambezi] waters rushing into a fissure or rent made right accross [sic] the bed of the river. In other falls we have usually a great change of level both in the bed of the river and ajacent [sic] country, and after the leap the river is not much different from what it was above the falls; but here the river, flowing rapidly among numerous islands ... meets a rent in its bed ... at right angles with its course, or nearly due east and west, leaps into it, and becomes a boiling white mass at the bottom.[2]

Livingstone later[3] estimated that the river, before dropping the equivalent of 95m, was 'a little over' a mile broad. Whereas the bottom of the crack into which it fell he felt (as a first impression) was less than 4m across. The crack went on for 30 miles, changing direction from left to right and right to left. So the river's 'course is changed also. It runs, or rather rolls and wriggles, from east to west untill [sic] it reaches what above was its left bank, then turns a corner, and follows or rather is guided by the fissure away in its usual route of S.E. and by E.'[4] Livingstone estimated that in places 'the lips of the rent' at the top of the fissure were between only 15 and 18.5m. As the river boiled and thundered through these narrow confines it sent up clouds of spray that looked like pillars.

The southern lip is straight & except at the west corner level with the general bed of the river above. Its wall is quite perpendicular. The northern lip is jagged, several pieces having fallen off, and five or six parts have the edge worn down a foot or two. In these, when the water is low, as it now is, the falls divide themselves, and from each ascends a column of vapour which rises from [62 to 77m]. Three of these falls throw more water each now, at low water, than the falls of Stonebyres do when the Clyde is flooded.[5]

To the head of one of these falls on the jagged northern edge of the drop they were taken by guides who knew how to avoid the submerged rocks in the river. In the lightest of canoes they sped 'swiftly down to an island situated at the middle and on the northern verge of the precipice over which the water roars. At one time we seemed to be going right to the gulph [sic], but though I felt a little tremour [sic] I said nothing, believing I could face a difficulty as well as my guides.'[6]

Gazing with awe into the boiling mass of water below, the men at the top tried to affect a kind of nonchalance.

My companions amused themselves by throwing stones into the gulph [sic] marvelling that a stone [2.5 to 5cm] in diameter should disappear before reaching the foaming waters … In peering down over the edge we could see only a dense white cloud with two rainbows on it.[7]

The ancient name of the falls, *Shungue*, was a reference to these rainbows. The reason the name had changed, however, was not far to seek.

A smart shower from the ascending columns falls [*sic*] when the wind shifted eastwards, and soon drenched us to the skin. This falls almost constantly on the southern lip, and a thick bank of evergreen trees enjoy perpetual showers. Several little streams are formed and run down that side, but never reach more than half way. The ascending vapour swills them up into the air with it. When the river is full, the noise is said to be terrific and the vapour seen ten miles off.[8]

From this phenomenon of vapour and noise came the contemporary African name for the falls: *Mosioatunya*, or 'the smoke that thunders'. Undaunted by the wild aspect of the scene and an abundance of hippopotami David decided to try a little botanical experiment. He revisited his precarious perch above the falls, a place which his companions called 'Garden Island'.

Returning with Sekeletu on the following day, I planted a lot of peach and apricot stones and coffee seeds on the island, which being already covered with trees seemed well adapted to be a nursery.[9]

After sharing their adventures thus far, Sekeletu parted with them at the falls.

Sekeletu had given Livingstone 114 men, mainly Tonga and a few Lozi. The chief men included Sekwebu, a Nguni who was a 'naturalized' Kololo, and they were joined at the falls by a Kololo headman who took charge of 'a large number' of the Tonga. So the party now numbered 115. David was again entrusted with a quantity of ivory, which he accepted as a means to 'promote legitimate commerce and work out the extinction of the trade in slaves carried on by the Mambari among the [Tonga] in the east'.[10]

In order to avoid tsetse fly, and to make contact with people recommended to him by Sekeletu, Livingstone's party made a detour to the north. The country, though parched, presented a pleasant contrast between 'the brilliant green of many trees' and 'the dark rufous green of the Mola', or cork tree, 'whose lovely shade & spreading oak form graces the scenery'.[11] They had reached the Tonga Plateau.

On Sunday 27 November David told the Tonga people 'for the first time in their lives that the Son of God loved them so that he came down from Heaven to save them'.[12] He could not help feeling that they were 'the most degraded-looking people' he had ever seen in Africa. It was the custom to knock out the front teeth on the attainment of puberty, and this was done especially to the women of marriageable age. 'Hard labour under a burning sun soon removes any little comeliness they possessed.'[13]

The men are not likely to improve either physically or mentally while addicted to frequent smoking of the Indian hemp. They like its narcotic effects, although two or three draughts are followed by a fit of violent coughing. This, which appears distressing and is in reality a most disgusting spectacle, is said to be pleasant. It ends often in rendering the victims liable to pneumonia ... I believe it was the proximate cause of [Sebetwane's] last illness.[14]

The Tonga were the last people owing allegiance to the Kololo. Beyond them lay 'No Man's Land', a beautiful country from which Sebetwane had been driven by the Nguni. 'It suited him exactly, both for cattle, corn, and *health*.' To discover healthy, elevated land was a key part of Livingstone's quest for possible mission centres. This area was now uninhabited.

'Rain is needed now, and appearances say it will not long be withheld. There are few trees. Large shady ones stand where the towns were formerly. The sight of open country now is very refreshing. The hills are low. Game abounds: buffaloes, eilands and zebras, with hartebeests, gnus and elephants. All are very tame.'[15]

Yet the people they came into contact with (on 4 December) were far from tame. The headman of 'the first village of rebels', or independent Tonga, appeared to be peaceable, but at dusk, the people of another village arrived and behaved differently. They began by trying to spear a young man who had gone for water. Then one came howling in the most hideous manner and at the top of his voice. His eyes were prominent, his lip covered with foam, and every muscle of his frame quivered. He came near me, and having a battle axe in his hand alarmed my men, but they were afraid to disobey my orders to offer no violence to any one. It seemed to me a case of extasy [sic] or prophetic frenzy voluntarily produced, as in the mysteries of the oracle priests of old. I felt a little afraid, but would not shew it before either my own people or strangers, and kept a sharp look out for the battle axe … I at last beckoned to the civil headman to remove him, and he did so, taking him by the hand and drawing him aside.[16]

Despite the good offices of the 'civil headman', as Livingstone and his party went further beyond the region controlled by Sekeletu, more and more people became suspicious of them. On 14 January 1856, at the meeting of the rivers Zambezi and Luangwa, it seemed that a fatal confrontation had come.

The people behave very suspiciously, collecting from all sides and keeping at a distance from us though professing friendship. They will have us completely in their power when we are parted in fording. They are silent as to the cause of the removal of the Portuguese hence, although we question them.[18]

Among the indications of previous Portuguese presence at the river confluence were signs of a worshipping community.

Here there are the ruins of an old church rudely built of stone. The bell (undated except I.H.S.+) lies broken by a dwelling house of the same materials, also the font in the edifice and the stand for the cross of wood. There are the remains of what may have been a fort, but all is occupied by gardens now.[18]

Among the ominous portents for the morrow was the fact that the people refused to provide more than two canoes for crossing the River Luangwa. Livingstone thought of evading this bottleneck tactic, but in the end rejected the idea.

I will not cross furtively by night as intended. It would appear as flight, and should such a man as I flee? Nay, verily. I shall take observations for lat. & long. tonight, though they may be the last. I feel quite calm now, thank God.[19]

Apart from the danger they were in, what troubled him was the thought of what people would say if he failed to make it to the coast. 'What an impulse will be given to the idea that Africa is not open if I perish now,' he thought. 'It seems a pity that the important facts about the two healthy longitudinal ridges should not become known in Christendom.'[20] He committed both his family and the events of the following day into the hands of God, and reminded himself of the promise of Christ, 'I am with you always, even unto the end of the world.' 'It's the word of a gentleman of the most sacred and strictest honour, and there is an end on't,' he decided.[21]

The following morning the Chief Mburuma's wife came from her village to visit Livingstone. She was forbidden to do so. All the women and children were sent away and armed men from the country all around came to surround Livingstone's camp on the left bank of the river. He was careful not to over-react, while keeping his wits about him.

Only one canoe was lent, though we saw two tied to the bank, and the part we crossed the river at, about a mile from the confluence, is a good mile broad. We passed all our goods first on to an island in the middle, then the cattle and men, I, occupying the post of honour, being the last to enter the canoe. We had by this means an opportunity of helping each other in case of attack.[22]

All the time the ferrying was going on armed warriors were

standing at David's back. He decided the greatest enemy was boredom, so he provided them with non-stop entertainment.

I ... shewed them my watch, burning glass, &c &c, and kept them amused till all were over except those who could go into the canoe with me. Thanked them all for their kindness and wished them peace. Perhaps after all they were influenced only by [the intention] to be ready in case I should play them some false trick. They have reason to be suspicious of whites.[23]

The day after David did not omit to send back gifts: 'a red baize cloth' for the chief 'and a few beads' for the warriors who had seen them across the river. Sekeletu had provided the cloth and beads for the purpose of buying a canoe. Even if they had only succeeded in borrowing one, it was worth leaving a good impression behind them. Mburuma and his men were 'highly pleased'.[24]

Livingstone found further evidence of an abandoned Portuguese settlement on the right bank of the river, and found out that the population had evacuated by boat on hearing of the approach of a Nguni force from the south. Sekwebu, it turned out, had been in that force. It had later attacked the Kololo and been defeated by Sebetwane. This probably explains why Sekwebu had been assimilated by the Kololo and later sent on the journey with Livingstone.

David certainly needed somebody with him who knew something of the land and its peoples. It was not long before he was again subjected to a nerve-jangling situation.

23rd January 1856. At Mpende's. This morning at sunrise a party of his people came close to our encampment, using strange cries and waving some red substance towards us. They then lighted a fire with charms in it, and departed uttering the same hideous screams as before. This is intended to render us powerless, and probably also to frighten us.[25]

Chief Mpende himself had so far not deigned to favour the newcomers with any direct message. He did, however, seem to be sending people to spy on them.

Parties of his people have been collecting from all quarters long before daybreak. It would be considered a challenge for us to move on down the river, and an indication of fear & invitation to attack if we went back, so we must wait in patience and trust in Him who has the hearts of all men in his hands.[26]

Patience and prayer were, it seemed, rewarded. One of Mpende's adviser's took the part of the newcomers.

Afternoon. After long discussion with his counsellors Mpende has been compelled to adopt peaceable measures. A man named Sindese-oa-lea was the chief advocate on our side. We passed him yesterday, and when we were parting he said to his people, 'Is that the man whom they wish to stop? After he has passed so many tribes, what could Mpende say to refusing him passage?'[27]

David was the more thankful for this outcome because he knew that the Tonga in his party were actually looking forward to a fight, and relished the idea of taking captives to carry the tusks for them. Once again, what troubled him was not so much personal danger as the detriment to his overall aim. 'I thank God heartily for this termination,' he wrote, 'for in the event of a skirmish I must resign my mission.'[28]

At this juncture Sekwebu proved invaluable. Livingstone had pacified his own men by giving them an ox, and sought to mollify Mpende by sending him a leg of it. That evening he sent Sekwebu to the chief to ask him to sell a canoe, since one of the men was too sick to walk. Sekwebu noticed that Mpende was momentarily disarmed by this admission of vulnerability. The chief remarked of Livingstone, 'That man is truly one of our friends, see how he lets me know his affliction.'

[Sekwebu] adroitly took advantage of the turn the conversation took and said, 'He highly appreciates your friendship and that of Mburuma, and as he is a stranger trusts you to direct him.' He replied, 'He ought to cross to the other side of the river, for this bank is hilly and rough and longer.' 'But who will take us accross [sic] if you do not?' 'Truly,' replied Mpende; 'I only wish you had come at midday, but you will cross. My people will ferry you over.'[29]

The friendly guidance of Mpende proved invaluable. Livingstone was continually surprised by the hospitality of the people they passed now. This made up a great deal for the fact that, by the beginning of February, all the riding-oxen were dead and the 'rich reddish-brown soil' was 'so clammy' it made walking very heavy going. Perhaps the soil's fertility encouraged the people to be generous.

I must express my admiration of the great liberality of these people to mine. They go into their villages and rarely return without some corn or maize. Some dance, and one, a natural bard, sings and jingles his bells, and never in vain. The real politeness with which presents of food are given through nearly all the tribes makes it easy to accept the gifts.[30]

However, as it was when approaching Angola from the east, so it was with entering the Portuguese settlements from the west: the nearer Livingstone got to tribes in actual contact with the colony, the harder dealings became with them. In the end, they had nothing to buy food with and little was offered. Livingstone's men were reduced to living on roots, and he became very weak and thin. On the evening of 1 March 1856,

Being pretty well tired out, I sent forward my letters of recommendation to the Governor of Tete ... At 3 in the morning we were aroused by two officers and a company of soldiers, who had been sent with the materials of a substantial breakfast for my use.

They also brought palanquins to take David to the town of Tete, which he reached on 3 March. 'A rest here will set me right again,' he wrote. 'Thank God who has brought me thus far.'[31]

Once again, Livingstone also had to be thankful for the ministrations of one person who went out of his way to aid his recovery. He was 'Tito Augusto d'Araujo Sicard, the name of the Governor of [Tete] who treated me with such extraordinary kindness and liberality. May Almighty God abundantly bless and reward him. 6th March 1856.'[32]

The Scot had become the first person to travel right across the continent of Africa while recording his route with an accuracy approaching the standards of modern mapping. Looking back, he was thankful to see how God's guidance and timing had protected him throughout the eighteen-month journey.

Livingstone only now found out that a war had been raging in this eastern region. When he had set out for the first time from Sekeletu's country in the centre of the continent, he might well have chosen to head for the east coast. The great River Zambezi flowed east and it seemed the easier route to the sea.

Instead, however, he had headed first for Luanda on the west coast. If he had gone to the east coast then he would have walked into the battle zone near Tete when the fighting was at its fiercest; but for now it was in abeyance. On the other hand, if he had given in to the temptation to go home from Luanda, and given up the possibility of travelling to the east, he could well have gone down with the ship that carried his papers.

Then again, he might never have tried to reach the sea at all if he had stayed to help Sechele and made it his mission to stay permanently with his people.

David's formidable father-in-law had spent a week with Sechele in June 1854, on his way to make contact again with Mzilikaze. Moffat had told Sechele that he regarded him as backslidden. 'I told him his reputed character and that his present circumstances rendered it impossible for him to be received into church fellowships.'[33]

Yet David had since heard that Sechele 'has, though unbidden by man, been teaching his own people. In fact, he has been doing all that I was prevented from doing, and I have been employed in exploring – a work I had no previous intention of performing. I think that I see the operation of the Unseen Hand in all this, and I humbly hope that it will still guide me to do good in my day and generation in Africa.'[34]

Now God had used him, he hoped, to open south central Africa to influences which would give an entry to that gospel which he had preached all along his route. With such an opportunity opened up, he now felt it right to go back to Britain and alert people to it.

Perhaps it was with a view to catching the interest of his countrymen that Livingstone now wrote to Lord Clarendon at the Foreign Office, suggesting a royal link with the greatest natural phenomenon he had seen on his transcontinental journey. 'I would fain call them the "smoke-sounding falls of Victoria",' he wrote, adding rather bashfully, 'but it smacks of impudence, rather, in a private person to make free with Her Majesty's name.'[35]

So it was that Livingstone sought to link the name of Mosioatunya with that of the chief of his tribe. The Kololo-led party would have understood that Livingstone needed to go back and see his chief, and the time it took to fulfil his promises would not have been the paramount factor to them that it would have been to westerners.

Yet the fact that he was leaving them at Tete did not mean that David could forget his responsibility to them. He committed himself to re-enter Africa at a point close to where he had left it, so that he could take them all back home.

9
Reunion and redirection

Sekwebu, having proved himself an invaluable travelling companion on the land journey, insisted on coming aboard the naval brig that was to take Livingstone to Mauritius. Hoping to see the Scot's native land, he was not prepared for the culture shock involved in seeing for the first time rolling seas, and the technology of a steamship which came out from Mauritius to tow them into harbour.

Sekwebu reacted by jumping into one of the lifeboats. David soothed his troubled mind by speaking to him of the familiar; they were going to see Mma-Robert. The Kololo, calmer than before, seemed to forget his threat to jump into the water. Nevertheless, the following night, he did just that, and was never seen again. David had not allowed the sailors to chain him, because that would have been to treat him like a slave. Sekeletu would not have forgiven him for putting one of his leading advisers under restraint.

Mma-Robert, the 'white African', had also been subjected to tremendous mental strain by going back to Britain. She too had not seen steam power before, although she handled train travel to Scotland better than Sekwebu could have done. The climate – it was an especially wet year in Scotland when she arrived – made her unwell, and it is unlikely that she could make head or tail of the broad Scottish dialect of David's parents in Hamilton. Culture shock for Mary was inevitable.

To Neil and Agnes Livingstone's consternation, Mary upped and went south with the children, without telling them where she was going. In fact it was to Hackney, where her father had friends. Finding lodgings was not easy, however, at a time when upheavals on the Continent were flooding London with refugees. When she did get them, there were many financial problems; although the London Missionary Society was sending her an allowance, it was not adequate for her needs. She was still an African, completely unused to the value and management of money and liable to incur expense for things (such as laundry) which would have cost her nothing but hard work in the past.

A move to Manchester, where her mother had friends, did nothing to ease the financial burden of looking after four growing children. Used to the open veldt, they did not take kindly to city life and Robert, in particular, was quite a problem. Tom was often ill, young Oswell needed attention and only Agnes seemed peaceful; she was to develop a closer relationship with her father, albeit by letter, than any of the others.

The strain told in a recurrence of the problem of Bell's palsy or semi-paralysis of the face, which showed that Mary was holding things in and not giving vent to her true feelings. In the end she found a haven with a Quaker family, called the Braithwaites, who lived at Kendal in the Lake District. Mrs Braithwaite had herself been involved in mission in America and understood what it was like to be separated from husband and family. In her care, Mary was able to let out her emotions. Aching for Africa and for David, she had a breakdown in the winter of 1853.

For two months she was also very ill physically, but as spring came she was able to go out and walk the narrow lanes. The countryside around Kendal reminded her of the landscape of Kolobeng, and she hoped so much to go to the Cape that year and rejoin David. When she heard that instead he had disappeared again from Luanda into the interior, she was sorrowful and set her face again to the south.

Recognizing that she would have to stay in England until the return of David from his journey along the Zambezi, she took rooms near Epsom in the summer of 1854. Though she wrote to David frequently, and he to her, by September 1855 he had still not received her letters (barring the first she had sent from Britain). Correspondence got through again once David reached Quelimane, a small Portuguese customs post on the east coast, at one of the mouths of the Zambezi. Coming to Cairo via the Red Sea, David was deeply affected to find that his father, Neil, had died before he could reach England.

Writing from the Bay of Tunis, David had to tell Mary that a storm had damaged the ship and he would have to make his way overland across France. He overtook the letter, however, so Mary was still at Southampton when he arrived by train at London Bridge on 10 December 1856. A day later, they were at last reunited. David had intended to take her back to Africa within a few months, but he had not reckoned with the claims of Victorian society.

Old friends such as William Oswell, who had paid for Mary to bring the children to England, were present at an official reception of the Royal Geographical Society on 15 December. Not only was David awarded their Victoria Medal, but also Mary was praised by Lord Shaftesbury. He described how she had encouraged and guided David as his companion during their life and work together in southern Africa. He spoke of the anguish she had suffered through separation from David during her time with the children in Britain, and of the positive way she had committed herself to this course of action.

Lord Shaftesbury's tribute to Mary had a distinctively Buxtonian flavour to it. He spoke of her spirit of sacrifice for the sake of both the advancement of 'civilization' and the progress of the gospel. For Livingstone himself, these three themes were bound together like a cord. His view of mission embraced every area of a national life. To him, the transformation of Africa and the building of Christian communities were inseparable. Since 'the end of the geographical feat' was 'but the beginning of the missionary enterprise'[1], it was quite natural to move from a meeting of the Royal Geographical Society to the London Missionary Society the following day, with one and the same Lord Shaftesbury in the chair.

It is possible that the LMS directors were less 'Buxtonian' than Lord Shaftesbury, for they had not shown the same enthusiasm for Livingstone's discoveries as he and Sir Roderick Murchison, the President of the RGS. When Livingstone had appeared at the mouth of the Zambezi, excited by the great river's potential as a highway to the interior, the LMS had written to say that they were in no position to finance any project in what they saw as untested, distant and demanding fields. The society was in the red; but what had really hit home was a warning that the LMS directors had no real mandate for supporting initiatives which they felt were only very tenuously linked to the propagation of the gospel.

If the LMS were really unable to take the wider view of mission, and sanction projects aimed at improving economic and political conditions on the ground, they could point to the failure of the Niger expedition[2] which Livingstone had seen launched in 1840. For Buxton, who had supported the project to try to undercut the slave trade, the loss of life through malaria and other causes which befell it was a terrible disappointment.

Livingstone knew, however, that there were those, such as Henry Venn, the General Secretary of the Church Missionary Society, who were still prepared to pursue a wider view of mission than that subscribed to by the LMS. It would not be long before he began to correspond with Venn. For the time being, however, he maintained his relationship with the LMS, who agreed to consider a mission to the Kololo.

Meanwhile, David took Mary north to Hamilton in Scotland to see his widowed mother, Agnes, and to gaze upon Neil Livingstone's empty chair. As he had told his mother, there was no-one he would have liked better to have recounted his adventures to than his father.

David felt certain his duty lay in Africa, but first John Murray, the publisher, persuaded him to write an account of his life and service there. Apart from struggling with the manuscript, David also found time for family life. He and Mary settled in a small house at Hadley Green, a village just north of London. Neighbours remarked how much he seemed to enjoy taking Robert, Agnes and Thomas into the Barnet woods whenever he got the chance.

The newspapers were treating his transcontinental journey much as the Apollo moon landing was seen more than a century later. The result was a whirl of social engagements that Mary was unused to, linked to a series of public lectures given by David. Following his lecture at the Society of Arts, for example, they were invited to a 'Photographic Soirée' at

King's College, by a naturalist called Professor Owen. It turned out to be a 'dress assembly in the Grand Hall'.

Mary innocently turned up wearing a straw hat of 1846 vintage, with a dress from the same fashion period. She became uncomfortably aware of what Professor Owen calls 'the extraordinary scrutinies of many fine ladies as they shrank at first from contact as far as the crowd permitted'. Yet when the news got round that the odd-looking couple with funny accents were Dr and Mrs Livingstone, 'what a change came over the scene. It was which of the scornful dames could first get introduced to Professor Owen to be introduced to Mrs Livingstone and the photographs were comparatively deserted for the dusky strangers.'[3]

While society feted the Livingstones and David was given the freedom of several British cities, the LMS was less certain about what to do with them. They had received a report from their southern committee recommending that the mission to the Kololo be started, on condition that at least one member of the Moffat family be involved. Yet they were unhappy about public subscriptions being taken up for the Livingstones over and above their LMS salary of £100 a year. David's book *Missionary Travels and Researches in South Africa* sold out the first printing of 12,000 copies on its publication in November 1857. Later printings were to sell another 58,000 copies, allowing David and Mary to set up a trust fund for their children. They offered some of the money to the LMS, to help sponsor the expedition to the Kololo.

David's vision, however, was wider than the Kololo mission. He wanted to improve the conditions along the Zambezi where slave war was rife and where, he felt, trade needed to be encouraged. For these wider Buxtonian schemes the LMS had little time or enthusiasm. Quietly, David began to look elsewhere for support. Through a correspondence carried out by Sir Roderick Murchison of the RGS with Lord Clarendon at the Foreign Office, he was eventually offered a post as Honorary British Consul.

The idea was that he should lead a government expedition, which was to include a geologist, a naval officer, an artist, an engineer and a 'moral agent', to assess the potential resources of the Zambezi area for agricultural development, trade and communications. It was understood that Livingstone would also be on the look-out for healthy sites for mission centres.

The fact that Livingstone accepted the leadership of this expedition, thus making himself unavailable to the LMS to lead the Kololo mission, 'has to be seen in the light of his conviction that the Christian future of inland Africa was tied in with the whole complex of issues that his first great journey had revealed.'[4] Mission would succeed in the long term only if the slave trade, carried on by the Arabs and connived at by the Portuguese, could be displaced by normal commerce.

Where Livingstone might be criticized over his resignation from the LMS is not for any weakening of his sense of vocation, but for keeping them in the dark about the representations of Sir Roderick Murchison to the Foreign Office. Although nobody would normally want to give up one job before being sure of another, this was not a normal situation; the LMS had agreed to the Kololo mission on the condition that at least one Moffat would be included in it, and on the assumption that Livingstone would lead it. What he actually offered to do now was to visit the mission once he had found his way up the Zambezi; hardly the same degree of commitment.

Nevertheless, the lectures and writings of the Scottish pioneer were starting something much bigger than he, or anybody else, could control. In the wake of stirring speeches at Cambridge, both to the students of the University and to the merchants of the City Corporation, moves were afoot to found new missions and new trading ventures. On the whole, businessmen were slower to commit themselves than volunteers for missions, but Livingstone did not stay long enough to see the results of his appeal.

The effect on the students was, by all accounts, electric. His voice rose almost to a shout at the final phrase.

I beg to direct your attention to Africa; – I know that in a few years I shall be cut off in that country, which is now open; do not let it be shut again! I go back to Africa to try to make an open path for commerce and Christianity; do you carry out the work which I have begun. I LEAVE IT WITH YOU![5]

A lot of ink has been spilt by African historians on the meaning of the phrase 'commerce and Christianity', but perhaps the best way to interpret the commercial aspect is to refer to the speech David made the following day, 5 December 1857, to the merchants in the Town Hall.

I propose in my next expedition to visit the Zambesi [sic], and to propitiate the different chiefs along its banks, endeavouring to induce them to cultivate cotton, and to abolish the slave-trade: already they trade in ivory and gold-dust, and are anxious to extend their commercial operations. There is thus a probability of their interests being linked with ours, and thus the elevation of the African would be the result.[6]

This assumption that trade would 'elevate' the African through mutual interest would have rung strangely in the ears of the average LMS supporter, who read in the missionary magazines of the time constant complaints about the corrupting influence of European traders in southern Africa. There is little evidence that Livingstone and his contemporaries had any precise data on the economic links between the slave-trade and other forms of commercial activity.

Nevertheless, the drawbacks of alternative types of activity have to be set against the havoc wreaked by the slave wars, which had brought ordinary links between tribes and nations to an end. If the expectation of the beneficial effects of commerce was overly optimistic, it was tempered by the desire for deeper transformation through the gospel; Livingstone told his Cambridge hearers that his purpose was not merely to 'elevate' Africans, but also to open Africa in such a way that her people might become conscious of their need for the salvation of the soul.

The attraction of Livingstone's appeal was that it made ordinary working people feel that what they did had some relevance to Christ's kingdom. Normal working relations could help to counteract conditions of anarchy inimical to the peaceful proclamation of the gospel. 'Everyone can play a part' was his theme with the townspeople – including the vital work of prayer.

Parliament approved the provisions for the Zambezi expedition on a tide of public goodwill. Lord Palmerston was particularly sympathetic to the plan. Prince Albert was worried about the possible reactions of the Portuguese to Livingstone's activities, and in one respect he had cause to be. David at this stage secretly hoped to settle larger communities in healthy sites in Africa. Although the intention was to exercise a positive influence, its practical outworking would have a lot of potential for colonial rivalry. He outlined the idea to a close Cambridge friend, Professor Adam Sedgwick.

That you may have a clear idea of my objectives I may state that they have something more in them than meets the eye. They are not merely exploratory, for I go with the intention of benefitting [sic] both the African and my own countrymen. I take a practical mining geologist from the School of Mines to tell us of the mineral resources of the country, then an economic botanist to give a full report on the vegetable productions – fibrous, gummy and medicinal substances together with the dye stuffs – everything which may be useful in commerce. An artist to give the scenery, a naval officer to tell of the capacity of the river communications and a moral agent to lay the Christian foundation for knowing that aim fully. All this machinery has for its ostensible object the development of African trade and the promotion of civilisation but what I tell to none but such as you in whom I have confidence is thus I hope it may result in an English colony in the healthy highlands of Central Africa – (I have told it only to the Duke of Argyll).[7]

How Queen Victoria would have looked on such an aim at this stage in her reign is unclear. However, she showed more cordiality to David than did her consort. On 13 February 1858, one week after penning the letter to Adam Sedgwick, Livingstone called on her. She gave the Scot a good-humoured audience, in which they chatted about his travels.

David informed Her Majesty that it would be much easier to hobnob with Africans now that he could say he had seen his chief, as it always astonished them to hear that he had not. They would also want to know whether his chief was wealthy.

'Certainly, she is very wealthy,' he would reply.

'Well then,' the questioners would demand, 'how many cows has she got?'

At this point, attendants within earshot were startled to hear Queen Victoria burst out laughing.

The same evening, a farewell dinner was held, chiefly organized by RGS members, with Sir Roderick Murchison in the chair. Mary was in the gallery, with the ladies, far too hot in a hall crammed with more than 300 guests, but concentrating hard on the speeches. Her companion was Miss Coutts, granddaughter of the banker Thomas Coutts. Against the advice of her friend Charles Dickens, who regarded all effort in Africa by Europeans as wasted, she had taken an interest in the idea of cotton plantations which would draw money away from the slave-worked plantations in America.

Miss Coutts had also sent David the most modern microscope available for medical research. David was developing his own treatment for malaria, realizing that it was connected somehow with the kind of stagnant water that would be present near the mouth of the Zambezi. The cause of the disease – mosquito-borne parasites – was still unknown.

Mary kept her eyes fixed on David throughout the speeches. Miss Coutts was watching her reactions.

There is doubtless much activity of mind hidden under her extreme quietness. She betrayed by a slight twinkle in her dark eyes that she was gratified at the Duke of Wellington's speech about her, as the true helpmate of her honoured husband ... After the whole room had risen to salute her, and when the cheering and waving of handkerchiefs had subsided, I told her she ought to acknowledge the attention in some way and she did it at once with a calm curtsey.[8]

Mary was less restrained when it came to saying goodbye to Robert, Agnes and Tom at the Braithwaites' in Kendal, where she and David spent their last night in England. After chatting with each child in turn, the following morning it was time to go to the station. She wanted the last look she gave her children to be a smile, and made every effort to hold other emotions back. But she could not keep it up. Her train seemed to take an eternity to move and the tears welled up in her eyes before the last boy on the platform lost sight of her carriage window.

At Birkenhead, a new steam launch named after her, the *Ma Robert*, was loaded on board their ship, the *Pearl*. Oswell, now an energetic seven-year-old, sailed with them in rough seas and heavy snow. Both he and Mary were seasick all the way to West Africa.

Landing briefly in Sierra Leone, they discovered that Mary was not merely seasick; she was expecting another baby. Reluctantly, they decided that she would have to stop at the Cape. There was no way that she could go straight on with the expedition to the Zambezi.

Mary had her baby, Anna Mary, on 16 November 1858 at Kuruman. Missing David, she nevertheless did not lack for company. Her brother John Moffat and his wife Emily were there, making preparations for a move. Robert Moffat was due to take them on a mission to Mzilikaze and his section of the Nguni (which was to become known as the Ndebele people).

This was in addition to the fact that in the months following the birth, an experienced missionary couple, the Helmores, were preparing the expedition they were to lead to Sekeletu and the Kololo. Mary had agreed with David that by joining this expedition she would meet him in Kololo country. Mary and the Helmores were to be joined by Mr and Mrs Roger Price.

As the two expeditions prepared to go north, Kuruman became a hive of activity.

10
Trials and tears

David now had even stronger motives for keeping his promise to the Kololo to take them back, eventually, to Sekeletu's country. Not only had he helped to sponsor the LMS mission to go to the Kololo; he had also arranged to meet Mary herself on the Zambezi at the site of the new mission centre at Sekeletu's town. It was hoped that the chief would be willing to move away from the rather feverish low-lying area of his capital at Dinyanti, and use higher ground.

So Livingstone was involved in a two-pronged (and what later became a three-pronged)[1] assault on the Zambezi. The mission party, led by the Helmores, were to head north from Kuruman along the route that Mary had gone before to Sebetwane's country. At the same time the *Ma Robert* was to open up the river route from the coast to Tete and from Tete to Seshéké, in the centre of the continent.

The human responsibility Livingstone felt (let alone the visionary intention of a Buxtonian in seeing the Zambezi as 'God's Highway' to the interior) does much to explain his apparently unshakeable determination to force a way upriver. Yet his colleagues on the government expedition were less aware of what was at stake for him, and at times thought him fanatically keen to push on regardless of the consequences.

The first task for the expedition was to find for itself a navigable channel, which (with the help of the Navy) they did with the discovery of the Kongone entrance to the Zambezi. They got through the delta of the Zambezi, into the main channel of the river 30 miles inland.

At this point trouble flared up between rival naval personnel. The senior naval officer, Captain Bedingfeld, brought the *Ma Robert* alongside the *Pearl* which was in the care of Captain Duncan of the Merchant Navy. Bedingfeld leaped on board and quarrelled with Duncan. Livingstone responded by making it clear to Bedingfeld that his criticisms

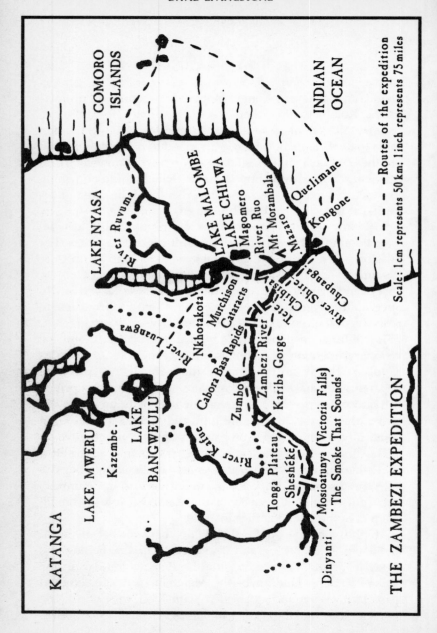

THE ZAMBEZI EXPEDITION

of Captain Duncan were unacceptable. The senior officer felt humiliated, and resigned.[2]

Bedingfeld's place as second in command of the expedition was taken by Dr John Kirk, the expedition's medical officer and botanist. Kirk was to prove far more loyal to Livingstone than Bedingfeld, who had a record of insubordination in the Navy.

The *Pearl* left the expedition and headed downriver on 26 June 1858, leaving the expedition's supplies on an island in the river. The *Ma Robert* was to be used to ferry supplies up the Zambezi to Tete. Getting there, however, was not a simple matter.

The river from Mazaro to the mouth of its tributary, the Shire (pronounced 'Shirry'), was controlled by a half-caste named Mariano, who was at war with the Portuguese. The Portuguese commander, Colonel José da Silva, was pinned down at Mazaro. The Scot was called upon to rescue him, under fire, from Mazaro and take him across the river to a house at Chupanga.

In the stone house, situated in a none-too-healthy mangrove area, the Scot treated da Silva for malaria. Under protest, the man took David's quinine-based pills and recovered. This was a real opportunity to show goodwill. Da Silva was the Governor of Quelimane, the Portuguese port of entry into the Zambezi. The Portuguese authorities were suspicious of the expedition, but it happened that two of the gentlemen present were old friends of Livingstone. Colonel Nunes of Quelimane, like Major Tito Sicard of Tete, had been hospitable to the Scot when he reached the Portuguese settlements at the end of his transcontinental journey two years previously. Now both helped him again by sending men to cut wood for the boiler of the *Ma Robert*.

The new steamer ate up fuel at what seemed to the members of the expedition a fantastic rate. It snorted so much that they dubbed it *The Asthmatic*.[3] Slow progress at the unhealthy time of year meant a drop in morale. 'Very curious are the effects of African fever on certain minds,' noted Livingstone. 'Cheerfulness vanishes, and the whole mental horizon is overcast.'[4]

These were the conditions in which Livingstone had to motivate a team which only succeeded in reaching the Portuguese town of Tete – the official starting-point for the expedition's work – ten months after leaving England.

Yet the Kololo were overjoyed when the *Ma Robert*, the expedition steam launch, reached Tete on 8 September 1858. As David came ashore in a small boat, they almost overturned it in their eagerness to rush through the water, neck-high, and greet their 'father'.[5]

They carried him ashore, singing in SeTswana. So many of the townsfolk had told them that their 'Englishman' (as the Portuguese and half-castes referred to the Scot) would never return. Now the doubters were proved wrong. 'Now our hearts will sleep. We have seen you,' cried out the Kololo. David was moved to tears at their reception. 'I am glad to meet you,' he said in SeTswana, but there is no [Sekwebu].'

Having explained the fate of his former companion, David then heard what had happened to those who had remained behind. Six men had been murdered by a suspicious chief; thirty had died of smallpox; and seventy-eight had survived.

'Poor fellows,' David wrote in his journal, 'how sad I feel when I think on those who have departed from this scene, and I pray, "Free me, O Lord, from blood-guiltiness." The principal men are here. "Grant, Lord, that I may be more faithful to them who remain".'[6]

The Zambezi was by now unusually low, giving the chance to test the truth of disturbing reports from the townspeople that there were formidable (and, so far as they knew, impassable) rapids upstream. The strategic significance of the rapids can be readily appreciated when we consider Livingstone's overall plan to turn the Zambezi into a 'highway into the interior'.

On his previous journey the Scot had mapped the route of the Zambezi from Seshéké for the greater part of its course towards the sea. He fervently hoped that that same route would now lead him in the opposite direction to the Kololo and to Mary. If the river proved to be navigable for its whole length, it would open up the possibility of a chain of mission (and, from the trading point of view, commercial) centres that could be supplied from the sea. Steamers with a shallow draught (that is, with keels that would not ground too easily on the river bottom) could enter the Zambezi at the newly discovered Kongone channel and not only reach Tete, but also get beyond the Portuguese-claimed area and go right up to the Victoria Falls.

The problem, however, was that in the final stages of his transcontinental journey Livingstone had left the course of the Zambezi and taken an overland route to Tete. So he did not know what the course of the river was like above Tete. None of the verbal reports he had heard prepared him for what he eventually found when the expedition pushed upriver to Cabora Basa. 'The scenery ... is quite remarkable and totally unlike anything that has ever been said of the rapids.'[7]

Livingstone recorded the first sight of this great obstacle to his plans on 10 November. Having got round the initial rapid, the *Ma Robert* got stuck at the second. A spur of conically shaped mountains hemmed the channel in. David estimated that this 'main channel' usually ranged from 37 to 46m in width. However, the channel ran into a deep fissure winding between a mass of huge rocks. The perpendicular rock

> makes the water branch off at some spots and there the main channel is as little as [19m] broad ... We saw abundant evidence that the water in flood rises more than [30m] perpendicularly and as the rise at the opening is not more than [9.25m] the rush of waters must be terrific.[8]

This was how the rapids looked at low water. Yet another disturbing report reached Livingstone's ears that there was more to come further upriver.

To finish the survey the Scot was on the point of pushing on by himself, leaving the less fit members of the expedition behind. Kirk remonstrated with him, and he agreed to take his second-in-command along with him and some Kololo. They had to cross the baking rock of a mountain spur on foot, before a sudden bend in the river gave them a glimpse of the new cataract at Morumbwa.

The Kololo were suffering from blisters on their bare feet, as they faced a steep climb of over 90m to get a view of the cataract. David reckoned the temperature to be 130°F (50°C), making it difficult to hold on to the sizzling rock. 'There we were,' he recalled, 'clambering up the face of the slippery promontory, certain that if one of the foremost lost his hold he would knock all the others down who came behind him.'[9]

The waterfall had a drop of not much more than 9m, and Livingstone hoped that the river in full flood would rise well above it. To free the channel, however, he predicted optimistically that a bit of rock-blasting would do the trick. A third visit to Cabora Basa confirmed that the Morumbwa cataract did disappear at high water, but the current was so strong that the Scot wrote to request a more powerful steamer to take it on.

While the new steamer, the *Pioneer*, was being built, Livingstone turned his attention to the valley of the River Shire, a tributary of the Zambezi that flowed out of higher ground that might prove suitable for mission settlement. As the *Ma Robert* progressed up the river, the Cewa tribe along its banks saw a steamer for the first time. Crowds crept along the river banks to track the expedition by day; by night guards kept watch with bows and poisoned arrows.

Livingstone was determined not to give in to intimidation, although he could not stop his petrified interpreter from begging permission to pass. We can compare Livingstone's analysis of the incident and the frustrations he felt, with Kirk's matter-of-fact account of how they muddled through.

When we got to a large village after dinner, we were hailed and ordered to stop ... There might be four or five hundred natives with their poisoned arrows all ready. We went on some little distance, then came on other groups who asked more civilly where we were going. Our interpreter made a mess of the whole thing by not sticking to what he was told.

One way and another, things looked bad. I saw all the arms loaded and the powder up and had the powder and rockets for the little ceremony at hand.[10]

While Kirk's role was to deter would-be attackers, Livingstone had to communicate their objectives. Generally he would try to convince a hostile chief that they came 'neither to take slaves nor to fight, but only to open a path by which our countrymen might follow to purchase cotton, or whatever else they might have to sell'.[11] However, on this occasion the message suffered from interference.

One man seemed to speak, from his gesticulations, so I stopped the engine to hear. He asked where we were going and, on my telling the interpreter to tell our objects, he began to entreat the man to allow us to pass instead. The headman, hearing this, ordered us to stop, and as it was vain to try and get this slave to speak what I said, I thought the best thing I could do was to go on and thereby demonstrate what I wished, namely, that we English did not want 'leave to pass'. About [275m] further on, another large party stood and as the headman spoke civilly, I stopped to talk, but this fool of an interpreter would do as his fears dictated. I told him to ask where the chief was; this he would not do, though I repeated my request again and again.

Only by offering a hostage could Livingstone coax the headman aboard to negotiate.

I gave him a present for his chief and two yards of calico to himself, shewing him at [the] same time our arms and telling him if we wanted to fight we had the means of doing so but were not anxious to quarrel.

Kirk was no doubt relieved to find the confrontation defused and concludes laconically, 'We parted friends as far as appearances went.' Livingstone, however, was extremely frustrated by the episode. The headman 'went off satisfied but

I was very much dissatisfied, as it appeared to him he had forced us to ask his leave to pass, and he shewed it by calling out to us, Go, go, go, when he reached the shore'.[12] The incident made him take a resolution to work hard on improving his cross-cultural communication, albeit at second or third hand. He would train his trusted companions to interpret for him.

The [Kololo] do not understand the [Cewa], but I intend to make them speak the [Tete] tongue to another man we have on board, and compel him to translate literally. I never was so badly off for means of communicating with the people.[13]

Although Livingstone felt that he had not been able to communicate effectively, he had shown that the expedition was both able to defend itself and unwilling to pick a quarrel. On the next journey up the Shire in March people were pleased to sell rice, poultry and grain to the expedition. This was something of a breakthrough, because the Cewa tribe had never allowed the Portuguese to pass through their territory.

Once past the formerly suspicious Cewa headmen, the main obstacle Livingstone faced was a natural one. There were cataracts up river on the Shire also, and David had called them the Murchison Cataracts after his friend at the Royal Geographical Society, Sir Roderick Murchison. Livingstone and Kirk were able to leave the *Ma Robert* in the care of Chibisa, a chief whose village was 10 miles below the Murchison Cataracts. With Kololo companions they passed north on foot through the Cewa area to find, on 19 April, a lake called Chilwa.

Viewing it from the base of Mount Pirimiti on the south-south-west side, Livingstone made a description of the area which he sent on 15 May 1859 to the editor of the *Intelligencer*, the Church Missionary Society magazine, as part of a series of reports published on Livingstone's discoveries.[14] Stressing that the country was high, cool and well-watered, David suggested that the CMS start a mission there. He also promised to put the proposal to Henry Venn, the CMS General Secretary.

Henry Venn would not have been surprised to know that Livingstone followed his letter to the CMS with another to James Aspinall Turner, a Manchester cotton manufacturer.[15] It was one of the material results of the survey of the Shire that plains on both sides of the river could well support agricultural projects, including cotton-growing. In fact, at one point the grass waved high above the heads of the party. Yet instead of using this rich soil to plant crops, the people were trying to make a living out of the slave-trade.

Following the River Shire to its source, the party sighted Lake Nyasa on 16 September. For the first time, European eyes looked out on the beautiful and seemingly endless stretch of water – to see it crisscrossed by the dhows of Arab slave-traders. A local chief who invited them to the village at the confluence of the river and the lake told them an Arab slave party was encamped nearby. Soon the leaders came over. They carried guns and, thought the Scot, 'were a villainous-looking lot. They evidently thought the same of us, for they offered several young children for sale.'[16]

The traders were following what was clearly a major slave route from the country to the west of the lake – Katanga and an area called Kazembe's – across Nyasa and down to the coast. Analysing the economics of their trade, Livingstone realized that the Arabs would not get enough for their slaves at the coast (or the market in Zanzibar) to pay for the food the gang would eat before reaching it. Only because the slaves were used as porters – usually carrying elephant tusks – was the trade lucrative. If, therefore, a cheaper way of carrying goods could be supplied, the slave trade would be made 'unprofitable'.[17]

This was a typically Buxtonian analysis; it was based on the principle that slavery is an economic institution, and must be countered by economic means. Applying this principle, the Scot came up with the idea of launching a steamer on Lake Nyasa. This would require building a road around the Murchison Cataracts – back-breaking perhaps, but feasible – and assembling the parts of the steamer on the lake.

The Scot's economic response to what he saw on the lake was to send Rae, the *Ma Robert*'s engineer, back to Britain to supervise the construction of a third steamer, the *Lady Nyassa*, that was to operate along the Shire above the Murchison Cataracts; while the *Pioneer*, the government-built steamer that was already on its way, would replace the ailing *Ma Robert* on the lower Shire and the Zambezi. He was prepared to pay for the third steamer himself, if the government were unwilling to do so.

Livingstone's missionary response to the survey of the Shire and the uplands beyond was to recommend that a new mission, whose existence he had heard of for the first time early in 1860, should settle on the banks of that river. David had never been denominationally minded, and the fact that the fledgling Universities Mission to Central Africa was definitely of a High Church Anglican character (having links with Dr Pusey and the Oxford Movement) worried him not a whit. The important thing was that they had responded to his appeal at Cambridge to risk life and limb in Africa.

The fact that they would be sending a bishop to lead them was also a plus point in Livingstone's mind. Knowing neither the language nor the culture nor the terrain, the UMCA would inevitably depend heavily on David's advice; yet he was already overstretched. The London Missionary Society had been bitterly disappointed that he could not personally lead their mission to the Kololo, but it was difficult enough to keep the government expedition together under his supervision.

David, who valued independence and assumed that his team members would not want to be interfered with too much in pursuing their duties, failed to supervise the younger members – such as the geologist, Thornton, and the artist, Baines – closely enough. Even his own brother, Charles, who had come over from America to join the expedition as a photographer and 'moral agent', felt at a loss to know exactly what was required of him.

In going to Nyasa he had left Baines, the artist and storekeeper, at Tete with his brother Charles and the young geologist, Thornton. Baines and Thornton had not got on well with Charles, who reported that both men had been negligent in their duties. Rae, the engineer, probably insinuated to Charles that Baines had misappropriated some of the stores. Livingstone sent Dr John Kirk, as second-in-command, to inspect Baines's boxes and to bring him to the Kongone, where a naval ship was expected. Kirk found no evidence against Baines, but noted that when questioned by Livingstone his replies were confused. There was no opportunity for a proper trial; Livingstone dismissed Baines, and Thornton too was suspended.

This was rough justice, and there is little doubt that under the strain of the demands made upon him, in an environment reminiscent of Joseph Conrad's book *Heart of Darkness*, a certain ruthlessness entered into the Scotsman's soul. Put to work in the mills as a boy, he had got his education only by dint of dogged determination, reading line by line as he passed a book stuck on his factory machine. With this kind of background, Livingstone found it difficult, if not impossible, to comprehend in any European anything less than complete and continual dedication to duty. After an unexpected outburst by Charles, David wrote:

My brother informs me that members of the Expedition did not get orders what to do, and were at a loss to know how to act ... All were willing and anxious to help if only I would have told them. He never told me this before ... On principle I abstained from multiplying orders, believing it more agreeable to men to do their duty in their own way.[18]

The result, in Baines, had probably been simple carelessness. Thornton redeemed himself, first by going on an expedition to Mount Kilimanjaro to the north, and then returning to the Zambezi on his own terms. Charles, however, having failed to produce photography of much value and having proved unreliable in his meteorological observations and magnetic readings, found that he had lost his brother's trust altogether. In his journal David wrote of Charles, 'as an assistant he has been of no value'.[19]

In his leadership of Europeans, it seems, Livingstone veered between expecting everything or nothing, a trait seen 'first, in putting too much trust in subordinates, and then in going to the other extreme by withdrawing his trust completely'.[20]

The contrast with his approach to Africans is striking. In the next phase of Livingstone's journeys he was to march overland to Seshéké and Sekeletu's country, to keep his promise to return the Kololo to their chief. This was also, as we have seen, his only chance to make contact with the LMS party led by the Helmores, in which Livingstone had suggested Mary should travel. In this journey, which began on 15 May 1860, David was back in his element, leading a group of Africans, in fulfilment of an obligation Africans understood.

It was without rancour that the Scot witnessed a number of Kololo desert early on in the march; he understood that they had married slave women at Tete, who had been forced to remain behind by their owners. 'We fully expected that all who had children would prefer to return to [Tete], for little ones are known to prove the strongest ties, even to slaves.'[21] If Livingstone had shown his European colleagues part of the sympathy he demonstrated for Africans, they too might have appreciated his leadership.

Charles, who came on the march, behaved bad-temperedly towards both his brother and the Kololo; Kirk, by contrast, won their respect. After the early desertions, the party held together. At Zumbo they saw (for the second time for Livingstone) the ruins of a trading-post.

The early traders, guided probably by Jesuit missionaries, must have been men of taste and sagacity. They selected for their village the most charmingly picturesque site in the country ... The Portuguese of the present day have certainly reason to be proud of the enterprise of their ancestors.

The site had been ideal for commerce, being at the confluence of the Zambezi and a tributary, the Luangwa, which ran in from the north. Yet it was long abandoned, along with the mission that had accompanied it:

The chapel, near which lies a broken church bell ... is an utter ruin now, and desolation broods around ... Thorn bushes ... rank grass ... and noxious weeds, overrun the whole place. The foul hyena has defiled the sanctuary, and the midnight owl has perched on its crumbling walls, to disgorge the undigested remnant of its prey.[22]

Was the fate of contemporary missions to be no better?

11
Blighted hopes

From the confluence of the Zambezi and the Kafue rivers, the party followed the Kariba Gorge into the country of the Tonga. The Tonga had been suffering from raids by Kololo and their Tonga collaborator, Moshobotwane. Livingstone's men

> made it known everywhere that we wished the tribes to live in peace, and would use our influence to induce Sekeletu to prevent the [Tonga] of Moshobotwane and the [Kololo] under-chiefs making forays into their country: they had already suffered severely ... In the character of peace-makers, therefore, we experienced abundant hospitality; and, from the Kafue to the Falls, none of our men were allowed to suffer hunger.[1]

The villagers welcomed them, and a local troubadour even followed them, making up verses in their praise.

> Our march resembled a triumphal procession. We entered and left every village amidst the cheers of its inhabitants; the men clapping their hands, and the women lullilooing, with the shrill call, 'Let us sleep', or 'Peace'.[2]

At Mosioatunya Livingstone once again made the perilous canoe journey to the island at the lip of the Falls. This time the man in charge, Tuba, failed to deflect the canoe from a rock quickly enough, and as the crew bailed out they blamed the incident on the man missing his breakfast![3] This was a light-hearted interlude for those who had been treated so well and heralded as peacemakers. Yet when they finally reached Sesheké, where Chief Sekeletu was residing, there was no peace.

The town that Livingstone knew was abandoned; the head-man, Moriantsane, had been put to death. His widow had been Sebetwane's only sister. As such, she was able to compare the ways of the former chief with Sekeletu's behaviour. She was able to tell David that the Kololo under-chiefs were acting alone and that Sekeletu 'now knows nothing of what his underlings do'.[4]

The new town was a quarter of a mile further on. They entered it on 18 August 1860 – but Sekeletu was not there. He had withdrawn to the opposite bank of the Zambezi, where he saw no-one. Strange rumours abounded. 'His fingers were said to have grown like an eagle's claws, and his face so frightfully distorted that no one could recognise him.'[5]

Sekeletu, in fact, had leprosy – but, believing himself to be bewitched, had executed the headman and some prominent families whom he suspected of casting the spell. Yet to Livingstone and Kirk, whom he invited to his wagon the following day, his manners were quiet and unassuming – like those of his father, Sebetwane. They found the rumours to be wildly exaggerated.

His face was only slightly disfigured by the thickening of the skin in parts, where the leprosy had passed over it; and the only peculiarity about his hands was the extreme length of his finger-nails, which, however, was nothing very much out of the way, as all the [Kololo] gentlemen wear them uncommonly long.[6]

From Sekeletu's own lips they heard the confirmation of tragic news of the LMS mission, that had spread throughout the country. The foreigners had died of fever at Dinyanti – first their wagon-drivers, then the Helmores who led the group, four of the children and Mrs Price. The sole adult survivor, Roger Price, had set off with two of the Helmore children only weeks before Livingstone's arrival, to go back to Kuruman.

Mary Livingstone had not been with them. In that fact the seeds of the tragedy had been sown.

Robert and Mary Moffat had prevailed upon Mary not to go with the mission party to Dinyanti, where Sekeletu had his headquarters at the time. It is doubtful whether Robert had ever been very keen either on the expedition to the Kololo or even to the Ndebele. When he received intelligence of a possible Boer attack on Kuruman, planned for May 1859, he threw all his energies into his first love – the defence of Kuruman. As he made representations to the Governor at the Cape, the threat receded, but the Helmore party set off to Sekeletu without Mary. The result was almost certainly deep disappointment on the part of Sekeletu.

In this pre-imperial period in sub-Saharan Africa foreigners entered African territory entirely on Africans' terms. This principle was well understood by David, who always took great care to treat Sekeletu with respect, even when he disagreed with his actions. The respect was mutual, but it was not only the chemistry of personal relationships that influenced Sekeletu in his decision-making. As an independent chief who had inherited a great empire from his father, he usually had a political motive in relating to outsiders. In this case, he was specifically interested in defending his crumbling dominions from the incursions of Mzilikaze.

The Moffats' influence with the Ndebele marauder was of incalculable political value to Sekeletu; he knew that as long as he had a Livingstone or a Moffat residing with his people, they would be safe from attack. Failing that, they trusted for their defence on the River Chobe and the swampy ground around Dinyanti, in which they could outwit Mzilikaze's *impis* (or legions). The problem for foreigners was that the marshy territory was extremely feverish. Numbers of the Kololos themselves had been cut down by fever. The mission could hope to succeed only if Sekeletu agreed to move his capital to the Tonga plateau.

This Sekeletu was still interested in doing – *if* he could get the kind of settlement that would protect his people. When Livingstone presented his credentials as consul – in other words, the Queen's representative to the African tribes of the region – this was his formal reply:

Sekeletu rejoices at the words of the letter that has arrived, but the country has disabled him while fleeing from [Mzilikaze]. He finds great affliction where he is. People perish, cattle perish. Is that not a great affliction! The country (called) Phori and Mpakane [highlands near the River Kafue] is beautiful, and people might dwell there properly, but how can I live alone? If I lived alone I should not even sleep in it. Had [Mma-Robert] come, then I should have rejoiced, because [Mzilikaze] would let her alone, and us, she being a child of his friend Moshete (Moffat). And Sekeletu says to the Lord [Queen] of the English, Give me of your people to dwell with me, and I shall cut off a country for them to dwell in.

A path towards the sunsetting has already been burst open by Monare (Dr L.) and a path towards the rising sun he is now bursting open, and the Lord [Queen] assisted Sekeletu by sending the iron ship. Will she not single out some of her people to live with him and hold intercourse? Thus the path would be burst open permanently. Then there would be sleep (or prosperity) to man.

The country of which we think is one of cottons and the [Tonga] tribes weave it. Subject tribes and the [Najoa] also sow cotton and use it.

Let there be friendship with him (Sekeletu) for ever so that we may mutually feel pleasure.

So speaks Sekeletu
SHESHEKE [*sic.*] 9th Septr 1860.

Signed in the Egyptian way with the finger dipped in ink by Sekeletu and his stepfather Mamire, the next in authority to himself in the tribe.

Witnesses:
D. LIVINGSTONE
JOHN KIRK[7]

As to the idea of English settlement, Livingstone (in consultation with Kirk) warned Sekeletu that it would sow the seeds of 'disturbances' in the future – a prophecy of what was to come in Rhodesia-Zimbabwe a hundred years later. Yet on the subject of Mary, David could only agree.

He did not, of course, know the full story of the Boer threat to Kuruman, where he wrote trying to point out that Sekeletu would move to higher ground if she came. Mary had, in fact, gone to Scotland with Oswell and baby Anna. Yet she would have been touched at the way that she, Robert, Agnes and Tom were still remembered by the Kololo women. 'Sekeletu's wives gently reproached me for not bringing [Mma -Robert],' David noted in his diary. To his surprise they could still quote some of his children's expressions. Were they to know nothing more than their names?

Sekeletu's wives had kept in safe custody at Dinyanti Livingstone's magic lantern, tools, books and medicine chest. His wagon too contained medicine, yet was left completely undisturbed, only a few hundred metres from where the Helmores had lain, desperately in need of the anti-malarial pills that were there for the taking. At least Livingstone and Kirk were able to treat Sekeletu for his leprosy. They had none of the medicines used at that time for skin diseases, and were forced to be inventive, with some success. At one point a skin condition affected their own hands, and they had to rub them with plenty of caustic to clean them. Sekeletu's skin began to clear 'and the deformity of the face disappeared'.[8]

Leaving Sesheke on 17 September 1860, Livingstone decided to take advantage of the downstream current to test the navigability of the Upper Zambezi. It proved to be feasible from below the Falls. When they reached the Cabora Basa rapids, the Scot decided to try to shoot them.

This last-ditch 'mad attempt',[9] as Kirk later called it, to conquer the obstacle that had so far frustrated all Livingstone's schemes for the Zambezi, very nearly came off.

Kirk's canoe went first. The torrent rushed hard against rock A, but the crew cleared it in style. The next danger was being carried against rock C. Turning the head of the canoe, the crew had given one stroke ahead when they saw Livingstone's carried up to rock A. There was a whirlpool at the partition between the two branches of the channel, and the canoe was drifting broadside into it. Charles's canoe, coming third, seemed about to run into his brother's. Kirk's men, instead of paddling on to safety, prepared to come to the rescue. A split second later there was a loud crack.

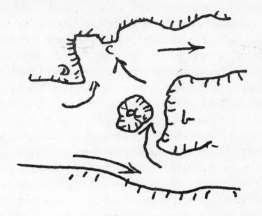

Dr. Kirk's canoe was dashed on a projection of the perpendicular rocks [C] by a sudden and mysterious boiling up of the river, which occurs at regular intervals. Dr. Kirk was seen resisting the sucking-down action of the water, which must have been [27 metres] deep, and raising himself by his arms on to the ledge, while his steersman, holding on to the same rocks, saved the canoe.[11]

Ironically, Livingstone's canoe, for which Kirk had predicted an imminent capsize, survived; a gap in the whirling maelstrom suddenly closed and there was enough water to carry him through. Kirk's chronometer and barometer, his journal for six months and his botanical drawings, were swept downstream. All his research on the resources of the interior – notably, fruit-trees – was lost. Kirk was so depressed by the loss of his work that he wanted to leave the expedition. 'We have kept faith with the Kololo,' David wrote to Sir Roderick when they finally reached Tete on 23 November 1860, 'though we have done nothing else.'[12]

Nevertheless, he was cheered by the news of the impending arrival of the *Pioneer*, the steamer ordered to replace the *Ma Robert*, with Bishop Mackenzie and the UMCA party. Kirk too was encouraged, and changed his mind about going home. Charles, who on the previous journey had been the 'demoralizing agent' rather than the 'moral agent', also stayed on. The die was cast for the next phase: finding an alternative route to Lake Nyasa north of the Portuguese influence, by an investigation of the River Ruvuma, which flowed into the Indian Ocean hundreds of miles north of the Zambezi delta.

This first attempt, at a time of year when the Ruvuma was quite shallow, was foiled by the depth of the keel of the newly arrived steamer. The *Pioneer*, with Bishop Mackenzie aboard, got no further than 30 miles upriver from the coast before having to turn back. Defeated by the sandbanks in the dry season, the expedition's next objective was to go to Lake Nyasa again up the Shire valley, and find out by exploration whether the Ruvuma came out of the north end of the long lake. On the way there, they would settle the UMCA mission along the banks of the Shire.

So the drama of the entry of the new mission into Cewa (pronounced 'Chewa') country began to unfold. Picking up the UMCA party from the Comoro Islands, where it had been waiting for the expedition's return from the Ruvuma, the *Pioneer* entered the Kongone again and ascended the Shire Valley. They reached Chief Chibisa's village, 10 miles below the Murchison Cataracts, on 8 July 1861. Rumours of war were in the air. A confirmation of this was that a Cewa slave gang had been seen crossing the river on its way to be sold to the Portuguese at Tete.

Setting off for the highlands a week later, the party came to a village where Livingstone hoped to hire more men. Speaking to an old friend, Mbame, he heard that more slaves were soon to pass through that village, heading for Tete. There were only a few minutes to discuss what to do, before a column of Cewa came into view under armed guard. The men had their necks caught in a fork of strong poles, 2m long, imprisoned by an iron rod riveted across their throats. The women and children were bound with thongs. The once proud and independent Cewa had lost hope; the guards, wearing red caps and blowing on a long tin horn, appeared brimming with confidence.

Yet at the sight of the mission party their African guards instantly turned tail and fled into the forest – all except their leader. A Kololo, who had come back with Livingstone from Sekeletu's country, caught hold of him by the hand. There was nothing for it but to set the captives free, using a saw found in the bishop's baggage. There were eighty-four men, women and children, some under the age of five.

They knelt and clapped their hands loudly, and as they were cut loose, began making a bonfire out of the slave sticks to cook a meal on. One small boy asked his liberators, 'The others tied and starved us, you cut the ropes and tell us to eat; what sort of people are you?'[13]

That question was going to be answered, one way or another, by Bishop Mackenzie. Having been out of sight taking a bath when the crisis occurred, he was doubtful about what to do with the freed Cewa. They could not go back into the war zone. He offered them the chance to go free or to stay with the mission. They all decided to stay.

Mackenzie did not lack courage, and his next priority was to talk to the tribe that was being used by the slave-hunters to capture the Cewa, the marauding Yao. He asked Livingstone to speak for him with their chief. Travelling with a party of Cewa, the two friends passed through a countryside ruined by war, including a village which two years before Livingstone had called the 'Paisley of the Hills', because so many of its people had been peacefully weaving cloth. At 2.00pm on 22 July they saw smoke rising ahead of them. They knelt and prayed fervently with battle-cries and wailing in their ears.

Just as they were getting back to their feet, a long line of Yao warriors, with their prisoners, came round the hillside. The headman jumped up on to an anthill on catching sight of the newcomers. Livingstone called out to him that they had come to talk to his chief. The Yao then heard the Cewa shout behind his back, 'Our *Chibisa* is come!'[14]

By doing this, the Cewa effectively pushed the bishop and his party into battle with the Yao. Chibisa was famous as a conjuror – and a general.

'*Nkondo! Nkondo!*'[15] screamed the Yao, scattering. It was their war-cry. Armed men came running up from the Yao village below. In a few seconds the warriors were all around the bishop's party, taking aim from behind rocks and long grass. A poisoned arrow struck a Cewa through the arm. The party began to move back up the hill, but warriors cut them off.

Then the Yao closed in. Some got within 40m, war-dancing as they came. An arrow fell between Mackenzie and Livingstone. Another whizzed between David and a Cewa. Four Yao with guns opened fire.

This was a moment Livingstone had hoped would never come. He had no gun on him and had never had to use one in anger, but now the bishop gave him his. If they made no defence now, they would all be wiped out. For the first and the last time in his life, Livingstone told his followers to fire.

Six of the Yao fell and the rest fled. They were safe, but the first step had been taken into inter-tribal hostilities. Having always tried to treat Africans with gentleness, this was a sad setback for Livingstone. Strongly dissuading the over-zealous bishop from pursuing the Yao, he recommended that the UMCA party keep out of African conflicts, even if pressed to join in by one tribe or another.

Given the unsettled situation, Mackenzie wanted to move further south, but Livingstone recommended Magomero, a peninsula created by a stream well away from the troubled Shire, but nearer Lakes Chilwa and Nyasa. This position was much easier to defend, and was as far as possible from the influence of the Portuguese agents at Tete who were provoking the slave war. The Portuguese, having found out from the expedition that the Kongone mouth of the Zambezi was navigable, had established a customs post there. So it seemed far better to find an alternative supply route up the Ruvuma valley to reach the mission via Lake Nyasa.

With this in mind the expedition, including Dr John Kirk, Charles Livingstone, and some Kololo, carried a gig 40 miles past the Murchison Cataracts. Reaching Nyasa, they found the lake being pirated and terrorized by a Nguni group called the Mazitu. Livingstone did manage to map quite accurately 200 miles of the western shore of the lake. In a solitary sortie he reached the point on that side opposite the course of the Ruvuma. There was, however, no way of getting round to the eastern side to discover whether or not the Ruvuma was connected with the lake. The chaos reigning in the area stopped the party in the gig from passing the northern section of the shore. Having been abandoned by the frightened Kololo, Kirk, Livingstone and Charles reached an outlet of Nyasa on 26 October 1861.

The party crossed a lake called Malombe and descended the Shire River, slinging their boat on the branches of a tree at the head of the Murchison Cataracts in the hope of returning and reusing it. Arriving weak with hunger at the *Pioneer*'s berth at Chibisa's on 8 November, they were encouraged to meet a new UMCA missionary, Mr Burrup. He had come up the Shire by canoe, followed by a surgeon and his companion. They brought the news that a ship was due at the Cape. On board were the UMCA mission wives, James Stewart (surveying for the Free Kirk of Scotland's mission) – and Mary Livingstone.

David had written to Mary encouraging her to come, when he heard that again she was not coping well with their separation and life in Scotland, although this time she had been financially better provided for. They longed to see each other, and yet the country was in such a disturbed state. What would become of the UMCA women? Mackenzie, perhaps misunderstanding the promises David had made to the Cewa chiefs on his behalf, had effectively got involved in a war of liberation. When the bishop arrived at Chibisa's he was optimistic, however; the Yao were suing for peace.

The bishop aimed to go back to Magomero with Burrup and find an overland route from there to the mouth of the River Ruo, a tributary of the Shire, in order to rendezvous with the *Pioneer*. However, at Magomero he was prevailed upon to mount an expedition to free the captive husbands of some Cewa women. The expedition was successful, but in the process Mackenzie lost all his medicines. When he and Burrup finally reached their rendezvous at the junction of the Ruo and the Shire, the *Pioneer* had passed only a few days before, on its way downstream. By this time it was supposed to have reached the coast, picked up the UMCA wives and be ready to rendezvous with the bishop on its way back upstream. But the steamer had a deep keel and the level of the river had fallen unexpectedly early in the year.

Mackenzie caught fever; so did Burrup. When the bishop's sister and Burrup's bride came upriver by boat to look for them, it was to be told that the bishop was dead.

12
The shadow of death

On the day that Bishop Mackenzie breathed his last, David was exchanging signals with a naval vessel at the coast. The ship carrying Mary was waiting at the mouth of the Zambezi. To those on deck, it was a beautiful morning, in stark contrast to their experience of the voyage from the Cape. Mary's ship had been hit by a typhoon.

Now the sea was calm as the newcomers awaited the arrival of the *Pioneer*. A little cloud of smoke could be seen rising close to land. Next, the white hull of a paddlesteamer came into view. One of Mary's companions got out a telescope to watch. It was James Stewart, from the Scottish Free Church mission. He recorded her reactions in his journal for 1 February 1862.

About 8 o'clock the *Pioneer* glided in between the *Gorgon* and the brig. We thought she was going on board the *Gorgon* and Mrs. Livingstone's countenance fell. But she glided on and I could not help remarking to Mrs. Livingstone that the Doctor seemed to be a great swell. It must be confessed that in his white trousers, frock coat and naval cap he looked uncommonly smart and really had a commanding air ... I take my glass and though I have never seen him before have no difficulty in identifying the man. Mrs. Livingstone has not seen him and I disturb or perturb her by saying 'There he is'. I allow her emotion a minute or two to subside and then add, he is, etc. She gives me a gratified slap for so speaking of the great pioneer and prince of travellers on whom I have just set my admiring eyes, with much though apparently little reverence.[1]

Stewart's familiarity with Mary resulted from his prior acquaintance with her, not only during the voyage but also in Scotland. This inevitably had given rise to gossip, which, however, David was ready to discount. 'I think all that behaviour on their part was madness,' he said to Stewart, almost certainly referring to the scandalmongers. 'It seems to me that they were acting in the most nonsensical way imaginable.'[2]

Mary had longed for her husband ever since parting with him at the Cape three years and nine months before. She had gone back to Scotland to be with her older children, but felt much darkness of spirit. David had written her letters full of tenderness and Christian encouragement. He found that the inability of their eldest son to stick to his studies had been a source of discouragement to her.

> She was depressed on leaving England on account of Robert's unsettled state and that had an influence on inducing spiritual despondency but happily Mr. Stewart, an excellent man, was with her and she derived much benefit from his judicious counsels. It was a pity that Robert was not sent out with her – it would have done both mother and son good.[3]

Now Mary had the happiness of finding David alive and well. But she herself was not completely healthy; she was somewhat feverish. David was desperately anxious to get his wife and all the UMCA ladies out of the malarial low country to the uplands above the River Shire. However, the *Pioneer* kept getting stuck on the shoals of the river because she was loaded down with the separated sections of the *Lady Nyassa*. Livingstone had to call a halt while the *Lady Nyassa* was assembled and the engines of the *Pioneer* were repaired.

It took seven full days for the *Pioneer* to pass 80 miles of river. There were still 120 to go to the Ruo, and the rendezvous with the bishop. Captain Wilson of HMS *Gorgon*, the naval vessel that had escorted Mary's ship in, was trying to help Livingstone transport the *Lady Nyassa* to the Murchison Cataracts. He offered to take Bishop Mackenzie's sister and Burrup's wife ahead in the gig the remaining 120 miles to the Ruo. Dr Ramsey, the ship's surgeon, went too and Kirk followed in the whaler. After ten days of travelling, the whaler was sent back and Kirk squeezed in with the others in the gig.

At the rendezvous point at the mouth of the Ruo the local people denied knowing anything about what had happened to the bishop. In fact, Burrup had buried him at their insistence, under a mimosa tree on the small island in the river mouth. The only form of life there now was the crocodiles.

Five days later the party reached Chibisa's, to be told by the Kololo there that the bishop was dead. There were also letters from Magomero, where Burrup was headed, giving the impression that the mission there was in dire straits. Kirk, knowing the risks, set off with Wilson without medicine, proper food or sufficient cloth to barter for it – in the wet season. Within two days, both men were down with fever. Three men from Magomero met them with the news that Burrup, suffering from dysentery and fever, had died a week after reaching them.

Kirk noted, however, that the trio were themselves in pretty good condition (in fact, they had access to preserved meats, coffee and tea). It was Wilson who was in dire straits and Kirk had to nurse him back to health. Scudamore, one of the three, was made of sterner stuff than his fellows and was a great help to Kirk. Once Wilson was well enough to move, they took him to Chibisa's. Before he was fully recovered, Kirk took him downstream in the gig with the bereaved women. Stopping only to put up a simple cross on the bishop's grave, they reached the *Pioneer* on 14 March, where she was moored at Chupanga.

James Stewart later described Livingstone's numbed reaction.

It was difficult to say whether he or the unhappy ladies, on whom the blow fell with the most personal weight, were most to be pitied. He felt the responsibility, and saw the widespread dismay which the news would occasion when it reached England, and at the very time when the Mission most needed support. 'This will hurt us all,' he said, as he sat, resting his head on his hand, on the table of the dimly-lighted little cabin of the *Pioneer*.[4]

As the *Pioneer* headed swiftly downriver for the sea, the grief-stricken Mrs Burrup turned to Mary Livingstone for comfort. She had borne up remarkably well, but later collapsed from heat and exhaustion. On the night of her first wedding anniversary, she needed a shoulder to cry on. She and Miss Mackenzie were finally carried aboard HMS *Gorgon* on the crossed arms of the sailors, silently.

The *Gorgon*'s gunner, Mr Young, stayed with the expedition and organized the loading of the *Lady Nyassa*'s 2½-ton boilers on to the deck of the *Pioneer* and other machinery into the hold. This was the last stage of the shuttle of the sections of the lake steamer to Chupanga for assembly. On 14 April after an unusually fast run, they reached their destination – where David had nursed the Portuguese governor, da Silva, back to health.[5]

To his consternation, he was soon having to use his skills (with the help of Dr Kirk) to care for Mary. A week after their arrival at Chupanga Mary fell ill from an attack of malarial fever. She was brought ashore to a tent, and on 26 April moved into the long, low stone house, where David had treated da Silva. Four days later she was vomiting every fifteen minutes, giving no chance for medicine to stay in her stomach. In her feverish state, she began talking about Agnes and their other children, as if they were in danger.

Delirium gave way to silence. David was desperate to rouse her : 'My dearie, my dearie, you are going to leave me. Are you resting on Jesus?' He couldn't be sure if she heard, but 'she looked thoughtfully up'.[6]

On the evening of the seventh day, a Sunday, Livingstone called James Stewart into the sickroom. 'When I went into the room Dr. L. said that the end was evidently drawing near and he had sent for me,' Stewart recalled in his journal. He noted the medical facts. 'There was considerable stertor, fixedness of feature and eyes, and slight coldness of extremities.'[7] But it was Livingstone's reactions that most caught his attention.

He was sitting by the side of a rude bed formed of boxes, but covered with a soft mattress, on which lay his dying wife.

All consciousness had now departed, as she was in a state of deep coma, from which all efforts to rouse her had been unavailing ... The fixedness of feature and the oppressed and heavy breathing only made it too plain that the end was near. And the man who had faced so many deaths, and braved so many dangers, was now utterly broken down and weeping like a child.[8]

Those tears spoke to Stewart in a way the physical facts never could. 'I could not help feeling for him and found my own eyes full before I was aware. He asked me to commit her soul to her Maker by prayer. He, Dr Kirk and I kneeled down and I prayed as best I could. In less than an hour she was dead.'[9] Kirk was also present. As Mary's expression became settled in death, the watchers noticed it had changed. There was an extraordinary likeness to her father, Robert Moffat.

'For the first time in my life I feel willing to die.'[10] That was David's reaction to being left alone in the world by the only person whom he had felt to be a part of himself.

Oh my Mary, my Mary! How often have we longed for a quiet home, since you and I were cast adrift at Kolobeng; surely the removal by a kind Father who knoweth our frame means that He rewarded you by taking you to the best home, the eternal one in the heavens.[11]

The woman known through 1,800 miles of African territory as Mma-Robert had always been an African, yet had made the sacrifice of long separation from Africa and from her husband's side.

Although she had often appeared withdrawn to Europeans, David knew her as a companion with great zest for life. In an intimate moment only a few days before her fatal illness, she had said to him: 'You must always be as playful as you have always been, I would not like you to be as grave as some folks I have seen.'[12]

The men asked to be allowed to mount guard over her grave at Chupanga, which was built with bricks under a 'baobab-tree', which was 'sixty feet in circumference'.[13] The red hills and white vales of that area had struck Livingstone six years before as a beautiful scene. He could not help asking himself if some place he had already seen would mark his own grave.

> In some other spot I may have looked at, my own resting-place may be allotted. I have often wished that it might be in some far-off still deep forest, where I may sleep sweetly till the resurrection morn, when the trump of God will make all start up into the glorious and active second existence.[14]

Despite everything, there was only one thing he could do: press on. The *Lady Nyassa* was launched on 23 June, but the river was too low to try to take it up to the Murchison Cataracts. The mission at Magomero had been abandoned because of the slave wars, and its remaining members had retreated to Chibisa's village. The only aim that could be fulfilled now was a final check on the River Ruvuma.

On 6 August 1862, the *Pioneer* set off on the 600-mile journey from the Kongone mouth of the Zambezi to the Comoro Islands. There a naval ship, HMS *Orestes*, offered them a tow to the Ruvuma against contrary winds and currents. The towing hawsers parted in heavy weather and the *Pioneer* had to reach the coast under its own steam. A naval party went upriver with the expedition as far as the 30-mile mark to which they had penetrated before. Here Livingstone and Kirk went on in two boats, with Charles and some canoe-paddlers from the Zambezi.

It became apparent that the Arab slave-traders were using the Ruvuma as a slave route to the east coast. 'It is only where the people are slavers, that the natives of this part of Africa are bloodthirsty,' David noted later.[15] Confronted by a band of the Konde tribe armed with bows and muskets, they attempted to conciliate them. Yet in doing so David broke his principle of not paying tribute to pass through an area. Kirk saw him give

> some cloth to the man who seemed to be the chief and with some fine words, things seemed settled but no sooner had

we begun to move on than they danced and drew their bows. When close to the bank, which the water compelled us to be, a man took aim and fired his musket at us. It missed and the bowmen ran back, ready to run forward and take a snap shot. However being now past amicable settlement and their intention being evident, since after full explanation on both sides they had taken the first opportunity of actually firing, I at once picked out one of the two men on the bank at [139m] and killed him. Pierce, my coxswain, shot the other standing by him. After this, there were no more shots but they saw the distance our rifles could carry, as we fired several at full range. We have been driven to this and have fought in self-defence only. We must pray God to guide us in future. We have been doing his work in Africa and trust to his shield.[16]

Struggling on for another week past rocks and sandbanks, they reached a point 156 miles from the mouth of the river. Here they found out that it divided. One branch carried on westward toward the northern end of Lake Nyassa, but the most optimistic report said that if it flowed out of the lake, it ran in a small stream and down mountains.

In fact the Ruvuma rises 30 miles to the east of Nyasa. Livingstone's party had to turn back, knowing that the river was navigable by nothing bigger than a small boat. This knowledge had an important result. 'It had much to do with the decision of British missionaries and traders that, after all, the Shire was the only practicable approach to Nyasaland.' Indeed, the nation that became Malawi 'is largely the result of that negative but supremely important journey and ... in his uncouth way Livingstone showed finer qualities of leadership in pressing on against the wishes of all his men than in most of the other subsidiary journeys of this period.'[17] So Livingstone's perseverance – seen at the time by Kirk as madness – was, in retrospect, commended by geographers and historians.

The final task of the expedition was to return to the Kongone, tow the *Lady Nyassa* to the Murchison Cataracts and then build a road round them. The ultimate aim was then to carry the dismantled sections of the *Lady Nyassa* round the cataracts, reassemble the steamer and launch her on the lake.

The task was daunting. Livingstone had to coax his engineer, Rae, to commit himself to the project. At first he refused to install the engines of the *Lady Nyassa*; then he agreed to it if he could leave the expedition. Livingstone could not consent to this, and then had to cope with Rae's reaction, which amounted to a kind of persecution mania.

They only got the engineless steamer moving safely by lashing it to the side of the *Pioneer*. The ships then got stuck in a marsh. Morale was scarcely improved by the sight of corpses floating downriver.

Before Livingstone had gone up the Shire valley and won his way into the hearts of its people by gentleness and respect, the slave-hunters had never dared to go there. But by calling themselves his 'children', some had been able to follow him. Now the invasion of slavers and their tribal allies had had catastrophic results, at a time when the area was suffering from drought.

As the expedition continued up the Shire the number of dead bodies in the water increased so much that 'in the mornings the paddles had to be cleared of corpses, caught by the floats during the night'.[18]

Only eighteen months before this had been a well-peopled valley; now it was strewn with human bones. It had turned into a desert, filled with scenes that haunted David's memory for the rest of his life.

Wherever we took a walk, human skeletons were seen in every direction, and it was painfully interesting to observe the different postures in which the poor wretches had breathed their last …

Many had ended their misery under shady trees, others under projecting crags in the hills, while others lay in their huts with closed doors, which when opened disclosed the mouldering corpse with the poor rags round the loins, the skull fallen off the pillow, the little skeleton of the child, that had perished first, rolled up in a mat between two large skeletons.[19]

It turned out that this devastation was made by Mariano, the man that the Governor of Quelimane had been fighting as a rebel. Yet ultimately it was caused by the Portuguese themselves, since their slave-traders were using Mariano as their agent.

An urgent appeal came from the UMCA remnant at Chibisa's. Scudamore had died of malaria and the mission doctor was in delirium. David and Kirk left by boat, only to reach the doctor a quarter of an hour after his death. The young geologist, Thornton, had returned from Kilimanjaro and rejoined the expedition. Finding the mission in need of fresh meat, he set out with one companion and successfully brought back a herd of goats. Yet the 200-mile overland journey had taken its toll; he collapsed from fever, and died.

The final straw for Kirk and Charles was a dangerous illness that led them both to request to give up their work and go home. Nevertheless, Kirk delayed his departure long enough to nurse Livingstone himself back to health. The Scot was left now with a few naval men, notably Lieutenant E. D. Young who had navigated the *Pioneer* upriver, Rae and some African hired men. Together they still carried on with the task.

After a few miles of the road were under construction, Livingstone tried to solve the labour shortage (caused by the drought and the war) by setting off with Rae, the engineer, to reclaim the boat that had been left above the Murchison Cataracts. The idea was to use the boat to look for food for the workers, but it proved to be burnt out. Next, they tried to carry up another boat past the Murchison Cataracts. Reaching the very last cataract, they put the boat for a short time in the water – and suddenly it was overturned and went away like an arrow back down the cataracts.

At this point, 2 July 1863, a message came from the British government: the expedition was recalled. In any case, Lieutenant Young estimated that 100 men would have been needed to build the road round the Murchison Cataracts and that the parts of the steamer were too heavy.

Another setback, which was a source of bitter disappointment to Livingstone, was that the mission was also withdrawing. Its new bishop decided to take those of the freed slaves who still survived to Mount Morambala, nearer the coast. Bishop Tozer was eventually to take UMCA off the mainland and make Zanzibar its base.

Livingstone was not able to withdraw immediately, because the river was too low for the *Pioneer* and would be so for months. He decided to make a last attempt to reach the northern end of Lake Nyassa overland. Several Africans and the steward of the *Pioneer* went with him.

So began a walk of 750 miles. Once they got lost in a wood for three days without food or goods to buy it with, but some Africans showed them kindness despite their own needs. Another time they could get no guides, although the country was difficult and deep ravines lay across their path.

Aiming to keep to the west of Lake Nyasa and so avoid the Mazitu (or Nguni) raiders, Livingstone wanted to check whether any large river flowed into the lake from the west; to visit a lake called Mweru if there was time; and to gather information about the great slave route, which crossed the lake at Nkhotakota.

Arriving at Nkhotakota bay on 10 September 1863, they were greeted by an Arab trader, Juma bin Saidi, whom Livingstone had met on the first exploration of Lake Nyasa. Juma was now busy building a dhow for the trade on the lake. Many refugees had fled from the fighting to his village.

Juma lent Livingstone a guide for the first day, as he set out on the slave route to Katanga and Kazembe's country. It was confirmed as such when on reaching a large town, they found it empty of all but skeletons. Approaching another village they met a dead body in the path with a wound in the back; then body after body in a startling variety of postures as if a painter had prepared a special study in the agonies of death.

Travelling westwards they began a steep climb to a table-land 1000m up. The air was invigorating to Europeans, but too cold for the Zambezians. Looking out over the gently undulating high landscape, Livingstone confirmed for the first time that there was a wide area suitable for settlement. Yet to the north, a slave war was raging.

Wanting to reach Lake Bangweulu, the Scot was forced to turn back in order to be sure of reaching the *Pioneer* before the river rose. Choosing a shorter route, they found all the villages deserted and the reeds along the banks of Lake Nyasa thronging with refugees.[20]

The expedition had exposed slavery at its fountain-head. First, the slave-grabbing by hostile tribes in the interior; second, the traders from the coast – the Arabs and the Portuguese half-castes – who incited African chiefs to collect slaves; and third, the parties sent out from Portuguese settlements and Arab coastal towns with cloth and beads, guns and ammunition. The destruction and killings carried out by these groups were 'the climax of the system'.[21]

Livingstone was determined to come back some day, via a route that would not be compromised by the colonial influence of the Portuguese. The Ruvuma valley (which later, by land and river, did prove of some economic value as a commercial route) was a possibility.

When he finally reached the *Pioneer* the river was rising very slowly. After a frustrating delay, the steamer set off down the Shire and Zambezi for the sea. On the way, thirty orphaned children and some widows were taken on board, on behalf of the UMCA mission engaged in withdrawing to Zanzibar. The rest of the freed slaves had been encouraged to become self-supporting, by forming their own agricultural settlement.

Others had refused to take the orphans for fear of offending the Portuguese, but Livingstone was in no mood for diplomatic niceties. He gave orders that anyone interfering with his African passengers was to be thrown overboard.

13
The calm before the storm

Once past the customs point at the Kongone mouth of the Zambezi, the *Pioneer* and the *Lady Nyassa* were taken in tow. The day after they set out, a typhoon passed over them. Often as David had been in danger before, he was never nearer the gates of death than now. He refused to abandon the little *Lady Nyassa*, which he personally owned, as long as there was any danger to it.

Suddenly the towing ship, the *Ariel*, was whirled right round in the storm. The wind was pushing her on to a collision course with the *Lady Nyassa*. 'I saw no hope of escape,' recalled the Scot, 'except by catching a rope's end of the big ship as she passed over us, but by God's goodness she glided past, and we felt free to breathe.'[1]

That night, 16 February 1864, the wind was furious. The watching crew of the *Ariel* expected the *Lady Nyassa* to sink; while those on board the *Lady Nyassa* could see the *Ariel*'s copper bottom exposed above the waves.

In the pitch dark, with the wind whistling overhead, the Africans on board the *Lady Nyassa* kept asking to go to the 'bank'. There were nine of them, almost all skilled in river navigation, but they had never seen the sea before.

They landed at the island of Zanzibar, site of the ancient slave markets, on 24 April 1864. Livingstone decided that if he was to stop the steamer from falling into the hands of the slave-traders, and at the same time raise money for his next journey into Africa, he would have to take it to a far distant port to sell. He decided on Bombay.

Since he had seen the *Lady Nyassa* stay afloat in rough weather, his decision could not exactly be called foolhardy. Yet it terrified the ship's engineer, Rae.

Having endured a harrowing experience following a shipwreck in 1860, Rae was in mortal terror of the proposed crossing to Bombay, and chose this opportunity to activate his plan of a few years to join forces with William Sunley in the Comoros and seek his wealth on a sugar plantation. For reasons not yet come to light, this plan 'fell through', and shortly thereafter Rae became associated with the firm of Smith, Fleming & Company of Zanzibar (which firm did not find favor [sic] with Livingstone due to its exploitation of Africans). October of 1865 found Rae back in Glasgow where, on the tenth of that month he married, only to die suddenly at home the next day.[2]

That loss left Livingstone with two trained seamen: Stoker First Class John Pennell and Quartermaster Charles Collyer. The carpenter, John Reid, was a civilian. Then there were nine African volunteers: Chiko, Susi, Amoda, Bizenti, Safuri, Nyampinga, Bachoro, Chuma and Wakatini. If seven of the Africans were rivermen, the Scot was 'a landlubber through and through'.[3] He had certainly never tried to cross the Indian Ocean, and he was going to do it in a riverboat.

When he left Zanzibar on 30 April 1864, he had only fourteen tons of coal for a journey of 2,500 miles. The nine African volunteers were about to find out just how far the opposite 'bank' of the ocean was. And the monsoon, Livingstone was told, was due to break in one month's time.

Among all Livingstone's exploits none was more daring than his ocean crossing in the *Lady Nyassa*. He expected to reach the Indian port of Bombay in eighteen days. But because of the unkindness of the winds the boat hardly moved for twenty-five days and the voyage became a dangerous race against time.

With violent monsoon storms due in May, a skeleton crew, not much fuel and a boat never designed for the open sea, no professional ship captain could have taken the risk. But David knew that if he sold the vessel in Zanzibar the slave-traders would take it over. To save the *Lady Nyassa* from such inhuman use, he was ready to sink her.

Indeed he had only providence to thank that the boat did not actually sink before the end of the forty-five-day

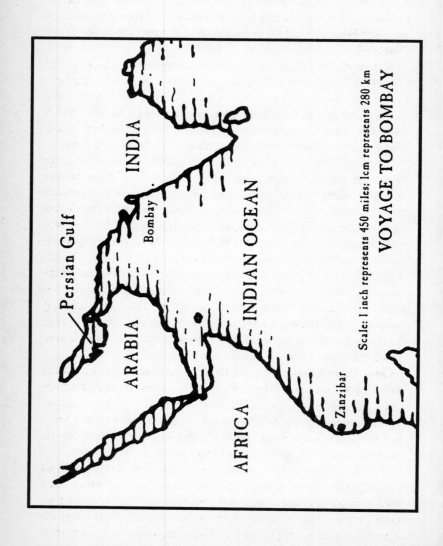

INDIA

Persian Gulf

Bombay

ARABIA

INDIAN OCEAN

AFRICA

Zanzibar

Scale: 1 inch represents 450 miles; 1cm represents 280 km

VOYAGE TO BOMBAY

adventure. Not only had the engineer left the ship before the voyage even began, John Reid, the carpenter, was already sick on the first day out from Zanzibar, and just as he began to recover, one of the two professional seamen was put out of action by fever and vomiting. The seven Zambezians on board and the two boys, Chuma and Wakatini, had never even seen the 'Big Water' before. So how could human skill see them through?

They had gone 1,000 miles without seeing any other boat and with only the dolphins for company, when the wind stopped. The sea was calm and without the necessary movement through the water, it was practically impossible to steer. When Livingstone came on deck at night he discovered John Reid asleep on watch and the helmsman steering the wrong way!

Next morning all was calm until suddenly there sprang up gusts of wind so violent that they tore up a sail. Afterwards it fell calm. Then soon after nightfall strong winds blew and rain lashed down, but only for a short time. For the rest of the night, there was a dead calm. 'Curious weather this – requiring much patience,' noted Livingstone in his journal. 'But we are in the hand of One who cares for us.'

The *Lady Nyassa* was only creeping along. All the crew were sick, so it was impossible to use the engines. The sails were practically useless. By 15 May 1864, fifteen days after setting sail, the wind was gone and the boat made no progress. A big, hungry shark and a school of dolphins circled round and round the vessel.

Once the stoker recovered they were able to steam along very slowly. Sometimes very light winds would touch the sails and then die away again. The shark was swimming along in the shadow of the boat. 'This very unusual weather has a very depressing influence on my mind,' David admitted to his diary. 'I feel as if I am to die on this voyage.'

The thought troubled him chiefly because he wanted to reach the outside world and tell the truth about what was happening in Africa: how its great potential was being blighted by slave wars. 'I have been unprofitable enough, but may do something yet, in giving information, if spared. God grant that

I may be more faithful than I have been, and may He open the way for me.'

That night there was not a breath of wind and next day the sea was 'glassy calm with a hot glaring sun and sharks stalking about us'. In the scorching heat, with not a speck of cloud in the sky except a fringe down at the horizon, the crew were getting very bad tempered with each other, Livingstone included. Finding that the compass was damaged, he developed an awful suspicion that they might be completely off course.

Instead of brooding, David took his mind off the situation at sea by recalling the exhilaration of journeying by land. 'The mere animal pleasure of travelling is very great. The elastic muscles have been exercised. Fresh and healthy blood circulated in the veins, the eye is clear, the step firm, but the day's exertion has been enough to make rest thoroughly enjoyable.'

After reflecting on the positive influence that 'remote chances of danger' can have on the mind, and the possibility of being drawn into deeper fellowship with the companions who share those dangers, Livingstone began to set his mind on the situation at sea with the same vigour he would have done on land.

He now began to take observations about the ocean life round him just as he would do of wild beasts in the bush.

Very many flying fish rise before us … The dolphin pursues very swiftly but not so quick as they can fly. The dolphin has very bright colours – rims of brighter green than the rest of the body. This is one of the provisions of nature by which the prey is warned of the approach of the enemy.

Incessant activity is a law in obtaining food. It could be caught with ease and no warning given, races would have the balance turned against them and carnivora alone prevail. The cat shows her shortened tail and so does the rattlesnake shake his to give warning to the prey. The flying fish has large eyes in proportion to other fish, yet flies on board very often at night and kills himself by the concussion.

Dolphins 'leaped out of the water in sport'. A brown bird with a white rump seemed to catch food with his feet, bounding off the water 'like an Indian rubber ball'. A land bird came on board very sick and soon died, probably from drinking seawater. It was pursued by a squall, bringing rain with it.

At first the squall, which came on the twenty-fourth evening, speeded up the progress of the boat. 'But it chopped round suddenly to the south-east from the south-west and wave meeting wave was very disagreeable.' This frustrating check was overcome at midnight, however, when a good strong breeze prevailed.

Two days later the breeze was still blowing, but Livingstone's calculations made him doubt the advisability of continuing to head for Bombay. Even at their current rate of 70 miles a day, they were not going to reach port before fifteen days were up. In sixteen days, the monsoon was due to break.

Heavy thunderclouds had already closed in around them that day, their twenty-sixth at sea. Livingstone could see 'a few streaks of pea-green in the sky but in general only immovable masses of white clouds with fleecy ones still beneath'. The shark continued to stalk the boat through the choppy sea.

It seemed time to make a decision. But where could the *Lady Nyassa* go to escape the coming storms? David prayed for guidance. Having considered and rejected the idea of heading for Arabia, he tried to change course for the Persian Gulf; but it was clear that the wind was against them and it would be impossible to steam into it. There was nothing left to do but keep heading for India.

A check on the water supply revealed that there was only enough to drink for ten or twelve days, on a very small allowance. Before they reached Bombay, the crew might either die of thirst or be drowned by the monsoon. How were they going to make it in time?

The following day they noticed that their slow progress was being made even slower by screws and an iron belt sticking down from the bottom of the boat. The design of the hull was breaking up the flow of water past the vessel, creating whirlpools.

For the first time the barometer dropped and the air became chilly. Next day the sky was heavy with dense, still, brooding masses of cloud. An unidentified red mass passed by the boat, floating on the surface of the sea, followed by some jellyfish. Then 'at noon a dense black cloud came down on us from the north-east and blew a furious gale'.

The wind ripped into the sails and the riverboat rolled broadside-on to the gale 'and nearly rolled quite over'. Everything on board was thrown about, backwards and forwards, by the force of the storm. 'It was terrible while it lasted,' David confessed. 'We had calm after it and the sky lightened up. Thank God for his goodness.'

That was only a foretaste of the coming monsoon, but the *Lady Nyassa* had come close to capsizing. The full fury of the storm season would overwhelm them – and they were still 850 miles from Bombay! Only faith could write, 'we shall reach it'. For the next few days progress was painfully slow.

David felt more strongly, however, that God's hand was upon them. He gave time again to taking an interest in oceanic nature. 'The dolphins go with the ship exactly as a dog does with his master,' he quipped to his diary. 'He careers out from her after flying fish, then returns and walks alongside till he sees another fish, then off again.'

The crew, however, became increasingly edgy as May gave way to June. The sky grew murkier and the waves lashed up on to the deck. John Reid, ordered to bring up some canvas to protect the deck, began to protest. He got more and more vociferous, shouting that he would never have come on the voyage had he known that he (a European) would have such work to do.

He was given short shrift. The situation was too critical to indulge in tantrums. Captain Livingstone threatened him with the usual penalty for mutiny, pointing out that if they failed to take the necessary precautions for the safety of the ship, then everyone on board 'might as well all jump into the sea at once'.

It was the Africans who responded to Livingstone's leadership and rose to the occasion. Willing to go out on the end of a boom with the sea washing over it, they learnt to set the sails though they had no previous experience of them. Two of them had learnt how to steer. Chuma, despite his immaturity, was even now beginning to display some of the qualities that were later to make him one of David's most trustworthy followers and friends.

As the waves rose higher, the current grew more powerful, pulling the little steamer off course. After an unprecedentedly rough night on 4 June, the following day they looked in vain for the sun. It was nowhere to be seen, either on that day or the next. In the gloom, they noticed some locusts flying on board, but land was still 380 miles away.

The weather veered from one extreme to the other. Their tempestuous progress brought them within 170 miles of Bombay – only to find themselves becalmed. The wind dropped away completely, to be replaced eventually by a very gentle breeze. Nevertheless, there was a good deal of cloud about. From the south the rumbling of thunder could be heard. Time was running out.

They were almost within sight of land when the storm struck. During the night 'a furious squall came on and tore our fore-square sail to ribbons', David recalled. The rain poured down, the wind died down, and by the dawning of the next day, 10 June, the boat was completely becalmed again. They lay motionless and helpless.

Some might have seen it as a sinister sign when two poisonous sea-snakes swam past as a pair, although with different colours and markings. 'One was dark olive with light yellow rings round its flattened tail. The other was lighter in colour,' Livingstone noticed. There was also some seaweed in view.

The Africans, far from recoiling at these sights, danced with joy. These were things they recognized as belonging to the shore. Surely they could not be far off now?

That night they were passed by a big sailing ship, in full rig, going the same way. They saw it not only by its light, but also silhouetted by the flickering glare of bolt upon bolt of lightning. Again and again the blackness of the night was broken by the stark brightness of electricity.

The following morning the sky lowered at them. Great mountains of cloud were everywhere, with smaller fronds flying across the face of the bigger mass. The rain tumbled down incessantly. Livingstone managed to mend a piece of sail by sewing two cloths together, but the rest was beyond repair. The wind was blowing them too far to the east.

In the distance, the threatening noise of thunder could be heard again. Violent gusts and pelting rain drove in right against the direction of the wind. The sails were thrown backwards, making them a menace. Men wrestled with the rigging, trying to trim the sails to the other side. From this vantage point they caught sight of land, rising high above the level of the sea.

They were getting too close to the land mass for comfort, the wind working against them as they tried to hold course northwards. The sea was running very high with visibility poor due to haze. A heavy squall came off the land to the east at 8.00 pm, the wind whistling eerily through the rigging. They could make little headway steaming through it.

By 11.00 at night a good breeze sprang up and helped them on their way until midnight. In the darkness, white water showed up again and again. Did it betray rocky shoals? They steered clear of the tell-tale signs.

The scene at dawn revealed high land rising 160m above sea level. After the green vegetation of the Zambezi, the hills here seemed bare and brown.

Equipment broke down and the *Lady Nyassa* could no longer steam. Livingstone hoped to get into a harbour and find some fuel, but at 7.00 in the evening 'a furious squall came down off the land'. The crew hung on to their hats and peered around in the pitch blackness which engulfed them. All they could make out were the breaking crests of the waves, coloured by phosphorescence.

John Pennell had been working on the machinery for thirty hours without rest. Seeing that it was impossible to get into harbour, Livingstone put up some sails, shut down the engine and told the stoker to get some sleep. He was forced to keep steering for Bombay, despite the difficulty of making any progress in that direction. Flood waters from inland rivers were setting up a current against them.

Once gain the squall was followed by a dead calm and next morning the sea was 'as smooth as glass'. The surface was covered with a scum like dust and the land was blanketed in thick fog.

'It was so hazy inland we could see nothing whatever – then I took the direction by chart and steered right into Bombay most thankfully.' They had been brought safely over 2,600 miles of ocean in a riverboat with an untrained crew, entering the harbour only one day before the main monsoon was due to break. 'The vessel was so small, that no one noticed our arrival.'[4]

14
Planning the final campaign

In Bombay, Livingstone found places for the boys, Chuma and Wakatini, at the Free Church of Scotland Mission School. As for Susi and Amoda, grown men whom he had first employed at Chupanga to fit together the pieces of the *Lady Nyassa*, they were given jobs at the Bombay docks. These four who had shared with him the perils of the Indian Ocean were to be his companions in his final campaign for Africa.

What shape was this to take?

The depredations of disease, the climate and the terrain of the Zambezi region and the unsettled, often chaotic, conditions of the country converted Livingstone's thinking from that of a colonialist to a commitment to Christian transformation in African tribal society. This could be precipitated by carefully selected agents of change coming from overseas and playing key roles in the restructuring of the economy as well as being 'ploughmen' – preparing the ground for the reception of the gospel.[1]

There was plenty of time to reflect on this after he returned to England and began work on a book on the Zambezi expedition.[2] It was all the easier to concentrate on the book since the reception of the government, following the expedition's failure to extract measurable gain from African soil, had been cold. In any case, David had had little inclination to be hawked around London society. He was longing to see his family again.

Perhaps the hardest aspect of his long absence had been the fact that he had never seen his youngest daughter, Anna Mary, born three years before Mary went to rejoin David on the Zambezi. Her father gave her an African doll, but Africa was not in her upbringing; she would have preferred a European one.

David's mother, Agnes, could not even recognize him, but her namesake, his eldest daughter, became her father's confidante in her teenage years. From this time a pattern develops in his correspondence; whenever he writes a fresh batch of letters the first is nearly always to the youngest Agnes.

The one public engagement that he felt committed to (but nevertheless dreaded preparing a speech for) was the meeting of the British Association at Bath, where he went with Agnes on 15 September. The death of the explorer Captain Speke, occurred on the very day of their arrival, by the accidental discharge of his hunting-rifle. Speke had been due to debate the subject of the sources of the Nile with Burton, a rival explorer who held a theory of 'scientific racism' and discounted the idea that Africans could become Christians.

Some insinuated that Speke had committed suicide because he could not face the debate. Livingstone, who attended Speke's funeral on 23 September, did not subscribe to that view. Nor did he subscribe to the views of Speke, Burton or Baker (another contender in the controversy) on the sources of the Nile. Their perspectives differed, although all of them had been travelling in the northern sector of the East African Lakes region.

Livingstone's main concern at Bath had been to attack the slave trade while reporting on the Zambezi expedition. Judging by the extremely sensitive reaction of the Portuguese to his speech, this was indeed the main thrust. But he had also been asked to chair the debate between Burton and Speke. Despite the cancellation of that debate, he found himself drawn into the controversy. Speke had proposed that the Nile rose in Lake Victoria; Burton preferred Lake Tanganyika. In January 1865 Livingstone was asked to investigate the issue.

By this time Livingstone may have worked out a strategy which would turn his contemporaries' obsession with the problem of the Nile sources to advantage, in terms of his overriding aim of exposing the slave trade. Sir Roderick Murchison, the correspondent who offered him the task of exploring the lakes for the Royal Geographical Society, had only the geographical aim in mind. To him, mission would be something of a distraction. Richard Burton, who had proposed that the true sources of the Nile lay south of Victoria Nyanza, had the least enthusiasm for mission of perhaps any Victorian. Nevertheless, Livingstone was determined to stick to his vision of a Christian transformation of the African continent.

So instead of accepting Murchison's proposal as it was presented to him, namely, to go first to the northern part of Lake Tanganyika and check whether there was a river flowing out of it and into Lake Victoria, he decided to work further south where he knew the slave trade was strongest. His original plan had been to re-enter Africa on the east coast, along the northern bank of the River Ruvuma, thus keeping himself clear of Portuguese control while at the same time giving himself the opportunity to check the river's relation to Lake Nyasa, where the slave dhows were plying their trade.

This plan he decided to stick to, but to accommodate what was demanded of him, not only by Murchison but also by what might be called the 'spirit of the age', he would move north. He would pass around Lake Nyasa and find out if it was connected with Lake Tanganyika. But before moving to the northern end of Tanganyika, he would also explore unknown territory around Lakes Mweru and Bangweulu. In fact he felt it more probable that the sources of the Nile were in the south, but he was going to leave the final check on Burton's idea till last.

'The Nile sources', he confided to a friend, 'are valuable only as a means of enabling me to open my mouth with power among men. It is this power which I hope to apply to remedy an enormous evil.' In his journal for 7 January he records with almost curt brevity his response to the claims made on him by Murchison, who perhaps tried to wean him away from mission to purely geographical concerns.

Answered Sir Roderick about going out. Said I could only feel in the way of duty by working as a missionary.[3]

A longer-standing friend than Murchison was the Scottish industrialist Sir James Young, who had known David since his student days in Glasgow. To him David explained his priorities.

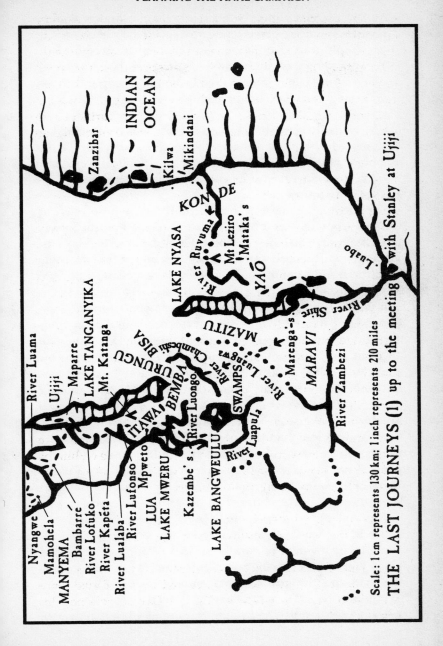

THE LAST JOURNEYS (I) up to the meeting with Stanley at Ujiji

Scale: 1cm represents 130 km: 1inch represents 210 miles

I am not sure but I told you already that Sir Roderick and I have been writing about going out ... I would not consent to go simply as a geographer, but as a missionary, and do geography by the way, because I feel I am in the way of duty when trying either to enlighten those poor people, or open their land to lawful commerce.[4]

The unlawful commerce he had in mind was the slaving operations which the Arabs were even then carrying further westwards into the African continent. Inevitably, it was Arab-Swahili traders with whom he would have to learn to deal on his last great journey.

Support for Livingstone's plan from those whose interests differed from his was muted. The Royal Geographical Society gave him only £500, despite their detailed requests for accurate astronomical observations. They demanded, in fact, more of his time and commitment than they were actually willing to pay for.

It was the same story with the government. At the Foreign Office Lord Russell, whose primary concern in the previous expedition had been to keep relations with the Portuguese on an even keel, was not unwilling to let Livingstone take his consul's cap into areas outside the Portuguese 'possessions'. But the fact was that Livingstone's agenda was almost antithetical to the government's cut-price policy of non-involvement overseas. Not only was the government grant no more and no less than that of the RGS, but it also came with the aggravating stipulation that he could expect neither a pension nor a salary. To try to sweeten the pill, Lord Russell wrote later – after Livingstone had left for Africa – to say that he could have a salary after all, if he 'settled' somewhere.

The donor closest to Livingstone's vision gave the most. James Young was both a convinced Christian and a businessman. As the inventor of paraffin he had resources that he was ready to commit to Livingstone's mission. He gave as much as the RGS and the government combined – £1,000, with no strings attached. It was time to go.

There were family considerations to think of first, however.

On 5 June David bought a tombstone for Mary's grave, 'to be sent out to the cape [*sic*]'. Two weeks later, 'A telegram came, saying that mother had died the day before. I started at once for Scotland.' David had visited his mother in Hamilton only the month before. Now he was there to bury her.[5]

David's next concern was to provide for his daughter Agnes's education. He travelled with her to Paris, where he installed her in a finishing-school. From Marseilles on 19 August 1865 he wrote to her, 'May the Almighty qualify you to be a blessing to those around you, wherever your lot is cast. I know that you hate all that is mean and false. May God make you good, and to delight in doing good to others. If you ask He will give you abundantly. The Lord bless you!'[6]

How much he wished that he had had as warm a relationship with his eldest son. Robert had repeatedly run away from the various boarding-schools he had been sent to in Scotland and in the end refused to continue studying. His father had encouraged him to come out to see him on the Zambezi, but the trustees who were supervising his education paid his passage only as far as Natal. There he had been kidnapped, taken to America and pressed into the Federal Army. This news had reached his father after his return to Britain. At the very time that David was planning to improve Agnes's education, Robert had met his death in the Civil War. He was buried at Gettysburg.

In a sense he had died fighting against slavery, but not in the way he or his father would have chosen. Nevertheless, from a military field hospital, prior to his final battle, Robert had written a letter to his father which showed great sensitivity. He described how he had tried hard to avoid taking life and, even in the heat of a bayonet charge, had taken his man prisoner. He regretted not having taken his education, and had changed his identity to avoid dishonouring (as he saw it) the family name. This correspondence tends to show that, had he experienced more parental love and security, he could in the end have been as close to his father as Agnes. As it was, he no longer claimed to have a filial character. He signed himself 'your quondam son, Robert'.

As for his two remaining sons, Thomas and Oswell, the bereaved father resolved not to interfere in their careers more than to pray for God's guidance for them. In fact, David's journey was to take him through the scene of his second son's early career; Thomas was to work for a mercantile firm, based in Cairo. At the time that his father travelled through Egypt, Lesseps was attempting to cut a canal for shipping.

Reaching Bombay, Livingstone was pleased to see how much progress Chuma and Wakatini had made at the mission school in his absence, particularly with their English. Retrieving Susi and Amoda from the docks, he had the core of his team. But many more volunteers were needed, and this was a problem. Although he hoped to pick up some of the reliable Kololo, in fact he would not be able to since his journey was north of their area.

The Governor of Bombay persuaded him to visit the Nasik school for freed slaves, where, however, there were only nine volunteers. Their background and motivation were largely unknown to the Scot. Two were Gallas, who had been enslaved in Somaliland, now called Simon Price, and Abraham Pereira. The others were Richard Isenberg, Reuben Smith, Andrew Powell, Albert Baraka, James Rutton, Edward Gardner and Nathaniel Cumba (called Mabruki). Most of them were in their early twenties.

The governor also assigned him eleven sepoys of the Bombay Marine Battalion, with their *naik* (corporal) and *havildar* (sergeant). These men, understood their terms of enrolment as providing military escort, not porterage. So Livingstone was still short of men, and went ahead with plans to hire porters from the Comoro Islands, despite their reputation for unreliability. Their leader was Musa.

The prospects for building up a stronger team were vitiated by the fact that the sale of the *Lady Nyassa* raised little over a third of its original value. Bad advice led Livingstone to invest the proceeds in a Bombay bank, which soon collapsed.

The Governor of Bombay was due to send a present of a steamer to the Sultan of Zanzibar, Majid. In order to encourage the sultan to assist Livingstone he asked David to deliver it.

The short, stocky Scot had to listen to a rendition of 'The British Grenadier' from the sultan's private band on arrival in Zanzibar! But the introduction had the desired effect. Despite the fact that Livingstone was working against the slave trade, which represented the major part of his customs revenue, the sultan gave him a 'passport' calling on all Arabs under his allegiance on the mainland to assist him.

Livingstone was going to need to deal as closely with the Arabs, whose interests were opposed to his own, as with the freed slaves, Comoros men and the Indians in his own party. Not long after landing at Mikindani, north of the Ruvuma, on 21 March 1866, Livingstone found his progress complicated by contrasting cross-cultural relationships.

At the beginning of the journey he had to pass through the territory of the Konde – the very tribe that had attacked Livingstone's party when he had gone up the Ruvuma with Kirk in 1862. Despite the memory of that encounter, David was able to win their confidence. He even found opportunity to teach the Konde about Christ. Livingstone tried to do this by using the youths from Nasik as interpreters. Although this method seemed to him to have failed, David's personal dealings with the Konde did have a positive effect. His party received hospitality from the tribe and was allowed through their territory without paying the usual *hongo* or levy.

This was despite the fact that the pack-animals they had brought with them, weighed down by their loads, damaged the Konde's corn. In fact, they were not, strictly speaking, pack-animals at all. David had brought with him a whole menagerie of animals – six camels, a donkey, two mules, three buffaloes and a calf. His aim was to discover which species would resist the bite of the tsetse fly better than others. The sepoys, however, did not have in view their experimental value. They saw them as pack-animals, whose presence would help to relieve them of the burden of porterage.

In contrast with free Africans such as the Konde, the Indians were culturally and linguistically an unknown quantity to Livingstone. For instance, he never appreciated the fact that for them, lifting burdens was beneath their dignity, which was why the sepoys transferred their loads to the animals. Not only did they overload them, but they also stabbed and wounded them to urge them on. By May 1866, when the camels started to die one by one, Livingstone could not be sure whether it was their wounds or the tsetse fly which killed them.

The freed slaves from Nasik began to be influenced by the dilatoriness of the sepoys. One of them, Reuben, was in fact seriously ill. But the others were probably playing up because the going was getting tough. Two hundred miles inland the party ran into an area hit by drought and Nguni raids, which interfered with agriculture. Food was very hard to get. The Nasik men, most of them a long way from the areas that they came from, were tempted to give up. On 2 June they and the sepoys tried to bribe the Somali guide, Ben Ali, to mislead the party so that they could get back to the coast.

One man David did consider hard-working was Abraham, whom he had sent back with cordials to look after the invalid, Richard. The Scot felt that Richard had resisted, as far as he could, the attempts of the sepoys to distract him from his duty. Within a fortnight from his ultimatum to the Nasik men, he heard from Reuben and Mabruki that Richard was dead. He was saddened that he had not been with him, to do what he could for him.

The following day, Livingstone happened on a telegram which had been sent to him saying, 'Your mother died at noon on the 18 June.'[7] This was the anniversary of her death in 1865. It was time to go through the grieving process, which he had barely had time for on the eve of his departure for Africa the year before.

A week later the opportunity offered itself of doing a good turn to a well-dressed African lady 'who had just had a very heavy slave-taming stick put on her neck; she called in such an authoritative tone to us to witness the flagrant injustice of which she was a victim that all the men stood still and went to hear her case'.[8] It turned out that she was a relative of the chief they had just passed, on her way to see her husband. Her old uncle had kidnapped her to sell her to the slave-traders!

The Scot bought her back with a cloth, and in a spirited

fashion she managed to retrieve most of her things from her uncle's house, in spite of having the door shut in her face. Askosakome, as she was called, rendered invaluable service to the party by giving them an introduction to her high-born relatives further along their journey. Her case illustrated the sad fact that Africans were selling Africans to the slave-traders. 'So many slave-sticks lie along our path, that I suspect the people hereabout make a practice of liberating what slaves they can find abandoned on the march, to sell them again,' Livingstone wrote in his journal.[9] There were all too many opportunities.

27th June. – To-day we came upon a man dead from starvation … One of our men wandered and found a number of slaves with slave-sticks on, abandoned by their master from want of food; they were too weak to be able to speak or say where they had come from; some were quite young.[10]

These sights moved David to begin pointing out the evil and injustice of slavery to the chiefs and their people. This was to become the hallmark of his visits to many hundreds of villages ahead.

At Chenjawala's the people are usually much startled when I explain that the numbers of slaves we see dead on the road have been killed partly by those who sold them, for I tell them that if they sell their fellows, they are like the man who holds the victim while the Arab performs the murder.[11]

Again his protest made its impact among the Yao people whom he met further on the road, whom he knew to be engaged actively in the trade. 'Some were dumbfounded when shown that in the eye of their Maker they are parties to the destruction of human life which accompanies this traffic both by sea and land.'[12] Being short of food, the party pushed on now on an eight-day march during which they would meet no other chiefs. 'We slept in a wild spot, near Mount Leziro, with many lions roaring about us; one hoarse fellow serenaded us a long time, but did nothing more.'[13]

Finally, after 'a weary march and long ... perpetually up and down',[14] the advance party reached Mataka's. It proved to be a well-ordered town of a thousand huts in an elevated valley, 370m above Lake Nyasa and near enough to it to ensure plentiful supplies of food. Before entering the town Livingstone encountered a courteous Arab called Sef Rubea, who presented him with an ox. It turned out that he was a slave-trader heading for Kilwa, a port south of Zanzibar. The Scot did not withdraw from relationships with Arabs, but rather learnt from the experience of interacting with them.

Before leaving for Kilwa the following day, Sef told the Scot that 100 traders of his caravan had died on their journey.

It struck me after Sef had numbered up the losses that the Kilwa people sustained by death in their endeavours to enslave people, similar losses on the part of those who go to 'proclaim liberty to the captives, the opening of the prison to them that are bound' – to save and elevate, need not be made so very much of as they sometimes are.[15]

There was cause for encouragement when it came to the attitude of the Yao chief, Mataka. Some of his people 'had, without his knowledge, gone to [Nyasa], and in a foray carried off cattle and people: when they came home with the spoil, Mataka ordered all to be sent back whence they came'.[16] Soon after giving these orders, the chief paid Livingstone a visit.

'I told him that his decision was the best piece of news I had heard in the country.'[17] Later, he gave Mataka a memento to mark his liberation. 'He replied that he would always act in a similar manner. As it was a spontaneous act, it was all the more valuable.'[18] The Scot had seen the liberated Nyasa people for himself: fifty-four women and children and a dozen boys who milked the cows, part of a herd of up to thirty cattle.

The magnanimity of Mataka contrasted with the scheming of the sepoys, who generally wore such sulky looks that the Yao had taken them for 'the slaves of the party'.[19] They had now killed the donkey and the young buffalo, but claimed to Livingstone that the latter had been attacked by a tiger. 'Did you see the stripes of the tiger?' he asked them.[20] They all said they had! This was the point of no return. Livingstone now discharged the sepoys from his service, not just because there are no striped tigers in Africa, but also because they had threatened, for the third time, to shoot Simon, his interpreter.

15
The search

Abraham recognized his uncle at Mataka's, but found that his
mother and two sisters had been sold to the Arabs shortly after
he had been enslaved. This dissuaded him from staying with
his relatives, so he set off with the Scot's party, minus the
sepoys, on the 40-mile march down to Lake Nyasa.

The ground was covered with quartz and small fragments
which were hard on the feet, but at the confluence of the
Misinje River they finally reached the lake. Livingstone was
ecstatic. 'It was as if I had come back to an old home I had
never expected again to see; and pleasant to bathe in the
delicious waters again, hear the roar of the sea, and dash in the
rollers ... I feel quite exhilarated.'[1]

He was less ecstatic about the carelessness of his cooks,
Chuma and Wakatini, who let Susi and Amoda eat all his
sugar and left a basin out at night to be stolen. They were
relieved of their culinary duties.[2] More seriously, the Scot was
unable to get a dhow to cross the lake to Nkhotakota. This
Arab settlement was run by Jumbe, a trader from Kilwa, who
did not in practice respect the authority of the Zanzibar
Sultan, Majid.

Not only did Jumbe avoid reading Sultan Majid's letter,
which requested aid for Livingstone, but also almost all the
Arab slave-trading parties shied away from the Scot's path as
soon as they heard of his approach. Heading south in order to
go round the lake, he entered a stretch of 100 miles of
depopulated country. All along the slaving routes were
scattered skulls and bones. One scene which he sketched into
his field notebook is particularly haunting: the genderless
skeleton of 'a slave tied to a tree dead & putrid & greatly eaten
by the Hyaenas [sic]'.[3]

David tried not to dwell on these sights, or to get morbid
about them; but when, on 13 September 1866, they came
within 3 miles of the end of the lake and got a clear view of the

River Shire, he could not help reflecting on what might have been. 'Many hopes have been disappointed here. Far down on the right bank of the Zambesi lies the dust of her whose death changed all my future prospects; and now, instead of a check being given to the slave-trade by lawful commerce on the Lake, slave-dhows prosper!'[4]

Determined to do what he could to turn the tide, he decided to visit Mukate, a Yao chief to the south who with two other chiefs still continued to raid the Cewa and was 'now sending periodical marauding parties to the Maravi ... to supply the Kilwa slave-traders'.[5] Mukate loved Arab cloth, but his headman drew David aside and urged him, 'Speak to Mukate to give his forays up.'[6]

There was little David could do beyond speaking forthrightly against the trade, and getting the people to think about their ultimate responsibility. 'Their forefathers never told them that after or at death they went to God ...'[7] There was more chance of making a lasting impression on the next Yao chief they visited – Mponda.

At Mponda's, Livingstone was able to inspect an Arab slave party, which consisted mainly of boys of eight to ten years old. The traders themselves confessed they would not make a great deal of money. 'I suspect that the gain is made by those who ship them to the ports of Arabia,' Livingstone concluded, 'for at Zanzibar most of the younger slaves we saw went at about seven dollars a head.'[8]

It was here that Wakatini, who had been freed in 1861 and baptized in Bombay, elected to stay. He had found a brother, and had the potential to influence his people in the long run by witnessing to what he had seen and heard. He promised the Scot that he would not obey an order from Mponda to hunt the Cewa.

I was sorry to part with him, but the Arabs tell the [Yao] chiefs that our object in liberating slaves is to make them our own and turn them to our religion. I had declared to them, through [Wakatini] as interpreter, that they never became our slaves, and were at liberty to go back to their relatives if they liked; and now it was impossible to object to Wikatani going without stultifying my own statements.[9]

Wakatini still had a part to play in the unfolding drama, and though Livingstone never saw him again, the influence that he had on that African teenager's life is testified to by a traveller who employed him as an interpreter nine years later. Though by then Wakatini had forgotten most of his English, he still sang, before going to sleep, a hymn that the Scot had taught him.

Eleven weeks later, on 6 December 1866, the British Consulate in Zanzibar received the melancholy news that Livingstone was dead, murdered by the Mazitu, a tribe of renegade Nguni, marauding from the Zambezi up to the northern shores of Nyasa.

Musa, the leader of the Comoros men who had been carriers for the Scot, explained that some days' march beyond the western shore of Lake Nyasa, the Comoros men were resting in the rear of the party. Musa had walked on ahead of them and heard Livingstone shouting that the Mazitu were coming. Catching sight of the Scot through the trees, he saw him shoot two Mazitu, only to be felled by an axe as he was reloading his rifle.

The Comoros men had fled, then crept back at sunset to find the bodies of several Nasik men lying near Livingstone, whom they buried. The baggage was all stolen and there was nothing they could bring back for identification. They had made their way back to Zanzibar via Kilwa, travelling with an Arab slaving party.

Although cross-examined by both the consul and Kirk, who had come to work with him on Livingstone's recommendation, no inconsistency could be found in the Comoros men's account. Flags were flown at half-mast both at the consulates and the sultan's palace. Sir Roderick Murchison, the president of the Royal Geographical Society, wrote to *The Times*, saying, 'if this cruel intelligence should be substantiated, the civilised world will mourn the loss of as noble and lion-hearted an explorer as ever lived.'[10]

The one person totally unconvinced by Musa's story was E. D. Young, the naval lieutenant who had known Musa on the Zambezi expedition. He offered to go to Lake Nyasa and check it out. Murchison supported him, and by 25 July 1867 the expedition arrived off the Luabo mouth of the Zambezi. Young had learnt the lessons of the Zambezi expedition, and had had an open steel boat built which drew only 46cm of water. It succeeded where both the *Ma Robert* and the *Lady Nyassa* had failed. By 19 August the boat, called the *Search*, was at the foot of the Murchison Cataracts.

Designed in sections small enough to be carried on men's backs, it was carried past the cataracts by 240 Kololo, who were delighted to do something to assist Livingstone. In the first week of September the *Search* was afloat on Lake Nyasa. Within a short time Young came across articles traded by a European traveller for food: a razor, a cartridge-case, a looking-glass. This was at the south-eastern corner of the lake, yet Musa had said that Livingstone crossed Nyasa at its northern end. When the *Search* went across at the southern end to the western shore (see map, p. 157), all doubt was removed. Young met some men who had served the Scot as porters and mimicked his method of taking observations.

What clinched the matter was Young's visit to Chief Marenga, at the south-western corner of the lake. Marenga had had words with Musa during Livingstone's two-day visit to him, trying to persuade him that there were no Mazitu on the path which the Scot had chosen, in a north-westerly direction away from the lake. Marenga had himself provided men to go with Livingstone several days' march in that direction; he introduced them to Young. But Musa had come back through his village, a short time after Livingstone had left, claiming that the Mazitu were ahead and that their term of service was over.

Young's final act was to go to the village where Wakatini had decided to settle. The fact that his brother lived there had persuaded him to stay. Young spoke with the brother, and although Wakatini himself was away, it was Young who was to employ him in 1875 when he returned to the lake to contribute to the realization of Livingstone's vision for that whole region.

Livingstone had not lost the opportunity at Marenga's to speak to his people 'through a volunteer spokesman, who seemed to have a gift that way' about the fatherhood of God and his love for all, and willingness to hear prayer. This to them was a revolutionary idea, since they had assumed 'the whole man rotted and came to nothing'.[11]

Arab slave-traders passing through the village spoke of Mazitu massacres of their brethren, and it was this that had terrified Musa and incited him to desert. In reality, however, these reports were signs of the Cewa themselves resisting their incursions. As the Scot realized, the Arabs attributed the loss of their slaves to the Mazitu purely for their reputation's sake. 'It is more respectable to be robbed by them than by the Cewa.'[12]

On 1 October 1866 Livingstone reached the Cewa chief, Kimusa, who not only remembered him from the Zambezi expedition but had actually taken his advice not to engage in the slave trade. The result was that the population of his village had tripled. Yet the chief did not trust his own people to buy ivory for him, and still used Arabs for this purpose.

Chuma had somehow persuaded himself that it was the Cewa who had sold him into slavery, when in fact it was his own Yao people. As a result, he very nearly became the victim of a confidence trick practised on him by a lady claiming to be his aunt. Livingstone dissuaded him from giving her yards of cloth, and he gave her a few beads instead.

Chuma had been only nine or ten when he and Wakatini were rescued by Livingstone from a slave gang in the Shire Highlands in July 1861. He had had time to forget what he had been delivered from, and his character was still very much in the process of formation. After the first rains came at the end of the month, the march grew difficult and food became scarce. It did no good to David's delicate digestion when the goats were lost, possibly stolen, on Christmas Day 1866. Their milk was vital to him.

It was in these circumstances, after Livingstone had no food left of any sort, that he was disappointed to find Chuma hoarding food for himself without sharing it.[13] This contrasted with the behaviour of Simon, who on 10 January gave the Scot the meal that he had and went without himself.[14] These were the kind of mixed results that Livingstone was experiencing all the time in his discipleship of the Nasik youths, who, since the desertion of Musa and the Comoros carriers, had realized that their leader was dependent on them.

A series of losses of a different kind now undermined David's position further. On 6 January 1867 his chronometers were damaged by the carrier's falling over twice. This was to put out Livingstone's measurement of longitude by a considerable margin. Nine days later, the party's poodle dog, Chitane (who had developed red hair on the march and fearlessly chased off village curs), drowned as they crossed a mile-wide ford. The guide had kept secret the existence of a narrower ford. The wetting and the 'real, biting hunger'[15] were taking their toll.

Five days further on, a real disaster occurred. Albert Baraka went off looking for mushrooms,[16] after exchanging his load with two Yao carriers, who subsequently absconded. Up to that point they had appeared to be trustworthy. It was clear that they had swapped with him in order to get custody of valuable cloth, but included in the bundle was 'what we could least spare – the medicine-box'. Memories of the ravages of malaria on the Zambezi inevitably flooded back, and Livingstone confessed, 'I felt as if I had now received the sentence of death, like poor Bishop Mackenzie.'[17]

Amazingly, in his more reflective moments, Livingstone was able to accept his vulnerability as God-given. 'Everything of this kind happens by the permission of One who watches over us with most tender care.'[18] Nevertheless, it was a shock to him a week later, 27 January, to notice how emaciated he had become. There was little prospect of improving his health as they pushed 'northwards, through almost trackless dripping forests and across oozing bogs'.[19]

By now they were across the Chambeshi River, and reached Chief Chitapangwa's on 31 January. Though Livingstone did not find the chief difficult to deal with, and even showed him woodcuts of biblical scenes from Smith's *Bible Dictionary*, he was embarrassed by the 'chirping, piping tone of voice' the young Nasik men adopted in his presence. Abraham, who interpreted, changed the Scot's words. 'It does not strike them in the least that I have grown grey among these people,'[20] grumbled David about his Nasik protégés, who still did not have the character to influence others. It seemed that they were willing neither to learn from him, nor to tell him frankly their own opinions.

Yet in spite of these impressions, something about their leader's character and acceptance of adversity did inspire respect. At this time the Scot's first attack of rheumatic fever came, with no medicine to deal with it. Whereas in the past he had led the march from the front, he now found that 'every step ... jars in the chest ... I have a constant singing in the ears, and can scarcely hear the loud tick of the chronometers'.[21] After facing with immense fortitude an attack from driver ants, Livingstone finally collapsed after reaching the goal of Lake Tanganyika.

'I had a fit of insensibility ... I found myself floundering outside my hut and unable to get in: I tried to lift myself from my back by laying hold of two posts at the entrance, but when I got nearly upright I let them go, and fell back heavily on my head on a box.'[22] It was then that his young followers showed a touch of delicacy (and perhaps, in Susi and Chuma's case, devotion) by hanging a blanket over the entrance of the hut, keeping their leader's helplessness hidden from the eyes of strangers.

In his debilitated condition David found solace in the views that were presented to his gaze.

After being a fortnight at this Lake it still appears one of surpassing loveliness. Its peacefulness is remarkable, though at times it is said to be lashed up by storms. It lies in a deep basin whose sides are nearly perpendicular, but covered well with trees; the rocks which appear are bright red argillaceous schist; the trees at present all green: down some of these rocks come beautiful cascades, and buffaloes, elephants, and antelopes wander and graze on the more level spots, while lions roar by night.[23]

Although Livingstone was intending to go up the western shore of Tanganyika, he was forestalled by a blood feud between Chief Nsama and Arab-Swahili traders, which also threatened to block his route to the next objective to the west – Lake Mweru. The Arabs used 'cabalistic figures' to divine whether or not to go to Nsama and make peace – a practice the Scot presumed pre-dated their prophet. In the end an uneasy peace prevailed, and Nsama agreed that Livingstone could pass him on the way to Lake Mweru.

An earthquake which struck on 6 June, although it caused no injuries, probably gave the *coup de grâce* to one of the chronometers. Although his observations were inevitably affected, Livingstone at least could obtain guides to go to Lake Mweru. These he requested from Tippu Tip, the Swahili trader who had been involved in the original incident with Nsama. When he met Tippu Tip on 29 July the trader 'presented a goat, a piece of white calico, and four big bunches of beads, also a bag of Holcus sorghum, and apologized because it was so little.'[24]

It was not until 30 August, 'after three months and ten days' delay'[25] from the beginning of the negotiations with Nsama, that the Scot's party of ten men was able to begin the march in earnest. As soon as they made contact with Tippu Tip, he again gave them a gift, 'a fine fat goat'.[26] Why was it that this powerful trader, who had built up hundreds of dependants through ivory and slaves, took an interest in helping a European who travelled only with ten companions?

Undoubtedly self-interest played a part. One use to which Tippu Tip put his slaves was to work on clove plantations in Zanzibar. He needed to keep in with the Sultan Majid, whose 'passport' Livingstone bore; but he also had to equip his expeditions with imported items (such as guns and powder) which he could get only with the goodwill of the European consulates on the island. In fact Dr John Kirk, at the British consulate, had Tippu Tip placed in confinement for letting off gunpowder in its vicinity. It was only after this that Tippu Tip went to Kirk with a letter which Livingstone had entrusted to him – in order to get Kirk to repent of putting him in prison.

Livingstone gave Tippu Tip not only a letter, but also, to Tippu Tip's way of thinking, one of his servants – Albert Baraka, who, soon after Livingstone set out again on 1 September, went back to Tippu Tip's village and entered his service for many years.

In fact the Scot could scarcely afford to lose another man, but he had noticed that since coming into close contact with Arab slave-traders the Nasik men had started to try to imitate them. Albert's desertion was only carrying this desire for emulation to its logical conclusion. Apart from the problem of their influence on his followers, Livingstone found that being bound up with an Arab caravan caused endless delay. 'Nothing can be more tedious than the Arab way of travelling,' he told his journal,[27] after authority was found in the Qur'an for yet another day's stop. 'There is no system in the Arab marches,' he noted two days later, after an inexplicable detour.[28]

Tippu Tip, by contrast, was perfectly happy to take his time, being quite ready to be away from Zanzibar between six and nine years, searching for trading opportunities. He knew no other motive for travel than trade, and the activities of Europeans were to him quite profitless. 'You busy yourselves with nothing but rivers, lakes and mountains,' he was to say some years later, 'and use up your life for no reason and purpose. Look at that old man who died in [Bisa]! What was he looking for so long that he became too old to travel? He was not rich, he never gave us presents. He bought neither ivory, nor slaves; yet he was a step beyond any of us – and to do what?'[29]

So much for exploration. If Livingstone had heard this speech, he might have replied that it was to open up Africa for the gospel; but the gospel too was a closed book to his Arab companions, in the sense that their Islamic teaching created barriers to accepting it. This was typified by such reactions as those of '[Sayed], who thinks that the sun rises and sets because the Koran says so, and he sees it. He asserts that Jesus foretold the coming of Mohamed; and that it was not Jesus who suffered on the cross but a substitute, it being unlikely that a true prophet would be put to death so ignominiously.'

Since they were not interested in lakes, the Arabs and Livingstone parted company as his party set out for the final march on Lake Mweru. Curiously enough, however, the Arabs not only escorted him some of the way, but Tippu Tip himself, as it turned out, took time later to have a look at the lake, Mweru, that this European was so curious about. When they reached it on 8 November, Livingstone saw it as a vital link in the East African watershed. 'The northern shore has a fine sweep like an unbent bow, and round the western end flows the water that makes the river Lualaba, which, before it enters [Mweru] is the Luapula, and that again (if the more intelligent reports speak true) is the Chambeshi before it enters Lake [Bangweulu].'[30]

Livingstone was concerned to find the southernmost sources of the watershed, before working northwards to discover whether the Lualaba would lead finally to the Congo, or to the Nile.

Meanwhile, the much reduced party of 'only nine persons in all' crossed a plain covered in red anthills to the village of Kazembe (which means 'general'). The current 'general' had recently ousted his predecessor, and the gateway was 'ornamented with about sixty human skulls'.[31] It was almost a relief to be greeted again by Arab traders; he met Muhammad bin Gharib (he had arrived seven days before with many slaves, and presented him with a meal of vermicelli, oil and honey) and Muhammad bin Salih, 'a fine portly black Arab, with a pleasant smile, and pure white beard'. He had 'been more than ten years in these parts, and lived with four [Kazembes]'.[32]

16
High noon

At Kazembe's, Livingstone unwittingly became entangled in the intrigue of Muhammad bin Salih, who saw him as a means to an end: that of getting free of Kazembe, who had held the white-bearded Arab under restraint for some time, suspecting him to have been involved with a plot against him.

On the one hand, the Scot was discouraged from carrying out his intention to visit Lake Bangweulu to the south, by fantastic tales of widespread elephantiasis among the people of the lake; without his medicine box, it seemed unwise to go to such an unhealthy region.

On the other hand, Livingstone was eventually manoeuvred into taking Muhammad bin Salih off with him in the opposite direction, to the north, to give the Arab a passport out of Kazembe's dominions. This was achieved by trading on the goodwill which the Scot, from his long experience of dealing with chiefs, had built up with Kazembe.

Bin Salih, after a long sojourn with four Kazembes, wanted to cut his losses and get back to Ujiji, the Arab entrepôt on the north-eastern shore of Lake Tanjanyika, where Livingstone too had asked supplies to be sent. But the territory into which he brought the Scot was highly disadvantageous; first, it was very wet at that season, and therefore very unhealthy (just as Lake Bangweulu had been made out to be); secondly, the prices were very high (much higher than they were in the south) and so Livingstone's stock of goods was running down too quickly.

On deciding to break with bin Salih and head back south for Bangweulu, Livingstone made an unpleasant discovery: the wily old man had also subverted his men. On 13 April 1868 they rebelled against his orders and refused to go south. Bin Salih tried to interpose himself as arbitrator; he 'demanded [to know] what I was going to do with those who had absconded'.[1]

This was the high noon of Livingstone's relationship with his followers who, in their prolonged exposure to the Arab slavers, both at Kazembe's and in the camps on the march, had succumbed to the temptations of what might be called an alternative lifestyle. One by one they came to him with their excuses for not going: 'Susi, for no confessed reason but he had got a black woman who feeds him. Chuma for the same reason.'[2]

Chuma, who was still a teenager, betrayed the fact that he had got mixed up with the drugs scene of the day. He 'came with his eyes shot out by *bange*'[3] or Indian hemp, or, as the Greeks called it, cannabis.

The Scot found himself in the position of a kind of foster-parent, faced with the first experiments of the youths under his charge with drugs and sex. 'They would like me to remain here and pay them for smoking the *bange*, and deck their prostitutes with the beads which I give regularly for their food.'[4]

In the extraordinary scene that followed, a kind of tug of love and war went on between him and his followers. 'Abraham had brought up some old grievance as a justification for his absconding. James said "He was tired of working." Abraham apologized and was forgiven. Susi stood like a mule.'[5]

It was Susi who had the potential to sway others, especially the younger Chuma. Seeing Abraham's change of heart, there seemed to be an intense conflict going on inside him. But he hardened as his 'father' made his appeal. 'I put my hand on his arm ... He seized my hand, and refused to let it go.'[6]

Physically seizing his leader in this way was tantamount to mutiny. The 'foster-father' became for a time a 'magistrate'. As soon as Susi did let his hand go, the Scot seized a pistol and fired at Susi. The shot missed, as it was intended to; but it was a sharp warning which served to bring some of the men to their senses.

Five men set out with Livingstone on the journey south. Amoda, who was among those who stayed behind, said he was 'tired of carrying',[7] but would go back to his leader once he had got an extra carrier to help from Muhammad bin Gharib. But Muhammad bin Salih (called 'Mpamari' by the Africans) 'told him not to return'.[8]

'I did not blame them very severely in my own mind for absconding: they were tired of tramping, and so verily am I,' confessed Livingstone. But Muhammad 'in encouraging them to escape to him, and talking with a double tongue, cannot be exonerated from blame. Little else can be expected from him, he has lived some thirty-five years in the country, twenty-five being at Kazembe's, and there he had often to live by his wits. Consciousness of my own defects makes me lenient.'[9]

In fact, even if this incident brought out the darker side of Livingstone's temperament – the determination that he 'would not be thwarted'[10] – it at the same time illustrates how mild the discipline he exercised had been: so mild, in fact, in comparison to that of the slave-drivers, that it had been in danger of breaking down altogether. His principle that his men were not slaves, and that they were therefore free to leave when they chose, had reduced his party drastically, while on the other hand the fact that he always forgave his men for their misdemeanours, and was generally gentle with them, ultimately aroused a profound attachment in those who remained.

Then it was back to Lake Mweru through black mud, ruts and foul water, on through an area where villages had been abandoned on account of 'ferocious wild beasts',[11] finally dealing with a suspicious headman who could not understand why he was coming back through the country he had left. Abraham went to Kazembe (or Muonga) and came back with a 'gracious' message[12] inviting them to return. Here they were to wait for guides to take them further south to Bangweulu.

On 11 June the party finally got off from Kazembe's and reached the River Luongo eleven days later. On the further bank, on 24 June, they were confronted by a strange sight. 'Six men slaves were singing as if they did not feel the weight and degradation of their slave-sticks. I asked the cause of their mirth, and was told that they rejoiced at the idea of "coming back after death and haunting and killing those who had sold them" ... Then all joined in the chorus, which was the name of each vendor. It told not of fun, but of the bitterness and tears of such as were oppressed, and on the side of the oppressors there was a power: there be higher than they!'[13]

The following day 'we came to a grave in the forest; it was a little rounded mound as if the occupant sat in it in the usual native way: it was strewed over with flour, and a number of the large blue beads put on it: a little path showed that it had visitors. This is the sort of grave I should prefer: to lie in the still, still forest, and no hand ever disturb my bones.' The Scot preferred the African style of grave to the British, which had no 'elbow-room'. His thoughts turned to where 'poor Mary' lay 'on [Chupanga] brae'.[14] Perhaps he would have been comforted to know that Lieutenant Young, on his journey up the Zambezi, had tended Mary's grave a year before.

It took ten days at the beginning of July to get a guide to take them further. They finally obtained one from Kumba-kumba, chief of a village of Banyanwezi, who traded in copper and was allied to the Sultan of Zanzibar. The Banyanwezi, though they often cheated the local people in trade, nevertheless gained influence in the region by defending it from the forays of the Mazitu.

In fact the party were often taken for Mazitu on their path to Lake Bangweulu. In one incident, a drunken group surrounded them. Yet Livingstone's experience was that 'there is usually one good soul in such rabbles', and so it proved. One man befriended them and retrieved their stolen goats, and they 'got away without shedding blood'.[15]

Livingstone had not, in fact, even loaded his gun. He was always thankful to avoid conflict. Perhaps he was also encouraged by the fact that in crossing yet another flooded area 'the young men volunteered to carry me across',[16] but, typically, he had already plunged in before the offer was made. After a couple of nights in the forest, they finally reached their goal on 18 July 1868. 'I walked a little way out and saw the shores of the Lake for the first time, thankful that I had come safely hither.'[17]

In an audience with Chief Mapuni at the lake he was asked by another traveller why he had gone through so much to get to this region.

I said … we were all children of one Father, and I was anxious that we should know each other better … I told him what the Queen had done to encourage the growth of cotton on the Zambesi [sic], and how we had been thwarted by slave-traders ... I showed them the Bible, and told them little of its contents.[18]

The only indication that the people had a sense of the existence of God (or Mungu) was the chief's comment that Mungu's footsteps could be seen on Lifungu Island, in Lake Bangweulu. Livingstone hired a canoe to see the islands and survey the lake, but on the second day the oarsmen confessed that they had stolen the canoe, and that the real owners were bearing down on them from another island. They naturally insisted on retreat and this, together with the damage to his chronometers, prevented an accurate survey of the lake. Even the depth could not be measured, since Amoda's absence meant that the plumb-line had had to be left behind.[19]

The lake, which was a deep sea-green colour due to reflection from the white sand on the bottom, was perfectly healthy and not a single case of elephantiasis was to be seen. But Livingstone left, anxious to make contact with a trading party going to Manyema. This was a region north-west of Lake Tanganyika – an area he wanted to explore, since such a journey would allow him to see if the River Lualaba flowed towards the Nile or towards the Congo.

As Livingstone marched north, however, he found the country riven by wars and rumours of wars. The Mazitu had made a foray and the Arabs had taken up Kazembe's cause against them. After this, however, Kazembe feared that the Arabs had grown too powerful. His ally, Chief Chikumbu, attacked Kumbakumba's stockade and now there was war between all the Bemba people allied to Kazembe and the Banyanwezi and Arab traders.

Although Kazembe wished to protect Livingstone, he and his party were once again surrounded, this time 'by a party of furious' Bemba. Once again 'one good soul helped us away – a blessing be on him and his'.[20]

The traders joined forces to escape and there was no other way for Livingstone to get out of the country except by going with them. A trader to the north, Sayed bin Habib, jeopardized the position of the party by fastening a dispute on Chief Mpweto, north of Lake Mweru, over runaway slaves, thus aggravating the Bemba further.

In these highly dangerous conditions, the deserters who had been influenced by Muhammad bin Salih came back to Livingstone. He readily forgave them. 'I have taken all the runaways back again; after trying the independent life they will behave better ... I have faults myself.'[21]

Using such influence as he had to moderate the behaviour of the slave-traders, the Scot protested when one, Sayed Majid, tied an old woman and her daughter to a stake. Both were released. Yet he could not persuade the party to give up the slaves which a Swahili, called bin Juma, had taken 'in revenge' on a local chief who had allowed a slave boy to escape through his territory. War broke out with 'the justly infuriated' Bemba.[22]

The Scot was impressed with the courage of the local Bemba tribe who, to the surprise of the Swahili, persisted in attacking with nothing but bows and arrows against the slave-traders' guns. 'Their care to secure the wounded was admirable ... Victoria-cross fellows truly many of them were! ... they had never encountered guns before.'[23]

Livingstone, whose sympathies were with the Bemba and the African cause, felt that Muhammad bin Gharib was putting him in an invidious position by turning to him to ask his advice once the war had already started. Bin Juma was one of bin Gharib's camp followers, but the Scot said they would never reach Ujiji with bin Juma among them. Fortunately, a degree of moderation belatedly prevailed. When two Bemba men came in offering not to fight if they were given back their captured wives, bin Gharib grasped the proffered olive branch and released six captives, including the two wives.

The march to Ujiji began on 11 December 1868. More slaves took advantage of the journey to make their bid for freedom. Two of bin Salih's slaves made off 'though in the yoke, and they had been with him from boyhood'.[24] As for bin Gharib's recent purchases, 'not one good-looking slave-woman is now left ... all the pretty ones obtain favour by their address, beg to be unyoked, and then escape'.[25]

The party caught up with Sayed bin Habib, the trader who had been to the north of them. Fortunately, he had also listened to counsels of moderation: the only mullah in the region had persuaded him not to pursue his quarrel with Chief Mpweto. If the trader had not backed down, the Bemba might well have had Mpweto as an ally when they attacked bin Gharib's camp, and their position would have been serious indeed.

Nevertheless Sayed bin Habib was now enmeshed in a long-term blood feud over his elder brother, Salem, killed in the Lua region further west. He vowed to despoil that whole country.

Meanwhile Sayed bin Habib had to mourn the death of another brother, and insisted that the Scot delay his march for the funeral. Muhammad bin Salih and four others went down into the grave, where the mullah made some inaudible prayers. 'We went to the usual sitting position, and shook hands with [Sayed bin Habib], as if receiving him back again into the company of the living.'[26]

The party then had to cross three branches and the main stream of the Lufonso River. The people were in the water up to the neck. Livingstone was probably pleased to see Susi leap in to help save two who were drowning, for he now calls him 'my man Susi',[27] as distinct from his usual way of referring to the more immature youths from Nasik as 'boys'.[28]

Marching round Mount Katanga on Christmas Day, they set a north-easterly course towards Lake Tanganyika. Reaching the River Kapéta, they 'slaughtered a favourite kid to make a Christmas dinner'.[29] This was a rare treat, but their usual fare was poor. On 30 December they reached the River Lofuko 'in pelting rain; not knowing that the camp with huts was near, I stopped and put on a bernouse, got wet, and had no dry clothes.'[30]

New Year's Day 1869 saw Livingstone sicker than ever before. 'I have been wet times without number, but the wetting of yesterday was once too often. I felt very ill, but fearing that the Lofuko might flood, I resolved to cross it. Cold up to the waist, which made me worse.'[31] Six weeks of pneumonia followed, which robbed him of the ability even to count the days of the week and month.

Too ill to walk, he was carried to Maparre on the west coast of Lake Tanganyika. 'I saw myself lying dead on the way to Ujiji.'[32] On the journey he thought often of his children. He was longing for letters, milk and medicine. When he did reach Ujiji, on the north-eastern shore of Tanganyika, it was to discover that both letters and supplies had been stolen.

Medicines, wine and cheese had been left at Nyanyembe, thirteen days march to the east, but the Ujijians told him that the way was blocked by the Mazitu, or renegade Nguni, on the rampage there. However, a gift of Assam tea had arrived from Calcutta, together with coffee and sugar. Despite his otherwise meagre fare, David began to recover some of his strength, and, on what he guessed was 28 March, managed to walk half a mile.

He realized that Sayed bin Habib would not let his men carry letters to the coast, since he suspected that the Scot would report on his depredations in the Lua area. Sayed himself arrived in camp 'with his cargo of copper and slaves' on 17 May,[33] which meant that Livingstone had to move house again. He was already hankering for the chance to be on his way again, since he felt stronger.

Another trader, Thani bin Suellim, brought goods from Nyanyembe on 26 May, but they had been ruined by damp. He, too, contacted other traders at Ujiji warning them not to take Livingstone's letters, of which he had written forty-two. Well might he fear their contents, since the Scot was by now provoked to anger at their proceedings.

'This is a den of the worst kind of slave-traders,' he wrote that same day. 'Those whom I met in Urungu and Itawa were gentlemen slavers: the Ujiji slavers, like the Kilwa and the Portuguese, are the vilest of the vile. It is not a trade, but a system of consecutive murders; they go to plunder and kidnap, and every trading trip is nothing but a foray.'[34]

Sayed bin Habib's forays against the Katala people, in revenge for the death of his brother Salem, had 'blocked up one part of the country'.[35] Livingstone planned to go north-west, to Manyema country, but it was now too late in the season to get porters. 'Two months must elapse ere we can face the long grass and superabundant water in the way to

[Manyema],' he predicted on 1 June.[36]

His aim in doing so was to 'trace down the western arm of the Nile to the north – if this is indeed that of the Nile, and not of the Congo ... The Manyuema [sic] are said to be friendly where they have not been attacked by Arabs: a great chief is reported as living on a large river flowing northwards. I hope to make my way to him, and I feel exhilarated at the thought of getting among people not spoiled by contact with Arab traders.'[37]

In fact, on all three counts Livingstone was to be disappointed. First the course of the River Lualaba was to prove to have so much westing that his doubts that it might be the Congo increased. Second, the great chief, Moenekuss or 'Lord of the Parrot' (so named because his country abounded with light-grey parrots with red tails) was dead. His sons were not of his stature, and in practice the entire Manyema country was ruled by headmen who were a law unto themselves, each in his own locality. Third – and most disturbing of all – the slave-traders were making inroads.

On 15 September, following days of uphill marching which had made him puff and blow because of the effect on his lungs of a previous attack of pneumonia, Livingstone encountered Dugumbé, a slave-trader who had entered this previously isolated territory. He was 'carrying 18,000 lbs of ivory, purchased in this new field very cheaply, because no traders had ever gone into the country beyond Bambarré or Moenekuss's district before'.[38]

A week later Livingstone reached Bambarré, where Moenekuss's two sons received the outsiders with some suspicion. 'They think that we have come to kill them: we light on them as if from another world: no letters come to tell who we are, or what we want. We cannot conceive their estate of isolation and helplessness, with nothing to trust to but their charms and idols – both being bits of wood.'[39]

The impression of isolation was strengthened when on 9 October, 'two very fine young men came to visit'.[40] Eventually the conversation came round to the topic they were most anxious to get information on. Did Livingstone's people die? Or, in their country, did they have a charm (buanga) against death? If they did die, who killed them? And where did they go after death?

'It is not necessary to answer such questions save in a land never visited by strangers. Both had the 'organs of intelligence' largely developed. I told them that we prayed to the Great Father, Mulungu, and he hears us all; they thought this to be natural.'[41]

In many ways there seemed to be a certain innocence about the Manyema. Not only did they not know the value of ivory, but they also would not steal, holding this to be totally against their customs and culture. When Dugumbé broke camp on 18 October, one of his party 'seized ten goats and ten slaves before leaving, though great kindness had been shown'.[42]

It was an ominous sign, and when Livingstone's party headed west for the Lualaba they were stopped on the banks of the River Luama, unable to get a canoe for love or money. This was the fruit of the depredations of Dugumbé ahead of them, as a result of which the Scot was forced to return to Bambarré on 19 December 1869.

It seemed that the 'age of innocence' of the Manyema was coming to an end. In Livingstone's absence, 'a large horde of Ujijians'[43] carrying 500 guns had passed through Bambarré. It was hopeless to attempt to go due west now. Livingstone decided to go north, to Mamohela, so as to avoid the path of the 'traders'.

17
The terrorists

Livingstone hoped to penetrate far enough north to make contact with another part of the Lualaba and buy a canoe. He found, however, that whereas previously he had passed through well-built villages in a fruitful land, the country to the north was difficult to penetrate, particularly in the rains.

Only an elephant could pass through the 'rank jungle of grass ... these are his headquarters', the Scot wrote, while resting from sickness in camp during 27–30 January 1870.[1] The fertility of the country could not disguise the health problems of its people, many of whom were albinos. Syphilis was prevalent. Yet it was not necessarily the healthier people who were more friendly.

> We came to a village among fine gardens of maize ... but the villagers said, 'Go on to next village' and this meant, 'We don't want you here' ... I was so weak I sat down in the next hamlet and asked for a hut to rest in. A woman with leprous hands gave me hers, a nice clean one, and very heavy rain came on: of her own accord she prepared dumplings of green maize, pounded and boiled, which are sweet, for she said that she saw I was hungry ... seeing that I did not eat for fear of the leprosy, she kindly pressed me: 'Eat, you are weak only from hunger; this will strengthen you.' I put it out of her sight, and blessed her motherly heart.[2]

In fact Livingstone was weak from loss of blood, and he had to rest at Mamohela from 7 February to 26 June. As happened before when they had got used to a place, some of his men now refused to continue and the Scot pushed on with only three: Susi, Chuma and Gardner. They struck north-west, but met followers of Muhammad bin Gharib who told them that the Lualaba was not in that direction. In fact it veered west-south-west.

It was imprudent to push on so far with only three attendants, particularly as Livingstone's feet were now ulcerated
and showed no signs of healing. He turned back, reaching
Mamohela on 6 July and 'limped back to Bambarré on 22nd'
July.[3] There he had to stay for eight months – a situation which
for the only time in his life led him seriously to consider giving
up his quest. 'The severe pneumonia in Marunga, the chol-
eraic complaint in [Manyema], and now irritable ulcers warn
me to retire while life lasts.'[4]

Finding that by rubbing a paste of malachite powder and
water into his sores a real improvement was made in his
condition, on 26 September he was at last able to 'report the
ulcers healing',[5] and on 10 October to come out of his hut.

After an eighty-day confinement, it was finally possible to
think of what strategy to follow. Tippu Tip, he had heard,
planned to cross the Lualaba at Mpweto's, north of Lake
Mweru, and to proceed north up the west bank. 'Much ivory
may be obtained by this course, and it shows enterprise.'[6]
Tippu Tip was actually on the way to carving out something
akin to an Arab state in the west (or what is now eastern
Zaire), whereas the hit-and-run tactics of the Swahilis usually
precluded them from settling.

It was also the intention of Dugumbé to open up the
Lualaba. Inevitably, Livingstone would encounter him. The
question was, how could he move without men? Simon and
Abraham had become what he called 'ringleading deserters'[7]
and had actually joined in with Arabs in slave-hunting – an act
which guaranteed that Livingstone would not take them back,
even though they hovered in his vicinity.

Yet Livingstone wanted to get to the Lualaba and, if possible, the Katanga district beyond, in his quest for the source of
the Nile. He had sent to Kirk for men some time previously,
but the death from cholera of thirty men in the camp did not
augur well for the possibility of their reaching him. A devast-
ating epidemic of cholera, radiating out from Mecca down to
Zanzibar and out along the caravan routes, was only too likely
to stop them from reaching him.[8]

The epidemic was also having a deterrent effect on one

aspect of the Manyema culture which Livingstone had at first been disinclined to believe: the custom of eating corpses, after they had been buried a few days. This may have arisen from their taste for eating *soko* – a forest ape – and for 'high' meat. It had given the Manyema men a reputation for cannibalism, which accounted for their extreme isolation from other tribes and, perhaps, for the very late entry of traders into their land.

The evidence Livingstone had gradually collected disabused him of his impression that the Manyema culture was a virgin one, innocent of violence until it was introduced by the traders. 'The evils inflicted by these Arabs are enormous,' he acknowledged (at one stage[9] he had passed through nine villages burnt for the attempted theft of a single string of beads), 'but probably not greater than the people inflict on each other.'[10] The men, for example, would go and kill a person from a neighbouring village for the privilege of being able to wear a red parrot feather.[11]

Both the cannibalism and the violence were brought home to Livingstone by the death of one of his remaining followers, James Rutton. Knowing the place to which Livingstone's men went regularly to buy food, Manyema men lay in ambush and shot James with an arrow. Although David did not record this, Susi was sure that the assailant not only killed James, but later ate his body. Whether or not this was James's fate, the sequel finally convinced Livingstone of the propensities of the people.

James had been lured into the ambush by a Manyema man who was apprehended. A rumour spread that he had been executed for his crime. On 12 February 1871 'crowds came to eat the meat of the man who misled James to his death spot ... they were much disappointed when they found that no-one was killed, and are undoubtedly cannibals.'[12]

Not for nothing did Livingstone read through the whole Bible four times while he was in Manyema country. It was one of his severest trials in terms of agonizing delay and, later, taut nerves and tension. It was faith alone that had enabled him to write, on 12 December 1870: 'It may all be for the best that I am so hindered, and compelled to inactivity.'[13]

Kirk's men finally reached him at Bambarré later in February. It turned out that he had got them off just before the cholera struck Zanzibar. But they had left their headman, Sherif, in Ujiji and had no intention of going further. They struck for higher wages. After dealing with the dispute, David was ready to go on 16 February, only to find Nathaniel Cumba claiming to be too ill to come. Muhammad bin Gharib propelled him after Livingstone, but also bundled out the deserters, Simon and Abraham. Neither bin Gharib nor Livingstone wanted them, and when they came up behind, the Scot deterred them only by threatening to use his gun.[14]

They reached Mamohela on 24 February, to be greeted respectfully by the Arabs; a letter was waiting for Livingstone from the Sultan of Zanzibar, as well as Dr Kirk. Now, at last, Livingstone was able to push on westwards to follow the great west-south-west curve of the Lualaba. 'I had to suspend my judgment, so as to be prepared to find it after all perhaps the Congo.'[15]

This time the problems came not so much from the terrain as from the recalcitrant nature of the ten new men in Livingstone's party. Although Kirk had sought to send freemen or at least freedmen, they insisted that they were slaves of their Banyan (Indian) master at Zanzibar and under his authority only. 'They refused to take their bead rations, and made Chakanga spokesman: I could not listen to it, as he has been concocting a mutiny against me ... so many difficulties have been put in my way I doubt whether the Divine favour and will is [sic] on my side.'[16]

Doubt and perplexity deepened when, having reached the market town of Nyangwe on the banks of the Lualaba, the goal for which he had been striving for so long, Livingstone found it impossible to hire canoes to get across to the far bank. His own 'Banyan slaves' spread reports that he would kill and plunder if he did so, since they wanted the Manyema to block his path and allow them to return. The Arabs warned Livingstone of their behaviour.

The traders were more polite than the Banyans, but the fact

was that they wanted to keep the ivory trade to themselves, and since they could hardly conceive of another motive for travelling in that territory, they hindered Livingstone from going there. The Arabs, therefore, while never actually refusing canoes, adopted delaying tactics, promising to consult with others to see what they could do. In the meantime, they even asked Livingstone questions about the Bible, and about how many prophets had appeared. Livingstone asked them in turn if they could tell how many false prophets had been in the world. 'It is easy to drive them into a corner by questioning, as they don't know whither the inquiries lead, and they are not offended when their [lack of] knowledge is, as it were, admitted.'[17]

As it turned out, however, Livingstone felt it to be a sign of God's protection that he did not get a canoe. On 14 June, Hassani, one of the Arab traders, hired nine canoes. Four days downriver disaster struck. A rocky ridge crossed the course, creating narrows. Unaware that the rocks ahead jutted out alternately, so that the mass of water rushed round one promontory after another, the lead canoe went into a powerful whirlpool and five lives were lost. If he had been allowed to go with the party, Livingstone well knew that Hassani would have insisted that he went into the lead canoe – ostensibly out of polite regard for precedence, but in practice to make a 'feeler' of him.

Two days after Hassani got his canoes, Dugumbé had passed through with 500 guns and many followers. He had brought his family with him and was clearly intent on setting up a power base in the region, sending back regularly to Ujiji for supplies as he opened up new fields for trade. In this, it seemed, he would brook no competition. When he discovered that Manilla, a slave of Sayed bin Habib, had fired eight villages and then 'mixed blood' with a number of headmen to bind them in an alliance under his protection, he publicly denounced him.

Livingstone also noticed that Dugumbé's men were trying to 'deal in the market in a domineering way'.[18] The market was a great institution among the Manyema and, just as their lawlessness was tempered by their antipathy to stealing, so their violent feuding between villages was mitigated by the principle that even in time of war, women could pass freely to and from the market without being molested. No Manyema would bear arms in the marketplace and, once there, the dealers felt secure.

It was the Scotsman's greatest source of entertainment to go to market. Everyone was pleased to answer his questions about their goods. Cassava, palm oil, fish, salt, pepper, cocks, pigs and pots were displayed. Potters slapped and rung their wares all around to show that there were no faults in them. If the buyers despised their goods, they would wrinkle their faces into expressions of withering scorn, expressing intense surprise at being doubted. Small girls ran about selling cups of water to refresh the combatants in their theatrical battle of words.

Such was the profound commitment of the people to the market that 1,500 people turned up on the day that Dugumbé decided to take reprisals against the villages that had allied themselves to Manilla. Who was Manilla to burn villages and make alliances? To teach the Manyema to deal with him alone, Dugumbé's men were setting fire to villages on the opposite bank of the Lualaba.

Livingstone was surprised to see three of Dugumbé's men in the market, with their guns. He wanted to rebuke them but, thinking that they must have been ignorant of local custom, he turned away in search of shelter from the heat of the sun. Before he had gone 9 metres two guns went off in the crowd. The sellers 'threw down their wares in confusion, and ran'.

At the same time that the three opened fire on the mass of people near the upper end of the market-place volleys were discharged from a party down near the creek on the panic-stricken women, who dashed at the canoes. These, some fifty or more, were jammed in the creek, and the men forgot their paddles in the terror that seized all. The canoes were not to be got out, for the creek was too small for so many; men and women, wounded by the [musket] balls, poured into them, and leaped and scrambled into the water, shrieking.

A long line of heads in the river showed that great numbers struck out for an island a full mile off: in going towards it they had to put the left shoulder to a current of about two miles an hour; if they had struck away diagonally to the opposite bank, the current would have aided them, and, though nearly three miles off, some would have gained land: as it was, the heads above water showed the long line of those that would inevitably perish.[19]

Livingstone felt that on that hot and sultry day he was in Gehenna. The crackle and flash of the muskets, 'the firearms pouring their iron bullets on the fugitives', was like 'burning in the bottomless pit'.[20] The Arabs admitted that 330–400 people were killed. Their slaves plundered those who fled on land. Those who took refuge with Livingstone's party, or under the flag that he sent out with some of his men, were saved. The Scot was able to restore thirty of the rescued to their friends the following day (16 July), but the carnage continued on the opposite bank until twenty-seven villages were destroyed.

An old man, called Kabobo, came for his old wife; I asked her if this were her husband, she went to him, and put her arm lovingly around him, and said 'Yes'. I gave her five strings of beads to buy food, all her stores being destroyed with her house; she bowed down, and put her forehead to the ground as thanks, and old Kabobo did the same: the tears stood in her eyes as she went off …

Many of the headmen who have been burned out by the foray came over to me, and begged me to come back with them, and appoint new localities for them to settle in again, but I told them that I was so ashamed of the company in which I found myself, that I could scarcely look the [Manyema] in the face. They had believed that I wished to kill them – what did they think now? I could not remain among bloody companions, and would flee away, I said, but they begged me hard not to leave until they were again settled.[21]

It was small consolation to Livingstone that the headmen now distinguished him from Dugumbé and from men of violence; for it was from Dugumbé and those same terrorists he had hoped to buy canoes and explore the west bank of the Lualaba. If possible, Livingstone hoped to go on to Katanga, where he hoped to find the rise of four rivers which (he had heard) came from a single mountain. This idea had made him dream of the 'four fountains' which Herodotus had spoken of as possible sources of the Nile.[22]

It was conditions of enforced inactivity in Bambarré that had allowed him to fantasize of such things. Now all these dreams were exploded, and the cruel reality of the massacre of defenceless market women reacted on his mind and spirit, filling him with 'unspeakable horror'.[23] He knew that for his own conscience's sake, even if the headmen pleaded with him to stay, he could not keep with Dugumbé, let alone travel with him. The shock of what happened sent him reeling on the road back to Ujiji.

As he had every reason to expect, by no means all the Manyema were able to distinguish between Livingstone's party and the perpetrators of the massacre. On 8 August 1871, three separate attempts were made on the Scotsman's life. Running the gauntlet through a dense forest, twice spearmen narrowly missed their mark. The first spear almost grazed his back, the second landing 'about a foot in front'.[24]

Breaking into a clearing, he caught sight of a gigantic tree, made still taller by growing on an anthill twenty feet high; it had fire applied near its roots; I heard the crack which told that the fire had done its work, but felt no alarm till I saw it come straight towards me.'[25]

Livingstone's attendants 'scattered in all directions'.[26] The tree came crashing down, breaking into several sections. Looking back, they saw their leader completely covered in dust, standing only a metre from the leading piece of trunk. They came running back, calling out, 'Peace! Peace! You will finish all your work in spite of these people, and in spite of everything.' 'Like them, I took it as an omen of good success to crown me yet, thanks to the Almighty preserver of men.'[27]

When they finally got out of the forest, they were met by the local chief, Muanampunda, 'walking up in a stately manner'.[28] He had heard the gunfire in the forest and came to ask the cause. Since, like many Manyema headmen, he had a feud with his neighbours, he presented ten goats and invited Livingstone to join him in a war of retaliation. His guest politely declined, saying that his assailants had mistaken him for Muhammad bin Gharib, and to take part in a 'feud would only make matters worse'.

This Muanampunda 'could perfectly understand'.[29] He escorted the party a long way onwards, pausing only to point out the spot where he and his men had killed a man and, afterwards, eaten his body.

Mamohela proved to have been abandoned by the Arabs; perhaps the tide was turning against their invasion. Livingstone became very ill with dysentery, but managed to keep going and 'crept into Bambarré' on 22 August.[30] There he found Muhammad bin Gharib with whom he had travelled in the earlier part of his exploration of Manyema. The final stage of the journey, to Lake Tanganyika, made Livingstone feel as if he were dying on his feet; 'almost every step was in pain, the appetite failed, and a little bit of meat caused violent diarrhoea, whilst the mind, sorely depressed, reacted on the body'.[31]

The now familiar angular fragments of quartz near the lake cut into his feet, while the dust of the path caused opthalmia, 'like that which afflicted Speke'.[32] By the time the weary traveller reached Ujiji (by his reckoning) on 23 October, he was 'reduced to a skeleton'.[33] But he hoped that rest and nourishment would restore his health. Sherif, the headman who had stayed at Ujiji with his supplies, came with all the Arabs to welcome him back.

One of the Arabs lost no time in confirming the impression of Livingstone's men, that Sherif had sold off his goods. 'We protested,' he said, 'but he did not leave a single yard of calico [cloth] out of 3000, nor a string of beads out of 700 lbs [pounds].'[34] When Livingstone challenged Sherif, he said that he had 'divined on the Koran, found that the Doctor was dead and then sold everything'.[35]

If the Scot had not had the foresight to leave a small quantity of barter goods with Muhammad bin Salih, 'in case of returning in extreme need',[36] he would have been completely destitute. As it was, he certainly felt like a traveller who had fallen among thieves. Where was the good Samaritan?

18
The Samaritan

A figure in a long white shirt came running like a madman to where Livingstone was sitting, outside his tent. It was Susi, his face under his turban lit up with excitement as he announced the arrival of a stranger. Then he dashed off to meet the newcomer.

'He turned out to be Henry M. Stanley, travelling correspondent of the *New York Herald*, sent specially to find out if I were really alive, and, if dead, to bring home my bones.'[1]

Stanley had found Livingstone against tremendous odds. War was raging in the country between Nyanyembe and Ujiji, the Arab traders *versus* the African resistance leader, Mirambo. Coming up from the coast, Stanley had not only to negotiate the war zone but also to outwit the chiefs on the road to Ujiji who were making extortionate demands for *hongo* to pass through their territory. He had reached Ujiji only after a dramatic moonlight dash through the jungle, which took strong discipline to achieve with a large caravan of porters.

The meeting with Livingstone, which may have been in the second or third week of November 1871, was the climax of a quest which Stanley had been ordered to make by his editor just over two years before, at a time when his quarry had dropped completely out of the public eye. True, Stanley was also given an extensive programme of foreign correspondence to do before seeking the Scot; but had he come earlier, he would have had precious little chance of finding him.

The moment came, the crowds parted, and Stanley 'walked down a living avenue of people' until he came before a 'semicircle of Arabs, which stood before the "white man with the grey beard".'

As I advanced slowly towards him I noticed he was pale, that he looked wearied and wan, that he had grey whiskers and moustache, that he wore a bluish cloth cap with a faded gold band round it, and that he had on a red-sleeved waistcoat and a pair of grey tweed trousers.

I would have run to him, only I was a coward in the presence of such a mob, – would have embraced him, but that I did not know how he would receive me; so I did what moral cowardice and false pride suggested was the best thing – walked deliberately up to him, took off my hat and said: 'DR. LIVINGSTONE, I PRESUME?'[2]

Stanley would never live those words down, and even today parodists still use them as the quintessence of emotional self-restraint. Yet the awkwardness was engendered by genuine uncertainty as to whether he would be welcome at all to a man who, Dr Kirk had assured him at Zanzibar, would put miles of swamp between himself and a journalist if he ever heard of his approach.

Yet Livingstone responded with a simple 'Yes',[3] smiled, and lifted his cap. The two sat down to an animated conversation that went on from noon until evening, and on into the night, with the 'roar of the surf'[4] of Tanganyika below them and a choir of insects around them.

Avidly reading letters from his children and listening eagerly to news of the outside world – the fall of Paris in the Franco–Prussian War, the laying of the transatlantic telegraph, the opening of the Suez Canal – Livingstone could not have been more appreciative. Quite sincerely he said to Stanley again and again, 'You have brought me new life. You have brought me new life.'[5]

Something in the chemistry of each man appealed to the other. Perhaps it was the similarities in their upbringings. Stanley's was harder, in that he had had to survive the rigours of a Welsh workhouse in his youth, and his family's rejection led to his eventual emigration to America. David had had a supportive family in what was considered a model project at the Blantyre cottonmill, but in reality his working conditions were hard and his hours long. Both recognized the awkwardness that these working-class conditions had given them as well as the spirit of determination with which they had carved their paths in life.

The combination of Livingstone's relief and gratitude to God for Stanley's timely arrival,[6] and Stanley's relief that he was so much welcomed and not regarded as an intruder, but given all the journalistic copy he could desire, inevitably led at first to the two men regarding each other with rose-tinted spectacles.[7]

'Here was the Good Samaritan and no mistake,' wrote David. 'Never was I more hard pressed: never was help more welcome.[8] He laid all he had at my service, divided his clothes into two heaps, and pressed one heap upon me; then the medicine chest; then his goods and everything he had, and to coax my appetite, often cooked dainty dishes with his own hand.'[9]

Stanley was an ambitious man, hardened by his wide experience of the world. He drove his caravan with a ruthlessness quite different in style from Livingstone's more conciliatory method. Although he would not adopt such an approach himself, he could not but be impressed with the genuine respect and gentleness with which the Scotsman treated all Africans – even those who deserted him were, sooner or later, sincerely forgiven. They were free men, free to choose whether to continue in his service or not.

Livingstone, certainly, had mellowed considerably since the days when Dr Kirk had worked with him, and Stanley, finding the reports he had heard of Livingstone's standoffishness and irascibility to be untrue, rejected everything negative he had ever heard about the fiery Scot. In doing so, he called into question everything Kirk had told him and suggested once too often to Livingstone that perhaps Dr Kirk had not exerted himself on his behalf as much as he should, and that in fact Kirk did not really care for him at all.

It was at precisely this point that Livingstone's armour was weakest. Six years of isolation from the outside world coupled with the painful consciousness of how vulnerable its lack of wholehearted support for his cause had made him, unbalanced his perceptions.

The longer Stanley lived with Livingstone (a period of over

five months) the more he began to notice that the older man still dwelt on the frictions of the past: the relationship problems of the Zambezi expedition, the meanness of the government which had at last voted him £1,000 in supplies, but only after it had been practically blackmailed to do so by Sir Roderick Murchison. In his isolation the Scot no longer knew whom to trust, and even began to suspect the motives of his staunchest supporters, such as Murchison and Kirk.

Since Stanley was overwhelmed by the mellow Livingstone whom he had first met, describing him as being as near to the likeness of 'an angel ... as the nature of a living man will allow',[10] he could not accommodate the anger and the hurt that the Scot also expressed when his mood changed. These impressions Stanley tried to drive from his mind, but confided to his diary (posthumously published) that the Scotsman's 'strong nature was opposed to forgiveness'.[11]

These contradictions in Stanley's observation can be summarized in a dichotomy that the journalist himself never recognized in writing: that Livingstone showed a great deal more appreciation of Africans than he did of Europeans, who tended to encounter the darker, more ruthless side of his nature. He was, after all, ruthless in self-criticism and unsparing of himself; perhaps unconsciously he applied the same standards to all Europeans. It would not be too far wide of the mark to say that the Africans experienced more of the 'saint', and Europeans more of the 'sinner', in their interaction with this visionary man.

Nothing could take away from the fact that, however complex Livingstone's character might be, Stanley could see that at any given moment he was hiding nothing from him. 'There is a good-natured *abandon* about Livingstone,' he wrote,[12] which made both his laughter and his storytelling infectious. He certainly held the attention of his helpers as he spoke to them in Swahili from the Bible on Sundays.

Stanley intimated to Livingstone that Sir Roderick Murchison was keen to know the configuration of the northern end of Lake Tanganyika. Indeed, David had known this from the beginning, but had been deterred from checking the area earlier by reports of the country being unsettled. Now Stanley offered to sponsor an expedition to the north of the lake.

Tribes along the route were in fact unusually unfriendly, and the journalist was amazed on several occasions by the calm and conciliatory way in which David dealt with situations in which Stanley would have resorted to bullets. The reward of their patience was that on 29 November 1871 they reached the River Ruzizi and found that it flowed into, not out of, the north end of the lake.

This discovery ruled out the possibility of Lake Tanganyika forming part of an eastern line of drainage for the Nile sources; but as far as Livingstone was concerned, it did not preclude its being part of a western line of drainage. 'The outlet of the Lake is probably by the [Lugamba] River into Lualaba as the [Luama], but this as yet must be set down as a "theoretical discovery".'[13]

Travelling north of the lake, on 7 December they 'passed the point where Speke turned'.[14] Speke, having found an outlet to the Nile from Lake Victoria, had failed to go all the way round it to check that Victoria itself was not supplied by a source further south. It was partly for this reason that Sir Roderick Murchison had asked Livingstone to make a thorough investigation of the interrelations of all the rivers in the East African watershed.

Within a week, Stanley was ill with fever and grateful for the medical treatment his companion was able to give him. He recovered sufficiently to start on the return march to Ujiji. On their way they passed through villages where the menfolk were being sent off to fight Mirambo, having made an alliance with the Arabs at Nyanyembe. 'Their wives promenade and weave green leaves for victory.'[15]

They reached Ujiji on 15 December. Stanley was by now thinking of returning to the outside world with his despatches and articles written by Livingstone for the *New York Herald*. He completely failed, however, to persuade Livingstone to accompany him. Although he urged on the older man the advisability of returning home, resting (and getting himself a new set of false teeth!) before resuming his work,

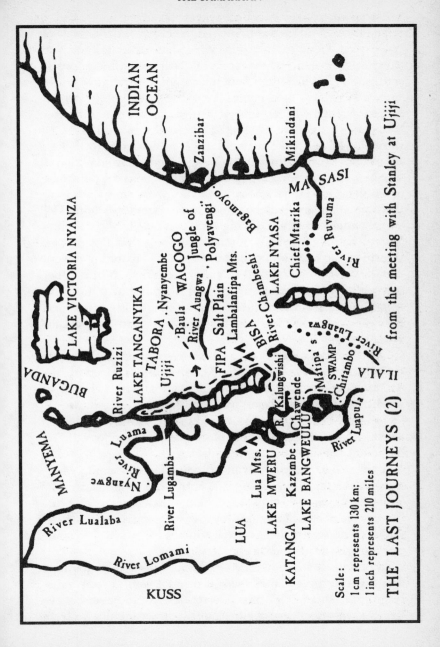

THE LAST JOURNEYS (2) from the meeting with Stanley at Ujiji

Scale:
1 cm represents 130 km:
1 inch represents 210 miles

the Scot was adamant that he would not.

In a sense, Stanley should not have been surprised, since he had sown the idea in Livingstone's mind that there was precious little concern for him and his cause in England.[16] To return now, Livingstone thought, without the solution to the mystery of the Nile sources for which the public craved, would result in being sent abroad again 'to an unhealthy consulate to which no public sympathy would ever be drawn'.[17] More than that, he had given his word to make a thorough job of the investigation of the sources, and above all else he would stick to his principle of doing what he promised.

Since both Livingstone and Stanley had stores awaiting them at Nyanyembe, they agreed to go together, leaving Ujiji shortly after Christmas. Livingstone was able to use a donkey Stanley had given him – for a time. However, on 27 January a swarm of bees attacked two of the donkeys, including the one David was riding. 'Instead of galloping off, as did the other, the fool of a beast rolled down, and over and over. I did the same, then ran, dashed into a bush like an ostrich pursued, then ran whisking a bush round my head.'[18] The animal died two days later.

Since Stanley suffered at times from severe fever, the march took fifty-four days. After arrival Livingstone received further encouragement from his daughter Agnes, who (as well as sending four flannel shirts) told him that much as she would like to have him with her, he should finish his work to his own satisfaction. 'A chip off the old block,' her father reflected.[19] He had plenty of time to work out his plans.

'I propose to go from [Nyanyembe] to Fipa [*i.e.* south west]; then round the south end of Tanganyika … then across the [Chambeshi] and round south of Lake [Bangweulu] and due west to the ancient fountains [south of Katanga] … This route will serve to certify that no other sources of the Nile can come from the south without being seen by me.'[20]

Although Livingstone nurtured a very human competitive spirit with respect to the Nile sources, not wanting anyone to beat him to them, the Arabs nevertheless could never believe that this was his primary aim. Indeed, they were not far from the truth. 'They all treat me with respect[21] and are very much afraid of being written against; but they consider my search for the sources of the Nile to be a sham; the true purpose of my being sent is to see their odious system of slaving, and if indeed my disclosures should lead to the suppression of the East Coast slave-trade, I would esteem that as a far greater feat than the discovery of all the sources together.'[22]

Indeed, the greatest weapon that Livingstone was now to bequeath to the antislavery cause was his description of the massacre of market women at Nyangwe on the banks of the Lualaba. His eye-witness account was to be carried by Stanley to the coast and was to reach Britain at an incredibly opportune time.

On 14 March Stanley and Livingstone 'ate a sad breakfast together'.[23] The two travellers could not bring themselves to part. Stanley intended to be off at 5.00 am, but three hours passed before they managed to say farewell to each other. The American fought back tears as he went on alone. This time he lost the battle to hide his emotions: Susi and Chuma raced after him to kiss his hands.

> I betrayed myself ... 'March! Why do you stop? Go on! Are you not going home?' And my people were driven before me. No more weakness. I shall show them such marching as will make them remember me.[24]

Meanwhile Livingstone was faced with a long wait until Stanley could send him men from the coast. Five days after his friend's departure, on the occasion of his fifty-ninth birthday, David renewed his faith. 'My Jesus, my King, my life, my all; I again dedicate my whole self to Thee. Accept me, and grant, O Gracious Father, that ere this year is gone I may finish my task. In Jesus' name I ask it. Amen, so let it be. David Livingstone.'[25]

In reviewing his progress, it was possible to see some purpose behind apparent setbacks. His retreat from Nyangwe after the massacre not only had been necessary to meet Stanley but, had he pushed on regardless, would almost certainly have meant death. An Arab trader who came to Nyanyembe told him that all 'those who went with Dugumbé were attacked near [Lua] …'

> We dare not pronounce positively on any event in life, but this looks like prompt retribution on the perpetrators of the horrible and senseless massacre of Nyangwe …
>
> This news shows that had I gone with these people to [Lomami], I could not have escaped the [Kuss] spears, for I could not have run like the routed fugitives. I was prevented from going in order to save me from death … how many more instances of Providential protecting there may be of which I know nothing![26]

Memories of the massacre and previous scenes of slaving came back to his mind unbidden, making him 'start up at dead of night horrified by their vividness'.[27] While he could still correspond with Stanley's caravan, Livingstone lost no opportunity to communicate his experiences. On 1 May 1872 he 'finished a letter to the *New York Herald*, trying to enlist American zeal to stop the East coast slave-trade'.[28] The concluding words were: 'all I can add in my loneliness is, may Heaven's rich blessing come down on everyone, American, English or Turk, who will help to heal the open sore of the world'.[29]

Yet this mission needed to be fulfilled for the purpose of empowering the African to improve his lot, not to aggrandize external powers. Hearing that Sir Samuel Baker had entered the service of the Khedive of Egypt to bring Sudan under his control, David expressed strong reservations. 'If Baker's expedition should succeed in annexing the valley of the Nile to Egypt, the question arises – Would not the miserable condition of the natives, when subjected to all the atrocities of the White Nile slave-traders, be worse under Egyptian dominion?'[30]

The presence in Nyanyembe of a delegation of Bugandans, from the dominions of the Mtesa north of Lake Victoria, provided food for thought. They had visited the Sultan of

Zanzibar with a present of ivory, which he had promptly sold in order to load them with gifts in return. These were being stored in the *tembe* at Nyanyembe while the delegation waited for the Arab war with Mirambo to die down.

Their headman, from whom Livingstone bought a milk cow, was a Muslim. 'He has been taught by Arabs, and is the first proselyte they have gained.'[31] Buganda, Livingstone felt, was a prime prospect for Christian mission. He cited 'its teeming population, rain, and friendly chief, who could easily be swayed by an energetic prudent missionary'.[32] But the prudent missionary would not come in with the paraphernalia of foreign provisions.

'The evangelist must not depend on foreign support other than an occasional supply of beads and calico; coffee is indigenous, and so is sugar-cane.'[33] Again Livingstone was ahead of his time in recommending a strategy close to the modern principle of tentmaking, or mission supported by working locally. 'When detained by ulcerated feet in Manyema I made sugar by pounding the cane in the common wooden mortar of the country,'[34] Livingstone recalled.

It is also clear that he did not envisage large numbers of Europeans descending on Buganda, but agents for change working singly, here and there. 'It would be a sort of Robinson Crusoe life, but with abundant materials,' he suggested.[35] Livingstone had lived long enough to sense that the idea of limited white settlement, which he had suggested as a means of addressing the problems of both the British and the African poor at a stroke, was not going to work. In fact, he would have been very shocked to see some of the consequences of such settlement where it took place.

Yet he encouraged the fainthearted to come into the hinterland of Africa, away from the coast. 'You have no idea how brave you are till you try. Leaving the coastal tribes, and devoting yourselves heartily to the savages, as they are called, you will find, with some drawbacks and wickednesses, a very great deal to admire and love.'[36]

For he certainly did want a counter-influence to operate against what was then dominating the interior. Tippu Tip, he now heard, had established himself further west in Katanga by marrying the daughter of a headman, and by this alliance was planning to conquer the country of Kazembe. If the gospel did not come, other influences would.

Yet the kind of white man who was needed was not the settler who related to the outside world, or even the trader (who, in Buxton's theory, should provide an economic alternative to the slave trade, but in practice gave rise to more complaints than plaudits). The sort of person that Livingstone could ultimately see contributing in Africa was the lonely missionary, who was willing to work to free himself as much as possible from foreign ties. Yet he was, in the nature of things, a temporary figure, since in the end everything was going to depend on the Africans themselves.

As time went on, the weariness of waiting for Stanley's reinforcements deepened his own sense of isolation and uncertainty. For one thing, he was well aware that there were flaws in his plans for seeking a western line of drainage for the Nile sources. 'The medical education has led me to a continual tendency to suspend the judgment ... I am even now not at all "cocksure" that I have not been following down what may after all be the Congo.'[37]

For another, he was only too well aware that although Agnes was behind him, the rest of his family was trying to take him away from his work. On 26 June he received a letter from Oswell, 'dated Bagamoio [sic] 14th May, which awakened thankfulness, anxiety, and deep sorrow'.[38] His son had been at Bagamoyo, a staging-post on the coast for caravans going west, with a search expedition that had been sent out to find his father.

Meeting Stanley's caravan returning from successfully carrying out that mission, Oswell, in common with other members of his expedition, had simply resigned and gone home. It was true that he would have had to make out by himself if he were to reach his father, but he confessed that his only motive in going out to meet him was to bring him back.

To the complex of feelings aroused by the tantalizing proximity of his son was added grief at a note which reached him a week later, although Oswell had penned it in April. It was the death of the very man who had set him the task which he had promised to fulfil: Sir Roderick Murchison, President of the Royal Geographical Society. 'Alas, alas! this is the only time in my life I ever felt inclined to use the word, and it bespeaks a sore heart: the best friend I ever had – true, warm, and abiding – he loved me more than I deserved: he looks down on me still.'[39]

Whether Sir Roderick was alive or not did not, in the end, alter Livingstone's determination to complete the work he had promised to do. Yet he could not but be conscious of the fact that the longer the wait went on, the more 'the best time for travelling passes over unused'.[40] He would have to face the marshes of Lake Bangweulu in the rainy season.

19
The last journey

At last three of the advance party of the men Stanley had sent from the coast arrived on 9 August. Livingstone appointed the leaders, Chowpereh and Manua Sera, to work together with Susi as a team.

Chuma, who was much younger than Susi, was beginning to enter into more responsibilities, particularly as a result of his recent marriage to Ntoaéka, a young woman who could have returned to the coast with Stanley's caravan but had elected to stay with Livingstone's party.

> When Ntaoeka chose to follow us rather than go to the coast, I did not like to have a fine-looking woman among us unattached, and proposed that she should marry one of my three worthies, Chuma, Gardner, or Mabruki, but she smiled at the idea.
>
> Chuma was evidently too lazy ever to get a wife; the other two were contemptible in appearance, and she has a good presence and is buxom. Chuma promised reform: 'he had been lazy, he admitted, because he had no wife'. Circumstances led to the other women wishing Ntoaketa [sic] married, and on my speaking to her again she consented.
>
> I have noticed her ever since working hard from morning to night: the first up in the mornings, making fire and hot water, pounding, carrying water, wood, sweeping, cooking.[1]

One person who had not immediately taken to Ntoaéka was Halima, Livingstone's cook. She quarrelled with her and ran away, but David forgave her for it readily enough, since she had been so reliable usually. 'I shall free her, and buy a house and garden at Zanzibar, when we get there,'[2] he promised himself – optimistically as it turned out.

As well as the porters sent by Stanley, there were, among the fifty-seven men and boys who arrived on 14 August, another group of six ex-pupils from the Nasik School. These had originally been sent from Bombay to join the now defunct search expedition, and included two brothers, John and Jacob Wainwright.

What Livingstone's feelings were on being sent another batch of freed slaves are not recorded, but he soon began to have the sort of difficulties he had had with the previous contingent, and this time they were dealt with more firmly.

The preparations for the march were plagued by a certain amount of confusion. On 16 August an earthquake struck the area and lasted a full fifty seconds. Mabruki Speke was too ill to travel and had to be taken to Sultan bin Ali at Tabora. But the least noticed hiatus turned out to be the most significant: the box of dried milk powder was left out of the packing.

The strategic value of this item was inestimable: the Doctor's digestive system depended on it. In areas where food was scarce, it was hard for him to subsist exclusively on rough maize and meal. The fact that he had bought cows from the Bugandans (now at odds with the Arabs for having detained them so long) was no insurance in the long term, since animals were prone to die from tsetse fly.

As if to underline this predicament, two Nasikers looking after ten head of cattle managed to lose one on 26 August, the first full day's march. It was 'our best milker'. Three days later 'the two Nassickers [sic] lost all the cows ... from sheer laziness ... Susi gave them ten cuts each with a switch'.[3] Although all the cattle were recovered except one, it was not a good sign. Within a month they would have to pass through a 'forest full of tsetse'.[4]

At the same time the Scot found that he had lost a good deal of his vitality. On 19 September he was 'ill with bowels, having eaten nothing for eight days'.[5] The shooting of a buffalo six days later assuaged the hunger, but not the tiredness. Since they were travelling so late in the season it was very hot among the rocks, and as they traversed the mountains they had to pass on the trek to Tanganyika. The constant going up and down made Livingstone 'very sore' in 'legs and lungs'.[6]

On 8 October they caught sight of the lake, but the people in the stockade nearby were too suspicious to let such a party in. More than sixty people then had to share the 'shade of a single palm'. After working round a series of bays they found, three weeks later, 'the mountains now close in on Tanganyika'.[8] Toiling up these heights the following day, they heard thunder and longed for the cooling rain.

Three days later they were led on a wild-goose chase by a guide, who having deliberately misled them, disappeared into a stockade. In these trying circumstances Livingstone was pleased to find that the porters Stanley had sent were up to scratch and, 'with one exception' the party was 'working like a machine'.[9]

The misfit was a confirmed cannabis addict who, the day after the escapade with the guide, joined with another man in shouting 'Posho! Posho!' as Livingstone came past. They were demanding extra rations. Perhaps the influence of Stanley showed in that the Scot dealt firmly with them, but not harshly, as the American might have done: 'the blows were given slightly, but I promised that the next should be severe'.[10]

Despite petty annoyances and the physically draining effect of climbing the broiling rocks of the lake mountains (his donkey was now ill), Livingstone never let go of his vision. 'The spirit of Missions is the spirit of our Master, the very genius of His religion,' he reflected.[11]

If this was the thought that remained to him when his strength was sapped and his mind drew its energy only from its most essential convictions, then it is reasonable to say that mission really was his heart's concern, however much he might speculate about the Nile sources, or troglodyte dwellings in Katanga, or whether Moses founded a city with his foster-mother, Merr. The fascination that isolation had given to such ideas in Manyema could not, now he was active and on the move, detract from his drive to be a disciplined disciple of Christ.

Nevertheless, his vision of mission was much wider than many missionaries of the later, colonial, period. 'A diffusive philanthropy is Christianity itself. It requires perpetual propagation to attest its genuineness.'[12] Spreading the influence of the gospel as widely as possible was his concern, and he could think about it even when 'ill and losing much blood'.[13]

Physically weakening through internal haemorrhaging, debilitated by haemorrhoids he had never had treated in England (through having been put off an operation, by the bad experience of a friend), David could still see providence at work. The fact that he had been delayed at Nyanyembe, waiting for men, meant that they had avoided coming into this area two months before, when war had been raging between two chiefs, M'toka and Zombe. Tippu Tip had also been raiding.

Nevertheless the consequence of the late start to the march was that after the hot phase they faced the soaking one. On 18 November they were 'overwhelmed in a pouring rain'.[14] The donkey, which had been kept forty-eight hours without water during the hot phase of the march, had finally succumbed to the bite of the tsetse fly two days before. Livingstone was thus footsore as well as soaked, but this did not prevent him from noticing and taking part in a drama of mercy.

One of the men picked up a girl who had been deserted by her mother. As she was benumbed by cold and wet he carried her; but when I came up he threw her into the grass. I ordered a man to carry her, and we gave her to one of the childless women; she is about four years old.[15]

Six days later, to take account of the conditions, Livingstone lightened the loads, much to the gratification of the men. They reached the River Lofu on 28 November and the following day encountered a fractious chief, who on being given a present eventually produced a goat, but grumbled again and again that he wanted more for it. Again, we see a more determined Livingstone, more like his younger self: 'on this, I returned his goat *and marched*'.[16] This decision was not taken lightly, since there was no food to be had in the countryside in consequence of the depredations of M'toka and – especially – Tippu Tip.

Tippu Tip's slaves had been out capturing people. 'A man came to us demanding his wife and child; they are probably in hiding … One sinner destroyeth much good!'[17] It turned out that Tippu Tip had outwitted Kazembe and killed him; his own people had kept the approach of the Arabs a secret from him until they were quite close. 'Having no stockade, he fell an easy prey to them. The conquerors put his head and all his ornaments on poles.'[18] Thus it was that Kazembe, who when Livingstone had first met him had had about sixty human skulls on his gateposts, met the same fate he had inflicted on others.

Tippu Tip's influence was far from being positive. People were suspicious, living on roots and berries, unable to trust any who passed. Guides misled the party into a detour. One vanished and they found themselves crossing the River Lampussi twice. Another, wishing to extract a cow for Nsama, the chief to the north of Kazembe who had been worsted by Tippu Tip, led them off on a diversion.

Positive action was necessary. 'Susi broke through and ran south, till he got a [south by west] path, which we followed, and came to a village having plenty of food.'[19] It did not do to be too malleable in such circumstances. 'The pugnacious spirit is one of the necessities of life,' Livingstone noted. 'The peace plan involves indignity and wrong.'[20] With regard to his own men, who were far from angels, the Scot could see that it was easier to control them in a village where people stood up for themselves.

No sooner had they crossed the Kalungwishi (on 19 December) when another attempt was made to mislead them, this time by men belonging to the brother of Chief Chama. David refused to follow a grass-covered path, as the guide bade them. The following day, 'we took quiet possession of their stockade, as the place that they put us in was on the open defenceless plain. Seventeen human skulls ornament the stockade.'[21] In making their escape, they carefully removed the arrows of Chama's brother, as insurance.

Perhaps the constant necessity of keeping his wits about him aided Livingstone a week later, when a 7ft snake, locally named a *Naia Hadje* 'reared up' before him and 'turned to fight'.[22] The Scot had to react fast to kill it. Yet perhaps sudden danger was more stimulating to deal with than what awaited them when they finally got near Lake Bangweulu.

The people near the lake were wary, at times terrified. A chief named Chungu declared that their real intention was to put his head on a pole, like Kazembe's! A great *kelele*, uproar, ensued and the stockade was shut against them. Chungu, like so many others, misled the party, sending them off in a direction that strayed too far towards the lake, into an angle formed by the rivers Mpande and Lopopussi.

The result was the beginning of the wettings, in that dampest of damp regions, which Livingstone was to find so debilitating. Chowpereh and Chuma carried him on their shoulders across spongy masses of waterlogged vegetation.

'Carrying me across one of the broad deep sedgy rivers is really a very difficult task,' David confessed to his journal on 24 January 1873. 'One we crossed was at least 2,000ft broad, or more than [600m]. The first part, the main stream, came up to Susi's mouth.'[23] Six men were needed to carry the Scot an average of 46m each, at the end of which they were quite out of breath. 'No wonder! It was sore on the women folk of our party.'[24]

Livingstone was losing a lot of blood which, however, did not alarm him since he thought of it as 'a safety-valve'.[25] He was unable to plot his position since cloud cover made observations impossible. To confuse matters further, the knowledge he thought he did have of the lake from his previous visit was compromised by the fact that his chronometers had been damaged at that time.

While he and the main group waited, Manua Sera went off with some scouts. On 30 January they returned after dark, having gone about eight hours to the south and sighted two islets in the lake. Rather than get into even deeper water than they were already, Livingstone decided to go back as far as the settlement of a headman called Chitunkubwe, who promised guides on to Matipa's.

'The water stands so high in the paths that I cannot walk

dryshod,'[26] Livingstone wrote of this trek. Seeing that in the prairies beyond the water was knee-deep, he sent two men on ahead to Matipa's to seek canoes to navigate with.

Waiting for them to come back proved to be no picnic. On 17 February there was a 'furious attack at midnight from the red *Sirafu* or Driver ants. Our cook fled first at their onset.'[27] At this point the Scot could have beaten a retreat too, but unfortunately he chose that moment to put a contemporary scientific theory to the test.

> I lighted a candle, and remembering Dr. Van der Kemp's idea that no animal will attack a man unprovoked, I lay still. The first came on my foot quietly, then some began to bite between the toes, then the larger ones swarmed over the foot and bit furiously, and made the blood start out.[28]

At this point the Scot called off the experiment and rushed out of the tent – too late. His followers saw him 'instantly covered' with ants 'as close as small-pox'. Some tried to pick ants off his limbs while others lit grass fires to drive the red marauders away. After this struggle had gone on for more than an hour the Scot was taken to a hut still free of the invaders. Yet the relentless *Sirafu* 'routed me out of there too!' The result? 'They took all my fat,' he recorded, simply.[29]

It was galling to discover that the men who had promised to go to Matipa had not gone at all. 'I have gone amongst the whole population kindly and fairly,' he asserted, 'but I fear I must now act rigidly, for when they hear that we have submitted to injustice, they at once conclude that we are fair game for all.'[30]

Next time a local man agreed to take the message to Matipa's, Susi and Chuma went with him. After four days, Susi came back with the good news that Matipa was willing to supply canoes to carry the party across to his brother, Kabende, on the south bank of the lake. This he would do in return for five bundles of brass wire which Livingstone had offered him.

Yet this too proved only to be a feint; Matipa made no move whatsoever, even after Livingstone had visited him. The

Scotsman's sixtieth birthday arrived on 19 March, with no sign of progress. He recorded a fervent prayer, which was also a question. 'Thanks to the Almighty Preserver of men for sparing me thus far on the journey of life. Can I hope for ultimate success? So many obstacles have arisen. Let not Satan prevail over me, Oh! my good Lord Jesus.'[31]

Some of that indispensable 'pugnacious spirit' returned to him. Early the next morning Livingstone put Matipa to the test. 'I made a demonstration by taking quiet possession of his village and house; fired a pistol through the roof and called my men, ten being left to guard the camp; Matipa fled to another village. The people set off at once and brought three canoes, so at 11 a.m. my men embarked quietly. They go across the [Chambeshi] and build a camp on its left bank.'[32] Reaffirming his determination to press on, David vowed, 'Nothing earthly will make me give up my work in despair. I encourage myself in the Lord my God, and go forward.'[33]

In crossing the Chambeshi River, which fed into the lake, one of the canoes sank and a servant girl of Amoda's drowned. The Scot sent canoes back to Matipa's to fetch everyone who remained. Another canoe was damaged by a donkey and a further five days' delay ensued, until seven men came back from Matipa's with another canoe. Kabinga, the chief on that bank of the Chambeshi, was biding his time. Eventually he sent men in an attempt to steal their canoes.

Livingstone decided to divide his people into a land party and a canoe party, which would try to keep parallel to one another. The system broke down on 6 April when a drummer called in the canoes, only for them to discover that the main land party had already moved on. At first the Scot thought this had been a foolish mistake, but the following day when a drum beat towards the east, leading them into 'stiff grassy prairies, [a metre or more] deep in water, for five hours'[34] he realized that it was yet another diversionary tactic by the denizens of the lake.

Not for nothing have Livingstone's wanderings been called 'a lonely and frustrating odyssey'.[35] It gave him a certain sensitivity to the struggles of other strangers – even animals. 'A lion had wandered into this world of water and ant-hills, and roared night and morning, as if very much disgusted: we could sympathize with him!'[36] By now they were reduced to dragging the large canoe along the shallow river in an attempt to find the land party.[37]

On 10 April the seriousness of Livingstone's condition really began to impinge on his consciousness. There is no more talk of a 'safety-valve'. 'I am pale, bloodless, and weak from bleeding profusely ever since the 31st of March last: an artery gives off a copious stream, and takes away my strength. Oh, how I long to be permitted by the Over Power to finish my work.'[38]

Perhaps he had a premonition that that prayer was soon to be granted. His men, seeing his condition, pressed him to allow them to carry him and two days later he gave in and allowed them to do it, albeit in relays. His mind was still very clear and at dawn on 13 April he was keenly aware of his surroundings, imparting to them a spiritual quality.

A blanket is scarcely needed till the early hours of the morning, and here, after the turtle doves and cocks give out their warning calls to the watchful, the fish-eagle lifts up his remarkable voice. It is pitched in a high falsetto key, very loud, and seems as if he were calling to someone in the other world. Once heard, his weird unearthly voice can never be forgotten – it sticks to one through life.[39]

The last romance of camping out, however, was shattered four days later when 'a tremendous rain after dark burst all our now rotten tents to shreds'.[40] Although defenceless against the elements, he tried to stop the bleeding with quinine (testing a novel hypothesis, that 'bleeding and most other ailments in this land are forms of fever').[41]

The bleeding did stop – temporarily and perhaps for reasons other than the quinine – but there is no doubt that Livingstone was now very, very weak. 'It is not all pleasure, this exploration,'[42] he observes, in what might pass as the understatement of the nineteenth century. He confesses that, were it not for his donkey, he 'could not move a hundred yards'.[43]

Indeed two days later the tired Doctor fell off the donkey and was taken back to the village of Chief Muanazawamba, who was quite ready to let him stay as long as he liked to recuperate. Yet the following day he insisted on continuing. Susi recalled that it was at this point they had made for him a *kitanda* or wooden litter, which had two side pieces over 2m in length, crossed with rails 1m wide. It was borne by Chowpereh, Chuma and two others. Frequently, when it was necessary to halt, Chuma had to stop the Doctor from falling out.

On 25 April, after marching for one hour south-west, they called a halt. While some men got to work building a hut for their stricken leader, he lay in a shady spot on the *kitanda* and sent a messenger to bring one of the villagers. A group of them came and he asked whether they knew of a hill on which four rivers took their rise. They did not; few people travelled much now that there was so much raiding going on.

Knowing perhaps, in his heart of hearts, that he was dying, David asked Susi the following day to buy two large tusks, which he could use to help pay their way back to Ujiji. On the 27th the Doctor 'sent to buy milch goats',[44] but his men were told that Mazitu marauders had taken everything. Nevertheless the chief sent a kid. A fruitless search for goats followed on the opposite bank of the River Lulimala, where they were camped.

To continue their quest meant breaking down the wall of the hut in order to get the Doctor back on to the litter, since he could not walk to the door. This done, they found the *kitanda* was too big to set down in the bottom of even the strongest canoe. The Doctor could not bear the pain of a hand passed under his back – yet he was determined to cross the Lulimala.

Beckoning to Chuma, in a faint voice he asked him to stoop down over him as low as possible, so that he might clasp his hands together behind his head, directing him at the same

[time] how to avoid putting any pressure on the lumbar region of the back.[45]

Once across the river they headed for the village of Chitambo. They kept stopping: the Doctor could not stand, yet if lifted he got drowsy. Mostly speechless, he nevertheless asked for water. Susi went ahead to Chitambo's village and sent some back. They stopped in some gardens outside the village, and then under the eaves of a hut.

Most people were out in the fields, in temporary huts, watching their crops, so there were few who observed the preparations being made to house the sick man. Next day Chief Chitambo came to pay his respects, but the Scot was too sick to see him. In the afternoon he asked Susi to bring his watch and showed him how to hold it, while Livingstone slowly wound the key. At about 11.00 pm shouting could be heard, and Susi was called again.

'Are our men making that noise?'

'No,' replied Susi, 'I can hear from the cries that the people are scaring away a buffalo from their dura fields.'[46]

Silence. Then Livingstone asked in Swahili if they had reached the Luapula. Susi told him they were in Chitambo's village, near the Lulimala.

'*Sikun' gapi kuenda Luapula?*' ('How far is it to the Luapula?') came the next question.

'*Na zani zikutatu, Bwana*' ('I think it is three days, Master').

A few seconds later, as if in great pain, Livingstone sighed, 'Oh dear, dear!'[47] and then dozed off. About an hour afterwards he called Susi again to give him some calomel and to pour out a little water into a cup.

'All right, you can go out now,'[48] the patient said in a low, gentle voice. A boy, Majwara, was placed at the door of the hut to be on call during the night.

At 4.00 am Majwara came to Susi, clearly agitated.[49] What Susi saw has been variously interpreted, but his verbatim account showed that he saw Livingstone on the bed, head buried in his hands upon the pillow. He was very still. When they touched him, his body was cold.[50]

He had finally been permitted to end his pilgrimage. Yet Susi had to summon urgently Chowpereh, Chuma, Manua Sera and another confidant, Matthew. Their pilgrimage was very far from over; for some of them, it was only just beginning.

20
Funeral march

At dawn the dead man's followers gathered to discuss what to do. First they made a careful inventory of all Livingstone's possessions. Then they appointed Susi, Manua Sera and Chowpereh to lead them. These men were to take them on an epic journey back to the coast, carrying the Scotsman's body out of the heart of Africa and seeing it safe all the way to its homeland. For Africans, it was unthinkable to bury a man they respected away from the land of his fathers.

Yet they buried his heart in African soil, for in Africa it had always been, ever since he landed on her shores thirty-two years before. Under a big *Mulva* tree they dug a hole over a metre deep, where the heart was reverently laid to rest, in a tin box that had formerly held flour. A Christian burial service was read out by one of the Nasikers who had been baptized and knew how to read: Jacob Wainwright. An inscription was cut in the tree in deep letters, representing the three leaders.

Chief Chitambo was solemnly adjured to protect the memorial, and he promised to keep away grass to save it from bush fires, although he imagined that the Mazitu might cut it down in one of their raids, to make a canoe. In case the tree did indeed suffer such a fate, the spot was also marked by two thick, high posts with a strong cross-piece, looking rather like a lintel and a door, which were coated in tar.

In fact the tree and the inscription in the bark were found and photographed many years later. It read:

LIVINGSTON

MAY 4   18 [not legible]

Yazuza   Mniasere   Vchopere

– names readily decipherable as Jacob's version of Susi, Manua Sera and Chowpereh.[1]

The remains of the body, little more than skin and bone,

were dried in the sun and then roughly embalmed with salt and brandy. The lungs were dried up and covered with black and white patches and it was particularly noticeable that a clot of coagulated blood was lodged in his left side, 'as large as a man's hand'.[2] David, in his final few days of life, must have endured excruciating agony. Death must, in the circumstances, have been a great mercy.

Such was the superstitious dread with which most Africans viewed the passing of a dead body through their village that a great deal of trouble had to be taken to disguise it. The limbs were drawn up to shorten the bundle which, when wrapped around with sailcloth and attached to a carrying pole, looked remarkably like a merchant's bale of cloth. Would this subterfuge work for a 1,500 mile journey? The triumvirate agreed to keep to the course the Doctor had set, since they were already almost half-way round the southern side of the lake. When they had reached its westernmost point, they would turn north-east for Tanganyika.

Within a few days of starting, a halt had to be called. Half the party were suffering from fever as a result of the interminable wading. Two of the women died and Susi became dangerously ill. It was a full month before the rains ceased and he and others were sufficiently recovered to press on round the south-western shore of the lake. Susi was again immobilized by illness at a border village.

At last they were able to leave the Ilala region and cross the broad River Luapula. The going got easier, but a lion took one of the donkeys and, at a stockaded village called Chawende, they came into conflict with the local chief. His people were in terror of the depredations of Kumbakumba. In the resulting fracas Susi's party had to resort to force, but determination saw them through. They had to press on, with Susi's wife, Chama, being carried in a *kitanda*.

John, one of the Nasikers, went missing and the ensuing search delayed them five days. The further they went in a north-easterly direction, however, the more the terror of Kumbakumba receded. They met Chief Chungu, who had affectionate memories of Livingstone and treated them well, allowing them to keep a buffalo they had shot. They were able to confide in Chungu, who threw off his natural superstition and treated the arrival of the Scotsman's body as a cause for genuine sorrow.

Since they were no longer trying to map the lake, Susi's party was able to avoid the punishing route Livingstone had taken along the rugged shore line. They also wisely decided to have nothing to do with Ujiji, and instead experimented with a route running directly north-east of Tanganyika through Fipa to the Lambalanfipa Mountains. Having traversed these, they encountered a salt plain. This gave way to a region covered in herds of game, especially giraffe and buffalo. Manua Sera was proving himself adept with the gun and they ate well.

This basically peaceful stage of the journey was tinged with suspense when a force was sighted approaching from the north. Precautions were taken, but it turned out to be a caravan from Nyanyembe. There, it seemed, the news of the Doctor's death was already known. What was more interesting was their report that 'Livingstone's son',[3] with two Englishmen and a quantity of goods, had reached Nyanyembe.

Such news gave added impetus to their journey, although minor obstacles still lay in their way. They had to pay taxes of four to six *dotis* of cloth to pass through more populated territories, but were grateful to reach the fresh water of the Aungwa River. Manua Sera improved relations with the people at the next town by opportunely killing another buffalo, and everyone took a three-day rest. More news of the English from another caravan spurred them on until they were doubling the speed of their outward journey.

They encamped at Baula, where Jacob Wainwright was commissioned to write an account of the Doctor's death. As soon as it was finished Chuma pressed on with three men to deliver it personally to the English. Meanwhile, the party followed on with the body cautiously, keeping the local Wagogo elephant hunters in the dark about the purpose of their journey.

Chuma reached Nyanyembe on 20 October, only to be disappointed to find that reports of Livingstone's son, Oswell, were untrue. Jacob's letter was read by the relief expedition's leader, Lieutenant Cameron, and Chuma was questioned in the presence of his two companions, Dr Dillon and Lieutenant Murphy. Chuma was anxious to get back to his comrades with cloth from the stores there so that they would have enough to pay *hongo* and get through to Nyanyembe. He rested only one day before taking the cloth, though Cameron demurred.

A host of Arabs and their slaves met the party when it finally appeared and accompanied the body as it was borne to the same *tembé* where Livingstone had waited so long before setting out on his last journey. Time seemed to have stood still at Nyanyembe, where the war between the Arabs and the African resistance leader Mirambo was still dragging on. Lieutenant Cameron was concerned too about the Wagogo elephant hunters to the east. He did his best to dissuade Susi's men from taking the body through their territory.

Susi refused point blank to leave Livingstone's body in Nyanyembe. He and the triumvirate had to be very firm in the face of Cameron's interference, but they did not prevent him from taking most of the Doctor's instruments out of their packages – instruments which had helped him make discoveries over a period of seven years. Aneroid barometers, compasses, thermometers, a sextant – all these were laid claim to by Cameron and were never to be seen again.

Four bales of cloth which Livingstone had left in reserve with Arab residents were reclaimed with no difficulty for the march down to the coast. Susi hatched a plan to deal with the problem of the Wagogo. He would avoid their main path by taking a ten-day detour through the jungle of Poliyavengi. There was a delay after the first day's march because Chowpereh's wife was ill.

A fracas now occurred between the triumvirate and Lieut-enant Murphy, who was going with them to the coast. He was unprepared for the very early start to the morning's march which Livingstone had trained his men to make, in order to make the best progress before the heat of the day. Susi and the triumvirate insisted on sticking to the same pattern, and in the end he and Murphy had to agree to differ. Dr Dillon had also left Cameron's expedition to return to the coast, but he was not to survive. Suffering intensely from dysentery, he shot himself in his tent at Kaseke'ra.[4]

Having safely circumvented Wagogo territory, the triumvirate held a consultation at Kaseke'ra. The route ahead ran through many villages, which had heard of the burden that they carried. The only way they could see of getting through was by an elaborate bluff. They decided to say that they would bury the body after all.

Unobserved by the villagers, they removed Livingstone's body from the bark case they had carried it in before, and buried the case. Next, they went into the nearby wood and stripped off a fresh length of bark from an *n'gombe* tree. The body was put inside and swathed in calico to look like an ordinary travelling bale.

Then a fake corpse was prepared by cutting *mapira* stalks into six-foot lengths and shrouding them with a cloth to imitate a dead body about to be buried. According to carriers' custom, a paper folded to look like a letter was put into a cleft stick. Six men with the right reputations for being entrusted with an important mission were detailed to take the corpse back to Nyanyembe to be buried.

The solemn procession set out from Kaseke'ra at sunset. Once they had got well out of range of the village they began quietly to throw stalk after stalk of the *mapira* far into the jungle. The same was done with the wrappings. Clear of their burden, first one man, then another, jumped clear of the path into long grass so as to leave no trace of their footprints. Each found his way back secretly to the camp.

The suspicions of the villagers were laid to rest and the brave band was able to smuggle the body all the way to Bagamoyo on the coast. There they committed it to the care of the acting British consul (since Kirk was away). As they handed over their precious burden a roll-call was made of the names of those Africans who had first set out with Livingstone eight years before. Only five were able to answer: Susi, Chuma and Amoda who had joined on the Zambezi back in 1864, and Abraham and Mabruki who had come from the Nasik School in India in 1865. The next two who had served longest were Ntoaéka and Halima, the women who had joined up in Manyema country and given such a good account of themselves.

It was, however, Jacob Wainwright, who had joined the expedition only at the time when Stanley sent his relief column to Nyanyembe, who was given the opportunity to attend the funeral at Westminster Abbey. The Church Missionary Society, which sponsored the Nasik School where he had trained, paid for his passage.

In Britain the body was identified by the false bone-joint which was the mark of the lion attack in southern Africa so many years previously. A day of national mourning was declared for 18 April 1874, and the greatest men of state came to Westminster Abbey for the funeral. Yet the service was as simple and straightforward as the Scot could have wished.

Some of those present remembered to the end of their days the emotion that swept the vast congregation when they sang David's favourite hymn:

> O God of Bethel ! by whose hand
> Thy people still are fed;
> Who through this weary pilgrimage
> Hast all our fathers led …
>
> O spread thy covering wings around,
> Till all our wanderings cease,
> And at our Father's loved abode,
> Our souls arrive in peace.[5]

The pall-bearers included Stanley, Jacob Wainwright, Kirk, W. C. Oswell and E. D. Young. Among them was the Revd Horace Waller who, as a UMCA missionary, had been present with Kirk at Mary's funeral in Chupanga. James Stewart, who had prayed with David in Mary's final hour, was also there in Westminster Abbey, as was Mary's father, Robert Moffat.

The Scottish industrialist, James Young, who had helped to finance Livingstone's last expedition, also paid for the passages of Susi and Chuma. They went to stay with Waller, who had been with Livingstone on the Zambezi expedition, to help him edit and make ready for the press *The Last Journals of David Livingstone*, which contain the following eulogium on their work:

Nothing but such leadership and staunchness as that which organized the march home from Ilala, and distinguished it throughout, could have brought home Livingstone's bones to our land or his last notes and maps to the outer world. To none does the feat seem so marvellous as to those who know Africa and the difficulties which must have beset both the first and the last in the enterprise. Thus in his death, not less than in his life, David Livingstone bore testimony to that goodwill and kindliness which exists [*sic*] in the heart of the African.[6]

Susi and Chuma later returned to East Africa and became much sought after as caravan leaders. It seems that a seed had been planted in Susi's heart in his nine-year knowledge of Livingstone. Thirteen years after the Scotsman's death, Susi was baptized and took the new name David, in memory of the man who had first shown him what it was to walk with Christ.

21
The fruits

What were the fruits of Livingstone's long pilgrimage? Did he traverse 29,000 miles of the African continent for nothing? Or was his faith that God would make everything 'come out right at last'[1] justified by events?

If it was true that during his lifetime he exercised most influence while at his weakest (at the mercy of the marauding lion, grief-stricken at the bedside of his dying wife, driven into deep depression by the massacre of the market women by the banks of the Lualaba), much more was this true of his death.

On 1 May 1873, very nearly the day that he died in Ilala,[2] the first blow was struck in a campaign to kill the slave trade. In response to public protest a British government mission arrived in Zanzibar to negotiate with the sultan. Negotiations broke down, yet within the space of one month the sultan's initial resistance was worn down and he issued a decree, banning the slave trade by sea.

Within three years he had banned the trade by land also. The ancient slave market on Zanzibar was closed for ever and a church was built on its site. The smugglers did their best to find new routes for their operations overland, even hiding their human cargo in dhow-shaped pits on Zanzibar. But the flow of groaning, oppressed humanity was reduced to a trickle. As a regular, organized business the slave trade was effectively stopped. Mission centres were set up on slave-smuggling routes.

In East Africa the confrontation took place on Lake Nyasa (now Lake Malawi). Lieutenant E. D. Young succeeded where his leader had failed, in launching a steamer on the lake. He named it *Ilala* after the region (in modern Zambia) where Livingstone died. It began the process by which the slaving dhows were undercut.

Within two decades of his death, Livingstone's vision to open up the area around Lake Nyasa to the gospel began to bear fruit. James Stewart, who had originally joined the Zambezi expedition to survey the area for the Free Church of Scotland, recovered from his initial disillusionment and was inspired to return. Both his mission and the established Church of Scotland worked in Nyasaland in the spirit of Livingstone, mixing evangelism, church-planting and Bible teaching with agricultural projects and industrial technology.[3]

Nevertheless, it has been said that 'Livingstone had fewer illusions about the difficulties that existed in realizing his goals for Africa than most of those who invoked his "legacy".'[4] In the case of the missions in Nyasaland, one was blind to the negative effects of commercialism, the other to those of paternalism.[5] Both struggled with the political consequences of their presence on the nexus of African and Arab trade routes – yet their work took root and grew.

In Central Africa the LMS recovered from the loss of the Kololo mission and found volunteers to fill the gap left by the Helmores. Sekeletu, however, had not survived his bout of leprosy: his appeal for settlers to come and live with his people on the Tonga Plateau fell on deaf ears, and when he died the great independent empire of his father Sebetwane died with him. However, the Tswana, under their great chief Khama, proved to exercise a great deal more influence in the ensuing history of the African church.

In West Africa Livingstone's influence was felt through Henry Venn, the General Secretary of the Church Missionary Society. Livingstone had been corresponding with him since his year in Britain in 1857, stimulating his concern to provide economic alternatives to the slave trade. Cultivating contacts with industry, Venn enlisted the support of a Christian manufacturer who agreed to import cotton at the minimum profit margin.[6]

This enabled Venn to set up the Nigerian cotton industry. In the event, the project coincided with the American Civil War (in which Livingstone's son, Robert, lost his life). The result was that an alternative source of cotton was made available from Africa at a time when supplies from the slave-worked plantations of the southern states of America were being disrupted. African chiefs thus had a viable economic alternative to the slave trade.

It is well to remember that the whole of the Livingstone-Venn period of Christian mission was carried out on Africans' terms. This was the pre-colonial era, when all mission endeavour depended on the goodwill of the people to whom the missionaries were sent – as it does today. The tendency to project imperial conditions back into Livingstone's day is an anachronism. His career stretched from 1841 to 1873, when people thought of Empire primarily as relations with Canada, Australia and other English-speaking dependencies.

Livingstone well understood that everything depended on the quality of his relationships with Africans. Chiefs such as Sekeletu would welcome him for their own reasons, as part of their foreign policy. Livingstone, for his part, would seek to win their influence for the gospel, for 'he never lost an opportunity of trying to impress the truths of Christianity upon the native peoples he encountered'.[7] This is demonstrated much more clearly by his private journals than by the books he wrote and published (such as *Missionary Travels*).

It is also confirmed by the contacts of those who followed him into areas he had pioneered. In 1877, four years after Livingstone's death, a representative of the Universities Mission to Central Africa made a journey in the valley of the Ruvuma and stayed for a while with the Yao chief, Matola.

While staying with Matola I was told that there was a man who wanted specially to see his English visitors, because he had known something of a white man in old days, and if we were all like him he would like to make our acquaintance. I desired that he might be presented to us. Forthwith he came, a pompous old man, who spoke in a dignified manner, and who evidently had some information to communicate. Over his right shoulder there hung an old coat, mouldy, partially eaten away, but still to be recognized as of decidedly English make and material. 'Whose was it?' I thought, as he began with much mystery to tell of a white man who ten years ago had travelled with him to Mataka's town.

Mataka's was the Yao settlement about 100 miles south-west of Mtarika's on the Ruvuma, where Livingstone had stayed a fortnight in 1866.[8] The man with the coat spoke of

a white man who treated black men as his brothers, and whose memory would be cherished all along that [Ruvuma] Valley after we were all dead and gone. Then he described him, – a short man with a bushy moustache, and a keen piercing eye, whose words were always gentle, and whose manners were always kind, whom as a leader it was a privilege to follow, and who knew the way to the hearts of all men ... Then he showed me the coat; it was ragged now, he knew, but he had kept it those ten years in memory of the giver, from whom it had been a legacy when they parted at Mataka's. To no one but an Englishman would he part with it, but he let me have it as one of Livingstone's brothers (he said).[9]

F. S. Arnot, a Brethren missionary who was brought up with the Livingstone boys, went into what are now Zambia, Zimbabwe and Katanga (Zaire) in the 1870s and 1880s.[10] Arnot heard Livingstone speak at a prize-giving when he was six. After the Arnot and Livingstone families became friends, he used to hear Livingstone's correspondence read out. It was through hearing by this means 'the horrors of the slave trade' that he committed himself to Africa. '"If God spares me I will go and help to right this wrong," was his reaction.'[11]

Arnot was indeed faced with the challenge of the slave trade. In August, 1894, he embarked on his third missionary journey from Durban to Chinde, at a mouth of the Zambezi, 'and from there to Tanganyika by river and lake'. Even at that late date he still found Arabs 'raiding the country for slaves and ivory'.[12]

Like David, he used a magic lantern to illustrate his themes, but the Africans who saw his pictures were a little disappointed. In their view, Arnot had strong 'power', but nowhere near as great as Livingstone's; for he could not bring back his parents from the dead.[13] Clearly, Livingstone had picked up the importance to his audience of his own ancestral background, and included pictures of his parents in his talk. As well as taking account of culture in communication, the Scot was also looking out for distinctively African ways of expressing Christian truth.

To do this, he asked questions, such as, 'What is holiness?' He records the answer of an African friend: 'When copious showers have descended during the night, and all the earth and the leaves and the cattle are washed clean and the sun rising shows a drop of dew on every blade of grass and the air breathes fresh – that is holiness.'[14]

The emergence of a distinctive African way of communicating the gospel is the fruit of Livingstone's primary vision, to see centres set up and staffed by African evangelists. Again, he was ahead of his time in this and adequate training facilities were long in coming. Today courses exist for African cross-cultural missionaries in Nigeria, South Africa, Kenya, Zaire, Ghana and Côte d'Ivoire.[15]

The growth of the church in sub-Sahara Africa is unique in the history of any continent. In 1900 those professing to be Christians were 10% of the population; by 1990 this had reached 57% and was expected to reach 61% by the year 2000.[16] Yet a lack of training centres creates in many parts of the continent a crisis of leadership. In Africa there is only one theological training school for over 250,000 practising Christians.

This is where the church of God worldwide can play a vital part. While the church is growing in Africa, finance and training are available in the West and in parts of Asia. Not only are expatriate Bible teachers and cross-cultural missionaries needed, but sometimes the finance to staff African Bible colleges with Africans.

In Africa's straitened circumstances, the development of alternative forms of training which are more economic than the three-year residential course is a key feature. Staying at work but meeting regularly with a tutor for theological education by extension is one such form; on-the-job training as a pastoral assistant is another.

Livingstone's conviction that 'to open African hearts to the message of Christian salvation it was necessary to help Africans develop economically'[17] finds its expression today in the concept of holistic mission – to meet the full range of human need in Africa.

The slave trade itself has not completely died out, re-emerging in recent times in parts of Sudan.[18] But the equivalent concerns in modern-day terms relate to the wider healing of society, whether through famine relief and refugee work, or projects aimed at constructing long-term employment oppor-tunities. The vital factor is whether such projects are linked in with the vision of the church for the transformation of society.

The fact that the gospel has been planted among so many African peoples does not render unnecessary the kind of comprehensive view of human need that Livingstone, in-spired by Buxton and others, took. The urban poor in the cities of Africa are not reached so easily, and there are still perhaps 700 ethnic and linguistic groups that remain untouched by the gospel (for example in the Sahel, parts of West and Central Africa, Ethiopia and Mozambique).

Indigenous churches, as David Livingstone foresaw, are doing a great deal of the cross-cultural pioneering work. Miss-ions from Nigeria, for instance, have shown great maturity in their approach; and others, such as those in Ethiopia, have reached out to unevangelized communities despite their own lack of resources. There is still ground-breaking work to be done, and still a need for those, who like David and Mary Livingstone, are prepared to be trail-blazers, to prepare people for their future reception of the gospel.

David Livingstone said: 'The fact which ought to stimulate us above all others is, not that we have contributed to the conversion of a few souls … but that we are diffusing a knowledge of Christianity throughout the world … We work for a glorious future which we are not destined to see … We are only morning stars shining in the dark, but the glorious morn will break – the good time coming yet.'[19]

Bibliography

Primary sources

G. W. Clendennen (ed.), *David Livingstone's Shire Journal 1881–1864* (Aberdeen: Scottish Cultural Press, 1992).

R. Foskett (ed.), *The Zambesi Journal and Letters of Dr John Kirk 1858–1863* (Edinburgh and London: Oliver and Boyd, 1965).

T. Holmes (ed.), *David Livingstone: Letters and Documents 1841–1872* (Livingstone: The Livingstone Museum, in association with James Currey, London, 1990).

D. Livingstone, *Missionary Travels and Researches in South Africa* (London: John Murray, 1857).

D. and C. Livingstone, *Narrative of an Expedition to the Zambesi and its Tributaries; and the Discovery of Lakes Shirwa and Nyassa, 1858–1864* (London: John Murray, 1865).

W. Monk (ed.), *Dr Livingstone's Cambridge Lectures* (Cambridge: Deighton, Bell and Co., 1858).

I. Schapera (ed.), *David Livingstone: Family Letters*; vol. 1, *1841–1848*; vol 2: *1849–1856* (London: Chatto and Windus, 1959).

————— (ed.), *David Livingstone: South African Papers 1849–1853* (Cape Town: Van Riebeeck Society, 2nd series, no. 5, 1974).

————— (ed.), *Livingstone's African Journal*; vol. 1, *1853–April 1855*; vol. 2: *May 1855–1856* (London: Chatto and Windus, 1963).

————— (ed.), *Livingstone's Missionary Correspondence 1841–1856* (London: Chatto and Windus, 1961).

————— (ed.), *Livingstone's Private Journals 1851–1853* (London: Chatto and Windus, 1960).

G. Shepperson (ed.), *David Livingstone and the Rovuma: A Notebook* (Edinburgh: Edinburgh University Press, 1965).

H. M. Stanley, *How I Found Livingstone: Travels, Adventures and Discoveries in Central Africa, including Four Months' Residence with Dr Livingstone* (London: Sampson Low, Marston and Co., 1872).

H. Waller (ed.), *The Last Journals of David Livingstone in Central Africa from 1865 to his Death. Continued by a Narrative of his Last Moments and Sufferings, obtained from his faithful Servants Susi and Chuma* (London: John Murray, 1874).

J. P. R. Wallis (ed.), *The Zambezi Expedition of David Livingstone 1858–1863*; vol. 1, *Journals*; vol. 2, *Journals, Letters* (London: Chatto and Windus, 1956). Central African Archives, Oppenheimer Series, no. 9.

————— (ed.), *The Zambesi Journal of James Stewart 1862–1863, with a Selection from his Correspondence* (London: Chatto and Windus, 1952). Central African Archives, Oppenheimer Series, no. 6.

Other works

F. Allshorn, *King Khama of Bechuanaland* (London: Sheldon, 1927).

W. G. Blaikie, *The Personal Life of David Livingstone* (London: John Murray, 1880, 2nd edn. 1881).

G. W. Clendennen and I. C. Cunningham, *David Livingstone: A Catalogue of Documents* (Edinburgh: National Library of Scotland, 1979).

R. Coupland, *Kirk on the Zambesi* (Oxford: Oxford University Press, 1928).

—————, *Livingstone's Last Journey* (London: Collins, 1945).

F. Debenham, *The Way to Ilala: David Livingstone's Pilgrimage* (London: Longmans, 1955).

J. J. Ellis, *Pathclearers of Central Africa* (London and Glasgow: Pickering and Inglis, 1928).

E. Healey, *Wives of Fame* (London: Sidgwick and Jackson, 1986).

D. O. Helly, *Livingstone's Legacy: Horace Waller and Victorian Mythmaking* (Ohio: Ohio University Press, 1987).

T. Holmes, *Journey to Livingstone: Exploration of an Imperial Myth* (Edinburgh: Canongate, 1993).

T. Jeal, *Livingstone* (London: Heinemann, 1973).

P. J. Johnstone, *Operation World*, 4th edn (Bromley: STL, and

Gerrards Cross: WEC International, 1987); 5th edn (Carlisle: OM Publishing, 1993).

K. K. Kinenge, *Tippo Tip, Traitant et Sultan du Manyema* (Kinshasa: Catholic Centre, 1979).

I. J. Knight, *Warrior Chiefs of Southern Africa* (Poole: Firebird Books, 1994).

J. Listowel, *The Other Livingstone* (Lewes: Julian Friedmann, 1974).

J. Macnair, *Livingstone the Liberator: A Study of a Dynamic Personality* (London: Collins, 1940).

G. Martelli, *Livingstone's River: A History of the Zambezi Expedition 1858–1864* (London: Chatto and Windus, 1970).

G. Seaver, *David Livingstone: His Life and Letters* (London: Lutterworth, 1957).

B. Stanley, *The Bible and the Flag: Protestant Missions and British Imperialism in the Nineteenth and Twentieth Centuries* (Leicester: Apollos, 1990).

A. F. Walls, 'The Legacy of David Livingstone', *International Bulletin of Missionary Research* (July 1987), pp. 125–129.

Notes

Full details of works cited are supplied in the Bibliography (pp. 233–235.)

Preface

1. Holmes (ed.), *David Livingstone*, p. xvi.
2. Blaikie, *The Personal Life of David Livingstone*.
3. Jeal, *Livingstone*.
4. Holmes, *Journey to Livingstone*.
5. Letter to the author, 15 August 1995.
6. Holmes (ed.), *David Livingstone*, p. xvii.
7. Helly, *Livingstone's Legacy*.
8. Livingstone, *Missionary Travels and Researches in South Africa*.
9. A line of enquiry suggested by Prof. Andrew Walls, formerly Director of the Centre for Studies of Christianity in the Non-Western World, New College, Edinburgh.
10. Holmes (ed.), *David Livingstone*, pp. xv–xvi.
11. Schapera (ed.) *David Livingstone: Family Letters; Livingstone's Private Journals 1851–1853; Livingstone's Missionary Correspondence 1841–1856; Livingstone's African Journal; David Livingstone: South African Papers*.
12. Holmes (ed.), *David Livingstone*, p. xvii.
13. 'I told Charles in answer to his invitation to turn Yankee that I am a missionary heart & soul. God had an only son, and he was a missionary and a physician. A poor poor imitation of Him I am or rather wish to be. In this service I hope to live, in it I wish to die. I would not exchange with his President.' Letter to his sister Agnes Livingston from Kolobeng, 5 February 1850, in Schapera (ed.), *David Livingstone: Family Letters*, vol. 2, p. 74.
14. Letter to James Stewart dated 26 January 1860, in Wallis (ed.), *The Zambesi Journal of James Stewart*, p. 206.
15. Martin Goldsmith, speaking in 1978 at All Nations Chris-

tian College, a centre for cross-cultural training in premises donated by the family of Thomas Fowell Buxton, whose vision of mission David Livingstone sought to emulate.

1. The clans

1. Blaikie, *The Personal Life of David Livingstone*, p. 2.
2. David's father changed the family name to 'Livingstone' (with an 'e') before December 1852. David did not consistently adopt it until December 1857, but began to use it much earlier. For the purposes of this book the date of the change is taken to be September 1855. (See below, p. 83.) For a discussion of this change, see G. W. Clendennen and I. C. Cunningham, *David Livingstone: A Catalogue of Documents*, Appendix 2, pp. 320–323.
3. Schapera (ed.), *David Livingstone: Family Letters*, vol. 1, p. 28, n. 2.
4. Walls, 'The Legacy of David Livingstone', pp. 125–126.
5. For a full discussion of Philip's activities, see B. Stanley, *The Bible and the Flag*, pp. 93–98.
6. Jeal, *Livingstone*, p. 31.
7. Schapera (ed.), *David Livingstone: Family Letters*, vol. 1, p. 35.
8. Letter to Mr and Mrs N. Livingston from Port Elizabeth, 19 May 1841, in *ibid.*, p. 36.
9. *Cf.* Gn. 9:22–27, esp. v. 25.
10. Schapera (ed.), *Livingstone's Missionary Correspondence*, p. 7, n. 2. *Cf.* Blaikie, *The Personal Life of David Livingstone*, p. 34.
11. Schapera (ed.), *Livingstone's Missionary Correspondence*, p. 4.
12. Letter to Janet Livingston from Kuruman, 8 December 1841, in Schapera, (ed.) *Livingstone's Missionary Correspondence*, vol. 1, p. 46.
13. Letter to J. J. Freeman from Kuruman, 23 September 1841, in Schapera (ed.), *Livingstone's Missionary Correspondence*, pp. 1–2. *Cf.* Blaikie, *The Personal Life of David Livingstone*, p. 34.
14. Livingstone, *Missionary Travels*, p. 9.
15. Just how vast became even more apparent later: *cf. ibid.*, p. 579 (Sebetwane's empire).
16. Letter to John Arundel from Kuruman, 22 December 1841,

in Schapera (ed.), *Livingstone's Missionary Correspondence*, p. 10.

17. Letter to Agnes Livingston from 'Bakuain (Kwena) Country', 4 April 1842, in Schapera (ed.), *David Livingstone: Family Letters*, vol. 1, p. 56.

18. The Kwena, 'one of the oldest Tswana tribes, had broken apart after the assassination (*c*. 1822) of Motswasele II, father of Sechele. One section, of which Motswasele's agnatic cousin Bubi became chief in 1828(?), ultimately settled at Dithubaruba, in the Dithejwane Hills, about 30 miles north-west of Kolobeng. D. L. was writing from there.' Schapera, *ibid*., p. 51, n. 3.

19. *Ibid*., p. 54 and n. 11.

20. Letter to J. J. Freeman from Kuruman, 3 July 1842, in *ibid*., p. 54. *Cf. Livingstone's Missionary Correspondence*, p. 16.

21. Livingstone, *Missionary Travels*, p. 9.

22. Letter to J. J. Freeman from Kuruman, 3 July 1842, in Schapera (ed.), *Livingstone's Missionary Correspondence*, p. 18.

23. Letter to J. J. Freeman from Kuruman, 3 July 1842, in *ibid*., p. 23.

24. David Livingstone states that he came back to the Ngwato after visiting the Kaa and the Kalanga (Shona) tribes; letter to J. J. Freeman from Kuruman, 3 July 1842, in *ibid*., p. 21. It is not clear exactly when this conversation took place.

25. Letter to J. J. Freeman from Kuruman, 3 July 1842, in *ibid*., p. 20.

26. See below, chapters 4 and 5.

27. Sekgoma I, who died in 1883, was chief of the Ngwato 'with two breaks' from *c*. 1834. 'He was the father of the famous Christian chief Khama, by whom he was ousted in 1875.' Schapera (ed.), *Livingstone's Missionary Correspondence*, p. 18, n. 1. A brief account of the career of Khama is given in Allshorn, *King Khama of Bechuanaland*.

28. Walls, 'The Legacy of David Livingstone', p. 126.

29. Letter to J. J. Freeman from Kuruman, 3 July 1842, in Schapera (ed.), *Livingstone's Missionary Correspondence*, pp. 23–24. *Cf*. letter to Mr and Mrs N. Livingston from 'Bakwain (Kwena) Country', 21 March 1843, in *David Livingstone: Family Letters*, vol. 1, p. 70 and n. 5.

30. Letter to Mr and Mrs N. Livingston from Kuruman, 26 September 1842, in *ibid.*, pp. 64–65.

31. Letter to Arthur Tidman from Kuruman, 24 June 1943, in Schapera (ed.), *Livingstone's Missionary Correspondence*, pp. 31–32.

32. Letter to Arthur Tidman from Kuruman, 24 June 1843, in *ibid.*, pp. 33–34.

33. *Ibid.*, p. 34.

34. Letter to Mr and Mrs N. Livingston from 'Bakwain (Kwena) Country', 21 March 1843, in Schapera (ed.), *David Livingstone: Family Letters*, vol. 1, pp. 70–71.

35. Letter to Arthur Tidman from Kuruman, 24 June 1843, in Schapera (ed.), *Livingstone's Missionary Correspondence*, pp. 34–35.

2. Mary goes north

1. Healey, *Wives of Fame*, p. 10.

2. See *e.g.* Knight, *Warrior Chiefs of Southern Africa*, pp. 7–49.

3. Johnstone, *Operation World*, 5th edn, Botswana section, p. 126. In 1986 the San were estimated to have forty dialects. See *Operation World*, 4th edn, p. 110.

4. For Mzilikaze's career, see *e.g.* Knight, *Warrior Chiefs of Southern Africa*, pp. 96–141.

5. Healey, *Wives of Fame*, p. 8.

6. *Ibid.*, pp. 8–9. See also chapter 5 below, p. 63.

7. Schapera (ed.), *David Livingstone: Family Letters*, p. 88–89.

8. Healey (who quotes Mma-Mary on the daily routine), *Wives of Fame*, p. 9.

9. David made this comment publicly at a farewell banquet in Britain on 13 February 1858 – by which time he had decided that Mary was '*always* the best spoke in the wheel' (italics added).

10. Healey, *Wives of Fame*, p. 9.

11. Letter to Mr and Mrs N. Livingston from Kuruman, 16 December 1843, in Schapera (ed.), *David Livingstone: Family Letters*, vol. 1, p. 88.

12. Livingstone, *Missionary Travels*, p. 12.

13. Letter to Mr and Mrs N. Livingston from Kuruman, 13

July 1842, in Schapera (ed.), David *Livingstone: Family Letters*, vol. 1, p. 59.

14. *Ibid*. Although David addresses it to 'my dear Parents', this comment comes at the end of the letter immediately after he sends 'My love to Mother & the sisterhood'.

15. Letters from Mabotsa to Arthur Tidman, 9 June 1844, in Schapera (ed.), *Livingstone's Missionary Correspondence*, p. 54 and n. 4.

16. MS 20312, folios 2–3, National Library of Scotland, Edinburgh.

17. Letter from Mabotsa to Arthur Tidman, 17 October 1845, in Schapera (ed.), *Livingstone's Missionary Correspondence*, p. 70.

18. Letter to Mary Moffat from Mabotsa, 12 September 1844, in Schapera (ed.), *David Livingstone: Family Letters*, vol. 1, p. 106.

3. A tale of three cities

1. Healey, *Wives of Fame*, p. 4.

2. Letter to Arthur Tidman from Lattakoo, 30 October 1843, in Schapera (ed.), *Livingstone's Missionary Correspondence*, pp. 46–51.

3. *Ibid*., p. 75, n. 2.

4. Letter to Robert Moffat from Mabotsa, 6 June 1845, in Schapera (ed.), *David Livingstone: Family Letters*, vol. 1, pp. 126–128.

5. *Ibid*., p. 130.

6. *Ibid*., p. 127.

7. Letter to Robert Moffat from Mabotsa, 13 August 1845, in *ibid*., pp. 138–141.

8. National Library of Scotland, Edinburgh, Acc. 1064. Letter from Kuruman to B. Pyne of Ongar, 28 January 1845, quoted in *ibid*., p. 17 and n. 20.

9. Moffat, *Missionary Labours*, p. 243, quoted in *ibid*., p. 192, n. 8.

10. Letter to Arthur Tidman from Kuruman, 24 June 1843, in Schapera (ed.), *Livingstone's Missionary Correspondence*, p. 36.

11. Letter to Robert Moffat from Mabotsa, 5 September 1845, in Schapera (ed.), *David Livingstone: Family Letters*, vol. 1, p. 143.

12. Letter to Robert Moffat, probably from Tshonuane, 1 November (?)1845, in *ibid.*, p. 154.

13. Healey, *Wives of Fame*, pp. 16–17.

14. Letter to Arthur Tidman from Kuruman, 17 March 1847, in Schapera (ed.), *Livingstone's Missionary Correspondence*, p. 95.

15. *Ibid.*, p. 96.

16. *Ibid.*

17. Schapera (ed.), *David Livingstone: Family Letters*, vol. 1, pp. 187 n. 7, 188.

18. Letter to Arthur Tidman from Kuruman, 17 March 1847, in Schapera (ed.), *Livingstone Missionary Correspondence*, pp. 95, 99.

19. *Ibid.*, pp. 99–100.

20. *Ibid.*, p. 99.

21. *Ibid.*, p. 101 and n. 1.

22. Letter to David Livingston from Arthur Tidman, London, 6 September 1847, in *ibid.*, p. 110.

23. Letter to Mrs N. Livingston from Kuruman, 4 May 1847, in Schapera (ed.), *David Livingstone: Family Letters*, vol. 1, p. 199.

24. *Ibid.*, p. 196.

25. Letter dated July 1847, in *ibid.*, p. 202.

26. Letter to Robert Moffat, Jr., from Kolobeng, 13 August 1847, in *ibid.*, p. 204.

27. *Ibid.*, p. 203.

28. *Ibid.*

29. Letter to Robert Moffat from Kolobeng, 29 September 1847, in *ibid.*, p. 211.

30. *Ibid.*, p. 212.

31. *Ibid.*

32. *Ibid.*, pp. 212–213.

33. *Ibid.*, p. 214.

34. *Ibid.*, p. 213.

35. Postscript to the same letter, dated 14 October 1847, *ibid.*, p. 219.

36. *Ibid.*, p. 222 and n. 44.

37. Letter to Robert Moffat, November (?)1847, in *ibid.*, p. 232.

38. Healey, *Wives of Fame*, p. 18.

39. Letter of 13 February to Watt, quoted in Schapera (ed.), *David Livingstone: Family Letters*, vol. 1, p. 235, n. 7.

40. Letter to Robert Moffat, March (?)1848, in *ibid.*, pp. 235–236.

41. *Ibid.*, p. 236.

42. *Ibid.*, pp. 236–238.

43. Healey, *Wives of Fame*, p. 18.

44. Letter to Janet Livingston from Kolobeng, 31 January 1849, in Schapera (ed.), *David Livingstone: Family Letters*, vol. 2, p. 18.

45. Letter to Charles Livingston from Kolobeng, 16 May 1849, in *ibid.*, p. 55.

46. Blaikie quotes a comment Livingstone made to this effect in 1870 while reflecting on his life among the Kwena: *The Personal Life of David Livingstone*, p. 97.

4. Sechele's decision, David's dilemma

1. See *e.g.* Knight, *Warrior Chiefs of Southern Africa*, pp. 50–95.

2. Letter to Robert Moffat from Kolobeng, November 1848, in Schapera (ed.), *David Livingstone: Family Letters*, vol. 1, p. 260 and n. 6.

3. Fragments of Kolobeng Journal, in Schapera (ed.), *Livingstone's Private Journals*, p. 300.

4. Letter to Arthur Tidman from Kolobeng, 1 November 1848, in Schapera (ed.), *Livingstone's Missionary Correspondence*, pp. 119–120.

5. Fragments of Kolobeng Journal, in Schapera (ed.), *Livingstone's Private Journals*, p. 298.

6. *Ibid.*, p. 298 n. 4.

7. *Ibid.*, p. 298.

8. Letter to Robert Moffat from Kolobeng, 2 September 1848, postscript (Monday evening), in Schapera (ed.), *David Livingstone: Family Letters*, vol. 1, p. 255–256.

9. *Ibid.*, p. 256.

10. *Ibid.*, pp. 260–261.

11. *Ibid.*, p. 261.

12. Schapera (ed.), *Livingstone's Private Journal*, p. 300.

13. Letter to Robert Moffat from Kolobeng, November 1848, in Schapera (ed.), *David Livingstone: Family Letters*, vol. 1, p. 261.

14. Letter to Arthur Tidman from Kolobeng, 26 May 1849, in

Schapera (ed.), *Livingstone's Missionary Correspondence*, p. 127.

15. *Ibid.*, pp. 127–128.

16. *Ibid.*

17. Letter to Robert Moffat from Kolobeng, 23 March 1849, in Schapera (ed.), *David Livingstone: Family Letters*, vol. 2, pp. 23, 24 n. 11.

18. See chapter 1 above.

19. Schapera (ed.), *David Livingstone: Family Letters*, vol. 2, p. 35 n. 5.

20. Letter to Robert Moffat from Kolobeng, postscript dated 14 October 1847, in *ibid.*, vol. 1, p. 219.

21. Writing to Robert Moffat from Kolobeng, 1 August (postscript) and 18 September 1850, in *ibid.*, vol. 2, pp. 91, 104.

22. Letter to 'Parents & sisters' from Kolobeng, 28 July 1850, in *ibid.*, p. 95.

23. An insight into the positive position taken by Livingston's successors on armed defence is given by the (non-Christian) chief of the Ngwato, Sekgoma. 'Asked if Christianity had made better or worse soldiers of his people, he replied: "If I wanted them for a raid, they would be of no use killing women and children; but if I wanted them to defend their country, they would fight as well as ever."' Allshorn, *King Khama of Bechuanaland*, p. 12.

24. Letter to Charles Livingston from Kolobeng, 16 May 1849, in Schapera (ed.), *David Livingstone: Family Letters*, vol. 2, p. 51.

25. *Ibid.*

26. Letter to Robert Moffat from Kolobeng, 11 April 1849, in *ibid.*, p. 30.

27. Mma-Bantshang later married, and went to live in the Ngwato area of the Shoshong Hills.

28. Letter to Robert Moffat from Kolobeng, 11 April 1849, in Schapera (ed.), *David Livingstone: Family Letters*, vol. 2, p. 31.

29. Letter to Arthur Tidman from Kolobeng, 26 May 1849, in Schapera (ed.), *Livingstone's Missionary Correspondence*, p. 130.

5. The lake and the desert

1. Letter to Robert Moffat, 4 May (?)1849, in Schapera (ed.), *David Livingstone: Family Letters*, vol. 2, pp. 43–44.

2. Letter to Arthur Tidman from Kolobeng, 26 May 1849, in Schapera (ed.), *Livingstone's Missionary Correspondence*, p. 130.

3. Schapera (ed.), *Livingstone's Private Journals*, p. 304.

4. Blaikie, *The Personal Life of David Livingstone*, p. 99.

5. Listowel, *The Other Livingstone*, p. 24.

6. Letter to Charles Livingston from Kolobeng, 16 May 1849, in Schapera (ed.), *David Livingstone: Family Letters*, vol. 2, p. 55.

7. Healey, *Wives of Fame*, p. 21.

8. Livingstone, *Missionary Travels*, pp. 61–62.

9. *Ibid.*, pp. 62–63.

10. Letter to Arthur Tidman from the banks of the River Zouga (Botletle), 3 September 1849, in Schapera (ed.), *Livingstone's Missionary Correspondence*, p. 132; *cf.* letter to Mr and Mrs N. Livingston from Kolobeng, 25 September 1849, in Schapera (ed.), *David Livingstone: Family Letters*, vol. 2, p. 66.

11. Letter to Arthur Tidman from the banks of the River Zouga (Botletle), 3 September 1849 (see n. 10 above), p. 135.

12. Letter to Mr and Mrs N. Livingston from Kolobeng, 25 September 1849 (see n. 10 above), p. 66.

13. *Ibid.* (postscript dated 12 October 1849), p. 67.

14. Letter to Agnes Livingston from Kolobeng, 5 February 1850, in Schapera (ed.), *David Livingstone: Family Letters*, vol. 2, p. 74.

15. Letter to Robert Moffat, probably from Lokakane Pan, 'about 80 miles by wagon road north-west of Shoshong', 8 July 1850, in *ibid.*, pp. 83 (and n. 1), 84.

16. Healey, *Wives of Fame*, p. 23.

17. *Ibid.*, p. 24.

18. Letter to Robert Moffat from Kolobeng, November 1848, in Schapera (ed.), *David Livingstone: Family Letters*, vol. 1, p. 259 and n. 1. Sebubi, a Thlaro tribesman, settled with the Ngwaketse. His descendants were still living at Tlhorong, his final mission centre, in 1959.

19. Writing to 'My Dear Livingstone', probably in April 1851; in Schapera (ed.), *Livingstone's Private Journals*, pp. 70 n. 2, 71.

20. Letter to Arthur Tidman from Boatlanama, 30 April 1851, in Schapera (ed.), *Livingstone's Missionary Correspondence*, p. 170.

21. Mrs Moffat quotes a letter from Mary as saying, 'I must

again wend my weary way to the far Interior, perhaps to be confined in the field.' Schapera (ed.), *Livingstone's Private Journals*, p. 70.

22. Letter to Robert Moffat from 'Banks of Zouga', 29 September 1851, in Schapera (ed.), *David Livingstone: Family Letters*, vol. 2, p. 137.

23. Schapera (ed.), *Livingstone's Private Journals*, p. 13. *Cf.* Livingstone, *Missionary Travels*, p. 79.

24. Livingstone, *Missionary Travels*, p. 89.

25. Listowel, *The Other Livingstone*, p. 51.

26. See chapter 2 n. 6 above, and Schapera (ed.), *Livingstone's Private Journals*, p. 18 n. 8.

27. *Ibid.*, p. 22.

28. *Ibid.*, p. 36.

29. *Ibid.*, p. 38.

30. Both Livingstone and the LMS originally applied the 'highway' epithet to the river flowing north out of Lake Ngami. See pp. 57–58 above, p. 109 below, and Buxton references in Index.

6. Do or die

1. Blaikie, *The Personal Life of David Livingstone*, p. 131, quoted in Schapera (ed.), *David Livingstone: Family Letters*, vol. 2, p. 182.

2. Parliamentary Papers 1854, XLIII, quoted and interpreted in Schapera (ed.), *David Livingstone: South African Papers*, pp. 43–44.

3. Schapera (ed.), *Livingstone's Private Journals*, p. 81, and *David Livingstone: South African Papers*, pp. 43–45.

4. Quoted in Holmes, *Journey to Livingstone*, p. 351.

5. Journal entry for 28 September 1852, in Blaikie, *The Personal Life of David Livingstone*, p. 139.

6. Schapera (ed.), *David Livingstone: South African Papers*, p. 49.

7. Adapted from *ibid.*, p. 145. *Cf.* Schapera (ed.), *Livingstone's Private Journals*, pp. 85–90.

8. Schapera (ed.), *David Livingstone: South African Papers*, pp. 176–177.

9. *Ibid.*

10. *Ibid.*, p. 64.

11. *Ibid.*, p. 51.

12. *Ibid.*, pp. 55, 59.

13. *Ibid.*, p. 50.

14. *Ibid.*, p. 146.

15. Schapera (ed.), *Livingstone's Private Journals*, pp. 146–147.

16. *Cf. ibid.*, p. 170, and Blaikie, *The Personal Life of David Livingstone*, p. 143.

17. Schapera (ed.), *Livingstone's Private Journals*, p. 137.

18. *Cf. ibid.*, p. 162.

19. *Ibid.*, p. 183.

20. *Cf. ibid.*, p. 184.

21. Blaikie, *The Personal Life of David Livingstone*, p. 143.

22. Schapera (ed.), *Livingstone's Private Journals*, pp. 200–201.

23. Blaikie, *The Personal Life of David Livingstone*, p. 144.

24. Schapera (ed.), *Livingstone's Private Journals*, p. 202.

25. *Ibid.*, p. 209 (entry for 14 August 1853). *Cf.* Blaikie, *The Personal Life of David Livingstone*, p. 146.

26. Schapera (ed.), *Livingstone's Private Journals*, p. 205.

27. Letter to Arthur Tidman from Dinyanti, 24 September 1853, in Schapera (ed.), *Livingstone's Missionary Correspondence*, p. 249.

28. Schapera (ed.), *Livingstone's Private Journals*, p. 232 (entry for 10 September 1853; see footnotes).

29. Letter to Arthur Tidman from Dinyanti, 24 September 1843, in Schapera (ed.), *Livingstone's Missionary Correspondence*, p. 250. *Cf.* Blaikie, *The Personal Life of David Livingstone*, p. 146.

30. Schapera (ed.), *Livingstone's Private Journals*, p. 277 (entries for 20–28 October 1853).

31. Schapera (ed.), *Livingstone's Missionary Correspondence*, p. 257 and n. 2. *Cf.* letter to Arthur Tidman from Dinyanti, 24 September 1853, in *ibid.*, p. 250.

32. Schapera (ed.), *Livingstone's African Journal*, vol. 1, p. 4. *Cf.* Schapera (ed.), *David Livingstone: Family Letters*, vol. 2, pp. 233, 273.

33. Schapera (ed.), *Livingstone's African Journal*, vol. 1, p. 8.

34. *Ibid.*, pp. 7–9.

35. *Ibid.*, p. 9.

36. *Ibid.*, pp. 9, 10, 24. *Cf.* Blaikie, *The Personal Life of David Livingstone*, p. 159.

37. Schapera (ed.), *Livingstone's African Journal*, vol. 1, pp. 13, 15.

38. See *ibid.*, p. 13, n. 3.

39. *Ibid.*, p. 57.

40. *Ibid.*, p. 59.

41. Blaikie, *The Personal Life of David Livingstone*, pp. 158, 159. Blaikie mentions that among the pictures was one of Abraham offering up Isaac. Did the audience see the knife coming towards them?

42. Schapera (ed.), *Livingstone's African Journal*, vol. 1, pp. 103–104. *Cf.* Schapera (ed.), *Livingstone's Missionary Correspondence*, p. 263.

43. Livingstone, *Missionary Travels*, p. 341.

44. Schapera (ed.), *Livingstone's African Journal*, vol. 1, p. 104.

45. *Ibid.*, p. 106. *Cf.* 2 Sa. 18:9.

46. *Ibid.*, p. 109.

47. *Ibid.*, pp. 122–123. *Cf.* Blaikie, *The Personal Life of David Livingstone*, p. 161.

48. *Ibid.*, p. 161.

49. Letter to William Thompson from Calinda (possibly Cabinda), 14 May 1854, in Schapera (ed.), *Livingstone's Missionary Correspondence*, p. 263.

50. Schapera (ed.), *Livingstone's Missionary Correspondence*, p. 264.

51. Blaikie, *The Personal Life of David Livingstone*, p. 154.

7. The promise

1. Letter from Gabriel to LMS, 4 July 1854, in Schapera (ed.), *Livingstone's Missionary Correspondence*, p. 266.

2. Letter to Arthur Tidman from Cassange, 14 January 1855, in *ibid.*, p. 269.

3. Schapera (ed.), *Livingstone's African Journal*, p. 150 and n. 2, and p. 151 n. 1.

4. Gabriel was born in 1821 and died in 1862. *Cf.* Schapera (ed.), *Livingstone's Missionary Correspondence*, p. 265 n. 1.

5. Schapera (ed.), *Livingstone's African Journal*, vol. 1, p. 145 n. 2.

6. Valdez, *Western Africa*, vol. 2, pp. 113–114, quoted by Schapera in *ibid*.

7. Writing from Tala Mugongo (near Cassange), 14 January 1855. In Schapera (ed.), *Livingstone's Missionary Correspondence*, p. 269.

8. Schapera (ed.), *Livingstone's African Journal*, vol. 2, pp. 150, 156.

9. *Ibid.*, vol. 1, p. 210.

10. Schapera (ed.), *David Livingstone: Family Letters*, vol. 2, p. 266, and *Livingstone's Missionary Correspondence*, p. 268 n. 2.

11. *The Times*, 8 August 1854, quoted by Schapera (ed.) in *Livingstone's African Journal*, p. 210 n. 3.

12. Letter to Sir Roderick Murchison from Tete, 4 March 1856, in *Journal of the Royal Geographical Society* (1857), p. 374.

13. It is also quoted in the *LMS Chronicle* (1857), pp. 7–8, and referred to by Schapera in *Livingstone's African Journal*, pp. xiii, 412, 422. *Cf.* Livingstone, *Missionary Travels*, p. 673.

14. Schapera (ed.), *Livingstone's African Journal*, p. 185.

15. *Ibid.*, p. 187 n. 1.

16. Stanley, *The Bible and the Flag*, p. 73 and n. 64, p. 191.

17. Schapera (ed.), *Livingstone's African Journal*, pp. 156 n. 2, 189.

18. Letter to Mary Livingston from Shinge, 20 March 1855, in Schapera (ed.), *David Livingstone: Family Letters*, vol. 2, p. 258 (quoted in Blaikie, pp. 172–173).

19. *Ibid*.

20. *Ibid.*, p. 259.

21. Schapera (ed.), *Livingstone's African Journal*, p. 278.

22. *Ibid*.

23. *Ibid.*, p. 276. Written at Luena, 25 July 1855.

24. *Ibid.*, p. 287.

25. *Ibid.*, p. 289.

26. *Ibid.*, p. 293.

27. *Ibid.*, p. 297 (entry for 13 September 1855).

28. See chapter 1, note 2.

29. Letter of 27 March 1854, in the National Archives of

Zimbabwe, Harare. In Schapera (ed.), *Livingstone's African Journal*, vol. 2, p. 297 and n. 1.

30. *Ibid.*, p. 295.

31. *Ibid.*, p. 297.

32. *Ibid.*, pp. 299–300 (entry for 23 September 1855).

33. *Ibid.*, pp. 300–301.

34. *Ibid.*, pp. 322–323.

35. *Ibid.*, p. 324.

36. Livingstone, *Missionary Travels*, p. 515.

37. Schapera (ed.), *Livingstone's African Journal*, p. 324. For an account of the wars, see Knight, *Warrior Chiefs of Southern Africa*, pp. 142–187.

8. No Man's Land

1. Schapera (ed.), *Livingstone's African Journal*, vol. 2, p. 326.

2. *Ibid.*, pp. 326–327.

3. In 1860, during his return visit to Sekeletu on the Zambezi expedition. See D. and C. Livingstone, *Narrative of an Expedition to the Zambezi*, p. 253.

4. Schapera (ed.), *Livingstone's African Journal*, vol. 2, p. 327.

5. *Ibid.*, p. 327 and n. 2: 'Stonebyres is one of the four falls of the River Clyde in the vicinity of Lanark, about 30 miles SE of Glasgow ...'

6. *Ibid.*, p. 326.

7. *Ibid.*, p. 327.

8. *Ibid.*, pp. 327–328.

9. *Ibid.*, p. 328. The incursions of hippopotami were to prove too much for the nascent seedlings. The name of the place was later changed from Garden Island to Livingstone Island.

10. *Ibid.*, pp. 331 n.1, 330.

11. *Ibid.*, p. 338.

12. *Ibid.*

13. *Ibid.*, p. 341.

14. *Ibid.*, p. 342.

15. *Ibid.*, p. 344.

16. *Ibid.*, p. 346.

17. *Ibid.*, p. 373.

18. *Ibid.*, p. 373 and n. 3. 'I. H. S.' stands for 'Iesus Hominem

Salvator' (Jesus Saviour of Men).

19. *Ibid.*, p. 374.

20. *Ibid.*, p. 373.

21. *Ibid.*, p. 374.

22. *Ibid.*

23. *Ibid.*

24. *Ibid.*, p. 375.

25. *Ibid.*, p. 381.

26. *Ibid.*

27. *Ibid.*, pp. 381–382.

28. *Ibid.*, p. 382.

29. *Ibid.*

30. *Ibid.*, p. 386.

31. *Ibid.*, p. 421.

32. *Ibid.*, p. 422.

33. R. Moffat, *Matabele Journals*, vol. 1, p. 166, quoted in Schapera (ed.), *David Livingstone: Family Letters*, vol. 2, p. 267 n. 19.

34. Blaikie, *The Personal Life of David Livingstone*, p. 195.

35. Letter of 19 March 1856, quoted in Parliamentary Papers 1857, Sess. 2, XLIV, 63, and in Schapera (ed.), *Livingstone's African Journal*, vol. 2, p. 326. n. 2. *Cf. Journal of the Royal Geographical Society*, (1857), p. 375: 23. v. 56 Murchison.

9. Reunion and redirection

1. Letter to Sir Roderick Murchison from Tete, 4 March 1856, in *Journal of the Royal Geographical Society* (1857), p. 374.

2. See chapter 1, n. 3.

3. Healey, *Wives of Fame*, pp. 34–35.

4. Walls, 'The Legacy of David Livingstone', p. 127.

5. Monk (ed.), *Dr Livingstone's Cambridge Lectures*, p. 24.

6. *Ibid.*, pp. 46–47.

7. Letter to Adam Sedgwick from 50 Albermarle Street, 6 February 1858, in Holmes (ed.), *David Livingstone: Letters and Documents*, pp. 49–50.

8. Quoted in Healey, *Wives of Fame*, p. 37.

10. Trials and tears

1. The third thrust would be to the north, to Lake Nyasa (via

the River Shire) and an attempt to reach Lake Tanganyika (via the River Ruvuma). See chapters 11 and 12 below.

2. Wallis (ed.), *The Zambezi Expedition of David Livingstone*, vol. 1, pp. 19–29.

3. D. and C. Livingstone, *Narrative of an Expedition to the Zambesi*, p. 33.

4. *Ibid.*, pp. 73–74. *Cf.* Foskett (ed.), *The Zambesi Journal and Letters of Dr John Kirk*, vol. 1, p. 137.

5. See above, chapter 6 n. 17.

6. Wallis (ed.), *The Zambezi Expedition of David Livingstone*, vol. 1, p. 42. *Cf.* p. 69 above.

7. *Ibid.*, pp. 60–61.

8. Martelli, *Livingstone's River*, p. 93.

9. Wallis (ed.), *The Zambezi Expedition of David Livingstone*, vol. 1, p. 70, quoted in Martelli, *Livingstone's River*, p. 98. See also Kirk's vivid description of the terrain in Foskett (ed.), *The Zambesi Journal and Letters of Dr John Kirk*, vol. 1, pp. 135–137.

10. *Ibid.*, p. 143.

11. D. and C. Livingstone, *Narrative of an Expedition to the Zambesi*, p. 76. Martelli sees no evidence that Tingane got such an idea from David Livingstone; *Livingstone's River*, pp. 104–105. Note however that Livingstone visited 'another chief also called Tingane', Wallis (ed.), *The Zambezi Expedition of David Livingstone*, vol. 1, p. 77.

12. *Ibid.*, pp. 77–78

13. *Ibid.*, p. 78.

14. The report and proposal were published in the *Intelligencer* for February 1860. A letter was also written to Henry Venn (General Secretary of CMS, 1841–73) from Lake Nyasa. See Church Mission Society Library MSS 0890 and 0942. National Library of Scotland copy no. 10779 (12).

15. Letter to James Aspinall Turner from Lake Chilwa, dated 30 May 1859. National Library of Scotland MS 0899.

16. D. and C. Livingstone, *Narrative of an Expedition to the Zambesi*, p. 124.

17. *Ibid.*, p. 128.

18. Wallis (ed.), *The Zambezi Expedition of David Livingstone*, vol. 1, pp. 163–164.

19. *Ibid.*, p. 164.

20. Martelli, *Livingstone's River*, p. 140.

21. D. and C. Livingstone, *Narrative of an Expedition to the Zambesi*, p. 159.

22. *Ibid.*, pp. 203–204.

11. Blighted hopes

1. D. and C. Livingstone, *Narrative of an Expedition to the Zambesi*, p. 233.

2. *Ibid.*, pp. 234.

3. *Ibid.*, pp. 250–252.

4. *Ibid.*, p. 273.

5. *Ibid.*

6. *Ibid.*, p. 274.

7. Wallis (ed.), *The Zambezi Expedition of David Livingstone*, vol. 2, pp. 395–396; *cf.* Martelli, *Livingstone's River*, pp. 149–150.

8. D. and C. Livingstone, *Narrative of an Expedition to the Zambesi*, p. 276.

9. Martelli, *Livingstone's River*, p. 151.

10. *Ibid.*, p. 152.

11. D. and C. Livingstone, *Narrative of an Expedition to the Zambesi*, p. 334.

12. Martelli, *Livingstone's River*, p. 154.

13. D. and C. Livingstone, *Narrative of an Expedition to the Zambesi*, p. 357.

14. *Ibid.*, p. 360.

15. *Ibid.*, p. 361.

12. The shadow of death

1. Wallis (ed.), *The Zambezi Journal of James Stewart*, p. 1.

2. *Ibid.*, p. 3.

3. Letter from Chupanga to James Young, 5 May 1862, in Holmes (ed.), *David Livingstone: Letters and Documents*, p. 75.

4. Quoted in Blaikie, *The Personal Life of David Livingstone*, p. 294.

5. See above, chapter 10, p. 111.

6. Healey, *Wives of Fame*, p. 50.

7. Wallis (ed.), *The Zambesi Journal of James Stewart*, p. 57

(entry for 'Sabbath, April 27th, 1862').

8. Blaikie, *The Personal Life of David Livingstone*, p. 298.

9. Wallis (ed.), *The Zambesi Journal of James Stewart*, p. 57.

10. Blaikie, *The Personal Life of David Livingstone*, p. 300 (journal entry for 11 May [1862], Kongone).

11. *Ibid.*, p. 299.

12. *Ibid.*, p. 301 (journal entry for 31 May 1862).

13. *Ibid.*, p. 299.

14. *Ibid.*, p. 300 (journal entry for 19 May 1862).

15. D. and C. Livingstone, *Narrative of an Expedition to the Zambesi*, p. 437. *Cf.* Wallis (ed.), *The Zambesi Expedition of David Livingstone*, vol. 2, pp. 222–223.

16. Foskett (ed.), *The Zambesi Journal and Letters of Dr. John Kirk*, vol. 2, p. 476 (entry for 19 September 1862).

17. Debenham, *The Way to Ilala*, p. 201.

18. D. and C. Livingstone, *Narrative of an Expedition to the Zambesi*, p. 449.

19. Blaikie, *The Personal Life of David Livingstone*, pp. 310–311. *Cf.* Livingstone's terse journal entry for 15 June 1863: 'Came to sleep at small water where some quite new huts were built. A child's skeleton wrapped up in a bit of mat and a man and his wife's bones lay side by side.' Wallis (ed.). *The Zambesi Expedition of David Livingstone*, vol. 2, p. 238.

20. See Blaikie, *The Personal Life of David Livingstone* (2nd edn), p. 319.

21. *Ibid.*, p. 324.

13. The calm before the storm

The journal for 26 March 1864 to 23 January 1866 has not yet been published. Written in Letts Diary No. 8 for 1863, it is kept on microfilm at the National Library of Scotland, Edinburgh (MS 10775 no. 4). Extracts are published in Seaver, *David Livingstone: His Life and Letters*, pp. 440–449. See Clendennen and Cunningham, *David Livingstone: A Catalogue of Documents*, p. 273.

1. Blaikie, *The Personal Life of David Livingstone* (2nd edn), p. 326. Letter to Agnes from Mozambique, 24 February 1864.

2. Clendennen (ed.), *David Livingstone's Shire Journal*, p. 89.

3. *Ibid.*, p. 89.

4. D. and C. Livingstone, *Narrative of an Expedition to the Zambesi*, p. 584.

14. Planning the final campaign

1. *Cf.* above, chapter 7 n. 13., and Helly, *Livingstone's Legacy*, p. 24, quoting Livingstone as saying, 'The idea of a colony in Africa, as the term colony is usually understood, cannot be entertained.'

2. D. and C. Livingstone, *Narrative of an Expedition to the Zambesi*. David collaborated with Charles and granted him the US rights for the book.

3. Blaikie, *The Personal Life of David Livingstone* (2nd edn), p. 350.

4. Letter to Sir James Young, 20 January 1865, in *ibid.*, p. 351.

5. Blaikie describes the deathbed scene: *The Personal Life of David Livingstone*, p. 355.

6. *Ibid.*, p. 360.

7. See above, pp. 154, 159.

8. Waller (ed.), *The Last Journals of David Livingstone*, vol. 1, p. 61.

9. *Ibid.*, p. 65.

10. *Ibid.*, p. 62.

11. *Ibid.*, pp. 62–63.

12. *Ibid.*, p. 67.

13. *Ibid.*, p. 70.

14. *Ibid.*, p. 71.

15. *Ibid.*, p. 74.

16. *Ibid.*

17. *Ibid.*

18. *Ibid.*, p. 75.

19. *Ibid.*

20. *Ibid.*

15. Search

1. Waller (ed.), *The Last Journals of David Livingstone*, vol. 1, pp. 90–91 (entry for 8 August 1866).

2. Field diary 17, entry for 14 August 1866, quoted in Helly,

Livingstone's Legacy, p. 151.

3. Field diary 17, entry for 4 September 1866, quoted in *ibid.*, p. 149.

4. Waller (ed.), *The Last Journals of David Livingstone*, vol. 1, p. 100.

5. *Ibid.*, p. 103.

6. *Ibid.*, p. 104.

7. *Ibid.*, p. 105.

8. *Ibid.*, p. 107.

9. Letter from David Livingstone to Horace Waller, quoted in *ibid.*, p. 109.

10. Letter of 7 March 1867, quoted in Coupland, *Livingstone's Last Journey*, p. 62.

11. Waller (ed.), *The Last Journals of David Livingstone*, vol. 1, p. 114.

12. *Ibid.*, p. 116.

13. Field diary 20, entry for 13 January 1867, quoted in Helly, *Livingstone's Legacy*, pp. 149, 151.

14. Waller (ed.), *The Last Journals of David Livingstone*, vol. 1, p. 172.

15. *Ibid.*, p. 179.

16. *Ibid.*, p. 229.

17. *Ibid.*, p. 177.

18. *Ibid.*, p. 178.

19. *Ibid.*, p. 184.

20. *Ibid.*, p. 192.

21. *Ibid.*, pp. 200–201.

22. *Ibid.*, p. 205.

23. *Ibid.*, p. 204.

24. *Ibid.*, p. 222.

25. *Ibid.*, p. 228.

26. *Ibid.*

27. *Ibid.*, p. 237.

28. *Ibid.*, p. 238.

29. Tippo Tip, speaking to H. M. Stanley in 1876. Quoted in Kinenge, *Tippo Tip*, p. 39. (Translated from the French.)

30. Waller (ed.), *The Last Journals of David Livingstone*, vol. 1, p. 243.

31. *Ibid.*, p. 247.
32. *Ibid.*, pp. 247–248.

16. High noon

1. Waller (ed.), *The Last Journals of David Livingstone*, vol. 1, p. 286.

2. Waller Papers 178.6, Rhodes House Library, Oxford, entry for 13 April 1868.

3. *Ibid.*

4. *Ibid.*

5. *Ibid.*

6. *Ibid.*

7. Waller (ed.), *The Last Journals of David Livingstone*, vol. 1, p. 287.

8. Waller Papers 178.6, Rhodes House Library Oxford, entry for 13 April 1868.

9. *Ibid.*

10. *Ibid.*

11. Waller (ed.), *The Last Journals of David Livingstone*, vol. 1, p. 290.

12. *Ibid.*, p. 292.

13. *Ibid.*, pp. 306–307.

14. *Ibid.*, pp. 307–308.

15. *Ibid.*, pp. 311–312.

16. *Ibid.*, p. 313.

17. *Ibid.*, p. 314.

18. *Ibid.*

19. *Ibid.*, p. 317.

20. *Ibid.*, p. 331.

21. *Ibid.*, p. 346.

22. *Ibid.*, p. 350.

23. *Ibid.*, pp. 349–350.

24. *Ibid.*, p. 356.

25. Waller Papers 178.6, Rhodes House Library, Oxford, entry for 13 April 1868.

26. Waller (ed.), *The Last Journals of David Livingstone*, vol. 1, p. 357.

27. *Ibid.*, p. 358.

28. See, *e.g.*, letter to J. Young from Chipeta, 10 November 1866: 'all of my [Comoros] men ... left me to face the terrible Mazitu with nine Nassick [*sic*] boys.' In Holmes, *David Livingstone*, p. 160.

29. Waller (ed.), *The Last Journals of David Livingstone*, vol. 1, p. 359.

30. *Ibid.*, p. 360.

31. *Ibid.*, vol. 2, pp. 1–2.

32. *Ibid.*, p. 2.

33. *Ibid.*, p. 9.

34. *Ibid.*, p. 11.

35. *Ibid.*

36. *Ibid.*, p. 13.

37. *Ibid.*, p. 15.

38. *Ibid.*, p. 24.

39. *Ibid.*, p. 27.

40. *Ibid.*, p. 29.

41. *Ibid.*

42. *Ibid.*

43. *Ibid.*, p. 36.

17. The terrorists

1. Waller (ed.), *The Last Journals of David Livingstone*, vol. 2, p. 41.

2. *Ibid.*, p. 41.

3. *Ibid.*, p. 47.

4. *Ibid.*, p. 55 (entry for 24 August).

5. *Ibid.*, p. 63.

6. *Ibid.*, p. 70.

7. *Ibid.*, p. 71.

8. See *ibid.*, p. 96 (entry for 28 January 1871). The full impact of this epidemic is described in Coupland, *Livingstone's Last Journey*, pp. 94–96.

9. Waller (ed.) *The Last Journals of David Livingstone*, vol. 2, pp. 46, 67–68 (entries for 30 June and 10 October 1870).

10. *Ibid.*, p. 97.

11. *Ibid.*, pp. 95, 98.

12. *Ibid.*, p. 100 (entry for 13 February 1871).

13. *Ibid.*, p. 87.
14. Waller Papers 265.8, Rhodes House Library, Oxford.
15. Waller (ed.), *The Last Journals of David Livingstone*, vol. 2, p. 102.
16. *Ibid.*, p. 110.
17. *Ibid.*, p. 113.
18. *Ibid.*, p. 132.
19. *Ibid.*, pp. 133–134.
20. *Ibid.*, p. 139.
21. *Ibid.*, p. 137.
22. *Ibid.*, pp. 65, 138.
23. *Ibid.*, pp. 139.
24. *Ibid.*, p. 146.
25. *Ibid.*, pp. 146–147.
26. *Ibid.*, p. 147.
27. *Ibid.*
28. *Ibid.*
29. *Ibid.*, p. 148.
30. *Ibid.*, p. 151.
31. *Ibid.*, p. 153–154.
32. *Ibid.*, p. 154.
33. *Ibid.*, p. 155.
34. *Ibid.*
35. Quoted by Coupland, *Livingstone's Last Journey*, pp. 99.
36. Waller (ed.) *The Last Journals of David Livingstone*, vol. 2, p. 156.

18. The Samaritan

1. Letter to Agnes Livingstone from Lake Tanganyika, 18 November 1871, quoted in Blaikie, *The Personal Life of David Livingstone*, p. 425.
2. H. M. Stanley, *How I found Livingstone*, p. 331.
3. *Ibid.*
4. *Ibid.*, p. 339.
5. *Ibid.*, p. 335.
6. *Cf. ibid.*, p. 331.
7. *Cf. ibid.*, p. 338. Note Stanley's 'violent reaction in [Livingstone's] favor'.

8. See note 1 above.

9. Quoted from 'a later letter' by Blaikie, *The Personal Life of David Livingstone*, pp. 425–426.

10. *Ibid.*, p. 422.

11. Stanley's diary entry for 3 March 1872, quoted by Jeal, *Livingstone*, p. 347, from D. Stanley (ed.), *The Autobiography of Sir Henry Morton Stanley* (London, 1909), p. 274.

12. Quoted from Stanley's *Autobiography* (see preceding note), p. 349, by Blaikie, *The Personal Life of David Livingstone*, p. 423.

13. Waller (ed.), *The Last Journals of David Livingstone*, vol. 2, p. 159.

14. *Ibid.*, p. 160.

15. *Ibid.*, p. 161.

16. See Jeal, *Livingstone*, p. 349. The brunt of Livingstone's sense of betrayal was taken by Kirk, as is shown by letters to W. C. Oswell from Tanganyika (6 Jan 1872) and James Young (15 March – July 1872) quoted in Holmes (ed.), *David Livingstone*, pp. 171–173.

17. Letter to Agnes Livingstone (see note 1, above) quoted in Jeal, *Livingstone*, p. 349. This was arguably the fate of David's brother, Charles. He was appointed consul in Fernando Po and died there of fever. See Holmes (ed.), *David Livingstone*, pp. 98–99.

18. Waller (ed.), *The Last Journals of David Livingstone*, vol. 2, p. 165.

19. *Ibid.*, p. 169.

20. *Ibid.*, p. 170.

21. *Cf.* Blaikie, *The Personal Life of David Livingstone*, p. 424.

22. Letter to Maclear and Mann, cited in Coupland, *Livingstone's Last Journey*, p. 222, n. 1.

23. Quoted by Coupland, *ibid.*, p. 175, from Stanley's *Autobiography* (see n. 11 above), p. 279.

24. Quoted by Jeal, *Livingstone*, pp. 351, 411, from Stanley's *Autobiography* (see n. 11 above), pp. 279–280.

25. Waller (ed.), *The Last Journals of David Livingstone*, vol. 2, p. 174.

26. *Ibid.*, pp. 178–179.

27. Quoted by Coupland, *Livingstone's Last Journey*, p. 222.

28. Waller (ed.), *The Last Journals of David Livingstone*, vol. 2, p. 181.

29. *Ibid.*, p. 182.

30. *Ibid.*, p. 185.

31. *Ibid.*, p. 181.

32. *Ibid.*, p. 191.

33. *Ibid.*, pp. 191–192.

34. *Ibid.*, p. 192.

35. *Ibid.*

36. *Ibid.*, p. 190.

37. *Ibid.*, p. 203.

38. *Ibid.*, p. 204.

39. *Ibid.*, p. 205.

40. *Ibid.*, p. 224.

19. The last journey

1. Waller (ed.), *The Last Journals of David Livingstone*, vol. 2, pp. 200–201.

2. *Ibid.*, p. 193.

3. *Ibid.*, p. 232.

4. *Ibid.*, p. 235.

5. *Ibid.*, p. 234.

6. *Ibid.*, p. 237.

7. *Ibid.*

8. *Ibid.*, p. 242.

9. Quoted by Blaikie, *The Personal Life of David Livingstone*, p. 439, from a letter to Stanley written near Livingstone's death.

10. Waller (ed.), *The Last Journals of David Livingstone*, vol. 2, pp. 244–245.

11. *Ibid.*, p. 246.

12. *Ibid.*

13. *Ibid.*, p. 247.

14. *Ibid.*, p. 249.

15. *Ibid.*

16. *Ibid.*, p. 251.

17. *Ibid.*, p. 252.

18. *Ibid.*, p. 253.

19. *Ibid.*, p. 255.

20. *Ibid.*, p. 256.
21. *Ibid.*, p. 258.
22. *Ibid.*, p. 260.
23. *Ibid.*, p. 269.
24. *Ibid.*
25. *Ibid.*, p. 270.
26. *Ibid.*, p. 275.
27. *Ibid.*, p. 276.
28. *Ibid.*, pp. 276–277.
29. *Ibid.*, p. 277.
30. *Ibid.*, p. 278.
31. *Ibid.*, p. 287.
32. *Ibid.*
33. *Ibid.*, p. 289.
34. *Ibid.*, p. 293.
35. Helly, *Livingstone's Legacy*, p. 197.
36. Waller (ed.) *The Last Journals of David Livingstone*, vol. 2, p. 297.
37. *Ibid.*, p. 294.
38. *Ibid.*
39. *Ibid.*, p. 296.
40. *Ibid.*, p. 297.
41. *Ibid.*
42. *Ibid.*
43. *Ibid.*
44. *Ibid.*, p. 303.
45. *Ibid.*, pp. 304–305.
46. *Ibid.*, p. 307.
47. *Ibid.*
48. *Ibid.*
49. *Ibid.*, p. 308.
50. *Cf.* Helly, *Livingstone's Legacy*, p. 111.

20. Funeral march

1. Helly, *Livingstone's Legacy*, pp. 115–117.
2. Waller (ed.), *The Last Journals of David Livingstone*, vol. 2, p. 316.
3. *Ibid.*, p. 336.

4. *Ibid.*, pp. 344–345.

5. 'O God of Bethel!' by Philip Doddridge and John Logan, as in *Scottish Paraphrases* (1781).

6. Waller (ed.), *The Last Journals of David Livingstone*, vol. 2, p. 346.

21. The fruits

1. See Preface n. 14, pp. 188–189 above, and H. M. Stanley, *How I found Livingstone*, p. 351.

2. Waller (ed.), *The Last Journals of David Livingstone*, vol. 2 , pp. 182, 308, gives 1 May as the day of his death; his tombstone gives 4 May.

3. Walls, 'The Legacy of David Livingstone', p. 127.

4. Helly, *Livingstone's Legacy*, p. 225.

5. B. Stanley, *The Bible and the Flag*, pp. 121–126.

6. For the significance of Livingstone's relationship to Venn, and comments on the political and economic dimensions of their thinking, I am indebted to an interview with Prof. Andrew Walls. *Cf.* Walls, 'The Legacy of David Livingstone', p. 125.

7. Schapera (ed.), *Livingstone's African Journal*, vol. 1, Introduction, p. xvii.

8. D. and C. Livingstone, *Narrative of an Expedition to the Zambesi*, p. 596.

9. Quoted in Shepperson (ed.), *David Livingstone and the Rovuma*, pp. 52–53, from Chauncy Maples, 'Masasi and the Rovuma District in East Africa', *Royal Geographical Society Proceedings* 11 (1880), pp. 344–345.

10. For a concise account of Arnot's life, see *e.g.* Ellis, *Path-clearers of Central Africa*.

11. *Ibid.*, p. 6.

12. *Ibid.*, p. 58.

13. Interview with Prof. Andrew Walls (see n. 6 above).

14. Macnair, *Livingstone the Liberator*, pp. 109ff.

15. Johnstone, *Operation World*, 5th edn, p. 39.

16. *Ibid.*, pp. 36–37.

17. Helly, *Livingstone's Legacy*, p. 224.

18. For example, the BBC Radio 4 'Today' programme broad-

cast on 20 March 1996 instanced slave raids carried out by Arabs from the Kordofan province of Sudan on southern Sudanese. The problem of child slavery was described as a 'major' one, 'involving many thousands' of both boys and girls being transported to northern Sudan.

19. Schapera (ed.), *Livingstone's African Journal*, vol. 1, pp. 57–58 (entry for 22 January 1854).

Glossary and index

Note: An asterisk (*) indicates those words that have a cross-reference elsewhere within this Glossary and Index. In the case of references of more than one word, the asterisk follows the term under which the reference is listed.